The Meaning of Life: Perspectives from the World's Great Intellectual Traditions

Jay L. Garfield, Ph.D.

THE
GREAT
COURSES

PUBLISHED BY:

THE GREAT COURSES
Corporate Headquarters
4840 Westfields Boulevard, Suite 500
Chantilly, Virginia 20151-2299
Phone: 1-800-832-2412
Fax: 703-378-3819
thegreatcourses.com

Jay L. Garfield, Ph.D.

Doris Silbert Professor in the Humanities
Smith College

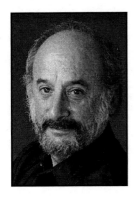

Professor Jay L. Garfield is Doris Silbert Professor in the Humanities, Professor of Philosophy, and director of the Logic Program and the Five College Tibetan Studies in India Program at Smith College. He is also Professor of Philosophy in the Graduate Faculty at the University of Massachusetts, Professor of Philosophy at Melbourne University, and Adjunct Professor of Philosophy at the Central University of Tibetan Studies in India. Professor Garfield received both his M.A. and his Ph.D. from the University of Pittsburgh.

Professor Garfield is the author, coauthor, or coeditor of 16 books, most recently *Buddhist Philosophy: Essential Readings* (coedited with William Edelglass; 2009); *Pointing at the Moon: Buddhism, Logic, Analytic Philosophy* (coedited with Mario D'Amato and Tom J. F. Tillemans; 2009); *Moonshadows: Conventional Truth in Buddhist Philosophy* (with The Cowherds, 2010); and *The Oxford Handbook of World Philosophy* (coedited with William Edelglass; 2010); all from Oxford University Press. He has also published nearly 100 scholarly articles and book reviews.

Professor Garfield teaches and pursues research in the philosophy of mind, foundations of cognitive science, logic, philosophy of language, Buddhist philosophy, cross-cultural hermeneutics, theoretical and applied ethics, and epistemology. He is currently collaborating on projects in developmental psycholinguistics and the history of 20th-century Indian philosophy. ∎

Table of Contents

Table of Contents

SUPPLEMENTAL MATERIAL

The Meaning of Life: Perspectives from the World's Great Intellectual Traditions

Scope:

This course explores answers to the question "What is the meaning of life?" from a wide range of intellectual traditions and across a vast historical sweep. It also introduces a number of profound texts to foster an appreciation of the diversity of approaches to this central question.

The exploration begins with the Bhagavad-Gītā, a classic of Hindu thought that is actually an episode from the great Indian epic *Mahābhārata*. The hero in the Gītā, Arjuna, finds himself on the eve of a battle in which he must lead his army against one led by many of his near relatives. The text counsels a life of action pursued with a certain kind of impersonal detachment in the context of a devotional attitude that allows one to understand one's role in the universe.

We then turn to ancient Greece, reading Aristotle's *Nicomachean Ethics*. Aristotle's answer to our question contrasts dramatically with that offered by the Gītā, locating happiness in the cultivation of a set of mundane virtues, such as courage, honesty, generosity, temperance, and the like, in the context of friendship and civic life. Aristotle develops a subtle moral psychology that paints an unusually detailed picture of the many dimensions of a meaningful life when understood from the human, as opposed to the cosmic, perspective.

A third approach is represented by the austere vision presented in the book of Job in the Hebrew Bible. Here, the puzzle regarding whether life can have any meaning is posed in the context of the possibility of divine indifference and a fundamentally cruel universe.

We then turn to the work of Lucretius and Marcus Aurelius, two influential Roman thinkers, both of whom meditate extensively on the problem with which we started: How can anything as fleeting and small as a human life mean anything in the grand scheme of things? Each focuses his meditation on the consequent significance of death and impermanence, making direct contact with each of the three traditions with which we began.

The fourth ancient approach we consider emerges from classical China. We begin with an exploration of *The Analects*, in which Confucius (Kongfuzi) develops an account of human perfection in terms of careful social cultivation in the context of social relations. We will see this view challenged by Daoism, grounded in the Daodejing and the *Zhuangzi*, in which meaning is to be found by harmonizing one's life with the fundamental structure of the universe. This requires not action or cultivation, as is suggested by the Confucian or Aristotelian approaches, but rather, a studied inaction and spontaneity.

The final ancient approach we consider is that of the Mahāyāna Buddhist tradition, the account of moral development and the goal of human life articulated by the 9th-century Indian philosopher Śāntideva. We will then explore the ways that Indian Buddhism and Chinese Daoist thought merge in the Zen tradition of China and Japan.

At this point, our attention shifts to modernity; we will discuss Hume's *Dialogues Concerning Natural Religion* and *Treatise of Human Nature*; Kant's "What Is Enlightenment?"; and Mill's *On Liberty*. We'll explore the view that the meaningful life is that lived autonomously, with active engagement in the public sphere, involving the free exercise of one's rights to thought and to speech, unfettered by religion or law.

Poignant critiques of this individualist, libertarian vision of modernity are offered by Tolstoy and Nietzsche. Tolstoy argues that modernity eviscerates life of spiritual values and interpersonal relations. Nietzsche, in *Twilight of the Idols*, argues that the central underpinnings of modernity are simply erroneous and defends a radically different view of the meaning of life.

The final section of the course looks at recent approaches to the meaning of life and their relation to those explored earlier. We consider Gandhi's concept of *satyāgraha*, or insistence on the truth, a challenging account of the demands of human existence, grounded simultaneously in the Gītā, in Buddhist principles, and in a modernist conception of individual dignity.

We then turn to the Lakota philosopher Lame Deer, who sees human life as gaining its meaning from a complex relation to the natural world in the context of which it is lived. We finish with the perspective of the 14th Dalai Lama, who integrates the views of Śāntideva with those of European modernity, defending an account of the meaningful life in the modern world that takes seriously such modern values as human rights, liberty, and a secular order but demanding the cultivation of compassion.

Although we may not conclude by answering the question of the meaning of life once and for all, we will find that our attempt to answer it in conversation with this array of scholars will yield rich insight and an appreciation for the value of addressing profound questions with intellectual rigor and seriousness of purpose. ■

After all, when we look at other lives and we ask which one is the most meaningful, we don't pick the one that's most sordid, the one that's most selfish. We pick the one that is most beneficial to others.

A t the end of the last lecture, we saw that there is a fundamental psychological block to meaningfulness—the fear of death—and to solve the problem of suffering, we need to remove that block. That subject is addressed in Śāntideva's *How to Lead an Awakened Life*.

In chapters 1 and 2, Śāntideva explores the motivation for cultivating virtue in order to make our lives meaningful. He begins by saying that he hopes to benefit others with his text and, in doing so, to become a better person himself. He points out that in our ordinary lives, we are overcome by motivations—greed, fear, selfishness—that make our lives sordid and meaningless, but we know that the cultivation of virtue and concern for others would make our lives more meaningful. If for a moment we have the motivation to cultivate moral development, we should seize it.

Śāntideva argues that the vicious life—the life replete with vice—is permeated by fear; the fear of death conditions our lives by animating confusion, attachment, and aversion, but despite its pervasiveness, this fear is invisible to us. In our inattention, we get caught up in motivations that we would never reflectively endorse. Vice is grounded in fear and it generates fear. Given that the two are so deeply interrelated, the only release we could possibly imagine from fear is the cultivation of virtue, which makes our lives peaceful, meaningful, and beneficial to others.

Recall, from our last lecture, that the first step on the bodhisattva path is the cultivation of aspirational *bodhicitta*, that is, the commitment to achieve awakening. Engaged *bodhicitta* is a goal that can be achieved only by cultivating all the perfections on the bodhisattva path, especially the perfection of wisdom. This perfection allows us to engage with reality as it is, not as it appears to us through the haze of ignorance. Engaged *bodhicitta* is the

According to the wheel of life, the biggest motivation for virtue is the fear of death. Virtue is something we cultivate in order to make our lives peaceful, in order to make our lives meaningful, and in order to make our lives beneficial to others.

spontaneous capacity, arising out of deep insight, to see things that have to be done and to do them. This idea coincides with those of Aristotle and the Daoists: The cultivation of deep insight generates the possibility of spontaneity.

In the remainder of the text, Śāntideva works through the structure of the perfections, beginning with generosity. This is the first of the virtues to be cultivated because giving enables us to reduce our attachment to things and to the self. The innate view that places us at the center of the universe is a distortion that generates pointless cycling through suffering instead of pointed altruistic aspiration.

The second perfection is that of mindfulness. From the Buddhist perspective, mindfulness is deeply moral because it keeps us focused on the virtues we intend to cultivate and on the degree to which our own activity reflects those virtues. Śāntideva gives us the image of unmindfulness as a mad elephant, stampeding and causing destruction wherever it goes. He further argues that our suffering is caused primarily by our own mental attitudes. For that reason, we can lead better lives, not by transforming the world around us, but by transforming our minds. This idea recalls the exhortation from Stoicism to focus only on what we can control.

Śāntideva then turns to the perfection of patience, an important virtue because it is the answer to anger and because it's a state of mind that can block attraction and aversion. It's also a necessary virtue for anyone who is seriously committed to moral cultivation, because self-transformation is an arduous path. The chapter on patience gives us numerous echoes of Seneca and Marcus Aurelius on the topic of anger. Anger destroys our ability to think rationally and to benefit others; a single moment of anger can devastate lifelong relationships or commitments. As Marcus Aurelius did, Śāntideva urges us not to become angry at people, who are driven by conditions, any more than we would become angry at a stomachache. Śāntideva also emphasizes the fact that anger isn't harmful to just others but to ourselves. Again, echoing both Seneca and Marcus Aurelius, Śāntideva tells us to respond to those who make us angry with pity and compassion. If we are going to benefit others, we must help them overcome irrationality, not pile our own irrational anger on top of theirs. The instrument for overcoming our own anger is thinking about it analytically and, in doing so, cultivating patience, which requires mindfulness, meditation, and wisdom.

In the cultivation of wisdom, we make the transition from aspirational *bodhicitta* to fully engaged *bodhicitta*. Wisdom is the dinstinction between just knowing analytically that anger is bad and patience is good and completely eliminating the superimposition of essences and independence. This leads to an engagement with things as interdependent, selfless, and impermanent, a spontaneous engagement that allows the virtuoso manifestation of compassionate action. ∎

Suggested Reading

Dalai Lama XIV, *A Flash of Lightning in a Dark Night*.

Śāntideva, *A Guide to the Bodhisattva's Way of Life* (three good translations: Crosby and Skilton, Oxford: Oxford University Press, 2008; Wallace and Wallace, Ithaca, NY: Snow Lion Publications, 1997; and Padmakara Translation Group, Boulder, CO: Shambhala Classics, 2006).

1. What is *bodhicitta*? What is the difference between aspirational and engaged *bodhicitta*, and why is this difference so important?

2. What are the six perfections? Why is each of them central to the cultivation of *bodhicitta*? How do they connect to the causes of suffering?

Śāntideva—Transforming the Mind
Lecture 19—Transcript

In our last lecture we saw that from a Mahāyāna Buddha's perspective the only truly meaningful life is a life motivated by compassion and committed altruistically to the benefit of others, and we saw that from this perspective that the conviction that that's the only meaningful life, is the only rational conclusion to draw from a real understanding of the omnipresence of suffering from interconnectedness and from selflessness.

We also saw a diagnosis of our ordinary human condition, the human condition that we might call the meaningless life, the life of being buffeted about. That was the diagnosis offered in the wheel of life in which driven by fear, driven especially by this background fear of death, we constantly cycle helplessly from emotional state to emotional state, and even the most pleasant of those emotional states is in the end a source of suffering.

We've seen that there's this fundamental psychological block to meaningfulness, and to solve the problem of suffering we need to solve that block. That's what Śāntideva's *How to Lead an Awakened Life*, *Bodhicāryāvatāra* is about. Śāntideva begins with a reflection on human imperfection, on what our current state of life is like, and how difficult it is to cultivate virtue and to make our lives meaningful.

He begins by trying to understand the motivation that we might have, nonetheless to cultivate virtue even in the grip of vice. The short way of saying what his answer is is that life without virtue—vicious life—is really bad. That in fact our only hope for happiness, for individual happiness and a meaningful life is to become morally better people.

Buddhism is a rich, textural tradition. The texts have their own flavor, so today we're going to get textural and work through Śāntideva's text, *How to Lead an Awakened Life*. We're going to begin with some discussions in Chapters 1 and 2.

Here Śāntideva is thinking about the motivation for moral progress and he begins by saying, in a kind of self-deprecating way,

There is nothing here that has not been said before,
Nor do I have any skill in composition.
Thus, I have no concern for others and
I have composed my text solely to cultivate my own mind.
Since my virtue is cultivated,
My faith thereby increases in power.
Nonetheless, if someone else with an outlook like my own
Sees this, it would be meaningful.

Now let's pause on that for a minute. Śāntideva is pointing out a couple of things. The first is that this text might be of benefit to others and that would be a very good thing. But the other thing that he's pointing out is that he himself hopes to benefit by writing this text. That by benefiting others he hopes himself to become a better person and to attain what might be a meaningful life.

He continues in Verse 4 of Chapter 1:

The time and opportunity, so hard to obtain,
Have been achieved, and they allow me to benefit the world.
If I fail to take advantage of this opportunity,
When will it arise again?
Thus, virtue is perpetually so feeble,
And the power of vice is so great and terrible.
If there were no bodhicitta, [remember that's this altruistic
aspiration for awakening]
What other virtue could overcome vice?

What's the point in these few verses? Śāntideva is pointing out that in our ordinary lives we are overcome by motivations that in fact make our lives sordid and meaningless, motivations of greed, fear, selfishness, averiis and so forth.

We actually know if we reflect on it even for a minute that the cultivation of virtue and a concern for others is what would make our lives more meaningful. After all, when we look at other lives and we ask which one is the most meaningful, we don't pick the one that's most sordid, the one that's most selfish. We pick the one that is most beneficial to others.

If for a moment we have the motivation to cultivate moral development. We should seize it. That's what Śāntideva is saying here. The primary purpose he identifies of moral development is to make our own lives better. But making our own lives better requires making the lives of others better. After all the problem of suffering that the Buddha identified is the problem of our own suffering. However, the Mahāyāna insight that we looked at in our last lecture was this: Interdependence means that the only way to solve the problem of our own suffering, to lead a good life, a life that we would care about for ourselves, is to solve the problem of the suffering for others.

Śāntideva then begins to really work on fear. He argues that the vicious life, the life that we ordinarily live full of vice, is permeated by fear and that the fear of death conditions our lives by animating confusion, attachment, and aversion. In these verses he really emphasizes that phenomenology of fear. He writes,

> How shall I escape?
> Rescue me quickly!
> Let death not steal upon me
> Before my vices have been eliminated!

> Thus, since I have not realized
> that I am ephemeral, [that is that I've passed over the truth of impermanence]
> Through confusion, attachment and aversion,
> I have committed many kinds of vicious deeds.

The point here is that despite or maybe even because of its pervasiveness. The fear of death is invisible to us. We don't pay attention to our momentary motivation and then we get caught up in these motivations that we would never reflectively endorse. Śāntideva continues that common sense suggests an obvious remedy. He says,

Now, having experienced the great terror, [that is, having really
    focused on the fear of death as opposed to just letting it
    unconsciously animate me,]
Heeding what you once told me, [here he's referring to the Buddha
    of course,]
I approach you for refuge so that you
Might quickly dispel my fear.
It makes no sense for me to enjoy the present day
Saying to myself, "I will not die just now."
The time when I will cease to exist
Will inevitably arrive.

What is this all about? Śāntideva has just diagnosed vice for us. He tells us
that vice is grounded in fear and it generates fear. That's the central idea
of that wheel of life. The biggest motivation for virtue then is the fear that
permeates that vicious life. That if we want to get rid of that fear, the only
way to get rid of it is by cultivating virtue, and that fear is grounded in the
primordial awareness of death. Since vice and fear are so deeply interrelated,
the only release we could possibly imagine from that horrible fear is the
cultivation of virtue. Virtue is something we cultivate in order to make our
lives peaceful, in order to make our lives meaningful, and in order to make
our lives beneficial to others.

Recall in our last lecture we distinguished two kinds of bodhicitta:
aspirational bodhicitta and fully engaged bodhicitta. The first step on
the bodhisattva path is the cultivation of aspirational bodhicitta. Even
though it's just aspirational it's no mere wish. It's already a commitment
to achieve awakening, and so it's already a personal transformation of
profound importance.

Engaged bodhicitta on the other hand is a goal that we can only achieve
by cultivating all of the perfections on the bodhisattva path, especially the
perfection of wisdom, because that's the perfection that allows us to engage
with reality as it is, not as it appears to us through the haze of ignorance.
Engaged bodhicitta is that spontaneous capacity to see things that have
to be done and to do them that arises out of deep insight. There's a neat
idea here that coincides with those of Aristotle and the Daoists. That we've

got this kind of deep insight that's cultivated that generates the possibility of spontaneity.

Śāntideva in the remainder of the text begins to work through the structure of these perfections beginning with generosity. That's the first of the virtues to be cultivated. That's because generosity, according to the Mahāyāna tradition, enables us to depersonalize. When we get used to giving, we get used to reducing our attachment to our things. When we get used to reducing our attachment to things, we reduce our attachment to self. As we reduce our attachment to self, we allow ourselves to stop seeing the world as me and everything else because that's a terrible distortion, that innate view that places us at the center of the universe. It's a distortion, because each of us has that view. They can't all be right and it's the distortion that generates pointless cycling through suffering instead of pointed altruistic aspiration.

Śāntideva writes,

> And so I will perform these deeds.
> Through the virtue I thereby acquire,
> May I completely alleviate
> All of the suffering of all sentient beings.
>
> May I be the medicine
> For all who are ill.
> May I be both medicine and physician
> Preventing the recurrence of illness.
>
> Through showers of food and drink
> May I alleviate the pain of hunger and thirst!
> At times of famine
> May I be both food and drink!

This is the generosity Śāntideva is talking about, a tremendous commitment to benefit others, but also a commitment that I be the person who is the cause of that benefit, a resolution to do it myself. It's a transformation that takes me out of egoism and into the realm of boundless altruism in which my life can be more than one of the petty lives led by four billion people on the planet.

The second perfection is the perfection of mindfulness. We don't always think of mindfulness as constant attention, as a moral matter, except maybe when we have special obligations, like say a surgeon has an obligation to be mindful while he's performing surgery. A guard has an obligation to be mindful while he's on sentry duty. But from the Buddhist perspective it's always deeply moral because it's mindfulness that keeps us focused on the virtues we intend to cultivate and on the degree to which our own activity reflects those virtues.

It forces us to reflect constantly on our motivations and to reflect on what's going on around us that may demand our moral attention. Mindfulness is a central, moral virtue to be cultivated. Śāntideva writes, "One who wishes to protect his practice should be careful to protect his mind. If one does not protect one's mind, it is impossible to protect one's practice" that is to protect that focus. Then he has this wonderful, wonderful metaphor. "The elephant of the mind causes much harm and degradation. Wild, mad elephants do not cause so much harm." That is, the image of the elephant here is something stampeding crazily around and Śāntideva has this vision that if we don't discipline ourselves, our minds just stampede from thing to thing causing destruction wherever they go. "Nonetheless, if the elephant of the mind is restrained by the rope of mindfulness, then all fear is banished, and every virtue falls into our hands." Note again that emphasis on fear. When we restrain our mind and focus just on what needs to be done, we are able not to dissipate the inevitability of death but to dissipate the constant effect that that background awareness of death has upon us.

There's another reason for mindfulness. Śāntideva argues that our own suffering is caused primarily by our own mental attitudes. For that reason, he argues, we can lead a better life not by transforming the world around us, but by transforming our minds. He has a wonderful couple of metaphors here. I want to take you through them. This is a fun one: "Who so purposefully forged / The implements of sentient beings' hell? / Who constructed the floor of burning iron?" Let's pause on that for a minute. What he's doing here is talking about the traditional Buddhist imagery of what a hell is like with all of these implements of torture on which the condemned are sitting on a floor of burning iron. He's pointing out that these are psychological constructs. There's not a literal hell, there's an experience of being tortured, an experience of living on a floor of burning iron and he asks, who purposely forged those? And then he asks weirdly, "and whence have those women come?" Now the commentaries tell us who those women are. These are these kind of hideous, ghostly women who torment us from trees in hell realms—I didn't make this up, I can't help you with that, but that's the imagery. But he's pointing out that these aren't made from outside. He says in the next verse:

> The Sage [that's the Buddha] has explained that
> The vicious mind gives rise to all of these.
> So, there is nothing whatever in the triple world
> More frightening than the mind.

The point here is that all of our suffering, our feeling that we're living in hell, our inability to be attentive to others isn't caused by the world around us. The world around us might give rise to adversity, but to transform adversity into suffering the mind has to get into action. Mindfulness can cause us to stop our minds from making that next move from adversity into suffering. Since vice on this view is a purely internal matter and that's the source of our unhappiness, we need to look to the mind as our source of unhappiness. That means if we only transform the mind, we can transform unhappiness into happiness.

Śāntideva gives us a wonderful recipe for that transformation. Śāntideva writes,

> My enemies, as boundless as space
> Cannot possibly all be defeated.
> But if I defeat the anger in my mind,
> That is to defeat all of my enemies.

No matter how bad things are outside, I can't do anything about that. Remember the idea in stoicism, the idea of the arrow. I can control the shooting of the arrow but not the hitting of the target. So focus on what I can control. Then Śāntideva introduces one of my favorite of his metaphors. He asks, at Verse 13 at Chapter five,

Where is there enough leather
To cover the entire world?

But when I put on my leather shoes,
That is to cover the entire world.

Just so, I cannot control external things,
But I can control my own mind.

What need is there
To control anything else?

It's a nice metaphor. The world is full of rocks and thorns and broken glass and stuff you don't want to step on. If what you want to do is to make the world a safe place for you to stroll, you can do two things. One is you could just buy a whole lot of leather, cover the whole world with it and things will be fine, take care of the external world. The other thing you could do though is just put on a pair of shoes. By putting on a pair of shoes, by taking care of yourself, you take care of the whole problem. For that reason, Śāntideva is saying, when we focus on suffering, whether my own suffering or the suffering of others, we want to focus not on the external conditions, but in order to transform suffering into happiness, in order to transform a meaningless sordid life into a meaningful one, the transformation has to be not an external transformation but the transformation of our minds.

Śāntideva then turns to another perfection, the perfection of patience. The chapter on patience is perhaps the best known of all of the chapters in *Bodhicāryāvatāra*, it's one the Dali Lama never tires of quoting and it's got tons of gorgeous poetry in it. Patience is a really important virtue from the standpoint of Mahāyāna Buddhism because patience is the answer to anger. If we're tempted to be angry with somebody, we want to be patient. If we're tempted to be angry with ourselves, we need to motivate patience. It's also a state of mind that can block attraction and aversion. I really, really want that chocolate, just be patient and think about what the consequences would be. I really can't stand this music, just be patient and listen to it, maybe I'll hear something in it that I like.

It's also a very necessary virtue for anybody who is seriously committed to personal cultivation, especially moral cultivation, of the kind proposed on the Mahāyāna path because that's an arduous path. Self-transformation is really difficult, it's really hard, and if you're impatient with yourself from a Mahāyāna perspective, you'll never get there. In a lot of Mahāyāna teachings, people distinguish two kinds of patience, patience with oneself and patience with others. They point out that patience with others, that's easy to cultivate. There's lots of ways you can convince yourself not to be angry with somebody else. Marcus Aurelius gave us some of those. Seneca gave us many of those but the hard one, this patience with oneself, is so easy because we see our own faults and we see our own failings to deprecate ourselves easier than you ever think and often more destructive, and cultivating patience with oneself is the most difficult thing of all.

Śāntideva really focuses on the dangers of anger and why anger is such a very, very bad thing. When we hear Śāntideva here in Chapter 6, the patience chapter, we are going to hear a lot of echoes of Seneca and Marcus Aurelius. There's no accident there of course. If you start thinking hard about anger and really ask the question, when is the last time anger was beneficial to you, you're going to have a hard time answering that. Anger takes us over. Anger destroys our ability to think rationally. Anger destroys our ability to benefit others. It turns our life into the life of an animal, not the meaningful life of a human being. That's what Śāntideva is going to emphasize in this beautiful chapter, so let's follow him along. Śāntideva writes:

> All of the virtuous actions
> Amassed over a thousand eons, such as
> Giving alms and making offerings to the tathāgatas,
> Are destroyed by a single instance of anger.

What does he mean by that? He means something very, very, very straight forward. Can you imagine a life that you've led very, very well, very happily. You've made a lot of friends. You've got deep personal relationships, think about what can happen in a moment of anger. You could harm somebody and never recover from that. You could destroy a friendship by a misplaced word and make the rest of your life one that you regret. You could alienate a child or alienate a parent. You could destroy a career by doing or saying the wrong thing. A single moment of anger can be so dangerous that no matter how much of a bank of positive commitment you've been able to build up, no matter how much success you've been able to achieve, you can undermine it instantly in a single moment of anger. That's why anger is so important to control. Śāntideva writes,

> There is no vice like aversion, and
> There is no aescetic practice like patience.
> When the thorn of aversion sticks in the heart,
> The mind finds no peace,
> nor can it achieve happiness or joy.
> Sleep does not come, and one's strength ebbs away.

That is Śāntideva saying when you're really bound up with hating somebody or you're bound up with dissatisfaction, you're bound up with feeling that the world is doing you wrong, you're bound up with seeking revenge, you don't get any happiness. You don't get any joy. You stay awake all night and you end up becoming a miserable creature. Anger doesn't benefit you. It's just like Seneca emphasized, right? It's not as though a little bit of anger is okay. A little bit of anger is a little bit of vice, anger is just never okay.

Śāntideva, again echoing Seneca, argues that anger is always irrational and he gives us some wonderful examples to show us that it's never reasonable to be angry. This is kind of nice because remember when we discussed compassion and we discussed the relationship between compassion and emptiness, between compassion and interdependence. We argued that if you really understand interdependence and you really understand how small a part of the world you are, and how vast a part of the world everybody else is, and how much your own happiness is dependent upon that of others, your own suffering on that of others. The only rational response is a commitment not just to alleviate your own suffering but that of others, because it's impossible to alleviate your own suffering without alleviating the suffering of others.

We saw that compassion or *karuṇā* is the only rational response to interdependence. Śāntideva now argues that anger is always irrational. He says,

I am not angry at such things as bile,
Although they cause great suffering.
Why be angry at sentient beings?
They, too, are driven by conditions.

So here's the point. We saw Marcus Aurelius say something very similar. If I've got a bad stomachache, my reaction isn't to be angry at my stomach, but to try to do something to alleviate it. I know that there's a cause for my stomachache and what I have to do is to find that cause and to alleviate that cause, and anger isn't going to help me do that. Suppose that somebody does something really mean to me, they say something terrible to me. They're insulting. They steal something of mine. They hit me, whatever. Let me think about their action. Let me think about why they did that. I don't need to think about whether it's justified or not, whether they were right to do it or not. That's beside the point. What Śāntideva points out in the last line of this verse—that's Verse 22 of Chapter 6 is they too are driven by conditions. The point there is that whatever they did, they were caused to do, perhaps by their own psychopathology, perhaps by their own ignorance, perhaps by their own confusion about things. If I'm not angry at my stomachache which has causes, why should I be angry at them? It's like being angry at the stick that somebody uses to beat you and not the person. Then Śāntideva continues,

Even without resolving,
"I shall become angry,"
People spontaneously become angry.
Similarly, without resolving,
"I shall arise,"
Anger just arises.

The point here is that anger doesn't come from a decision. Anger comes from a failure to make decisions. Anger arises from a failure of mindfulness, from not paying attention. It allows us to be driven by causes rather than to take control of our own lives. Again there's a nice echo here of the Gītā. Don't allow yourself to be driven by what's happening around you. When you get angry you are, so you're giving up on rationality.

Śāntideva emphasizes that anger isn't just harmful to other people, it's harmful to ourselves. It leads us to have accidents because we're not paying attention. I might be so bound up with thinking about what I'm going to do to that person I don't pay attention to what's happening on the road, or I don't pay attention to the fact that I'm walking down stairs. Anger leads to depression he points out, that people become so depressed that the rest of their lives become miserable. Anger sometimes leads onward to suicide because anger can be turned inward at ourselves. Remember that issue about patience, patience with ourselves is hard to cultivate. Anger with ourselves is easy to arise, and that can lead to suicide. Of course anger can also lead to the loss of our reputations as other people think less of us which then makes us less able to benefit others, because you can't benefit others unless they take you seriously. If they think that you are somebody who has no self control and who is just dangerous to yourself and those around you, you turn out to be totally worthless. Even to be effective as an agent you need to control anger.

Śāntideva writes,

> Since it is the nature of fools to harm others,
> My anger with them makes no sense,
> Just as it would make no sense to be angry at
> Fire, the nature of which is to burn.

Again if people have a particular kind of character or disposition, that might be a cause for compassion, a cause to do something to help them, but it's not a cause for anger. If you notice there's tremendous parallels here both to Seneca and to Marcus Aurelius, who when they think about others who harm them say, think about what's wrong with them. Respond to them with pity. Respond to them with compassion. It makes no sense to respond to them with anger because they're behaving irrationally. That's a harm to themselves. If we are going to be beneficial to them, it's to help them overcome that irrationality, not to pile our own irrationality on top of theirs.

Śāntideva argues that anger is both dangerous and it's irrational. It's also overpowering so it's something that we really have to deal with a great deal of effort. It appears to be spontaneous. If you want to avoid anger ruining your life, Śāntideva argues, the only thing you can do is assiduously cultivate patience. Śāntideva thinks that understanding anger, meditating on anger and thinking about anger analytically the way that we've been doing it now, is the real instrument for cultivating that patience. Only if you understand the anger that way and then internalize that understanding, make that understanding something that really motivates you, can you really overcome anger. Patience and compassion have to be settled into us as personality traits before they are real antidotes and that settling requires mindfulness and requires meditation to make them parts of us.

But, Śāntideva points out, it doesn't just require mindfulness and meditation. It also requires wisdom, real understanding, and it's in the cultivation of wisdom that we make the transition from the aspirational bodhicitta that gets us to begin the bodhisattva path, that gives us the motivation to cultivate these perfections or these virtues and engage bodhicitta, the bodhicitta we aspire to attain by the end of the bodhisattva path. That's the distinction between just knowing analytically everything that we know here that anger is bad, that patience is good, that others are driven by causes and conditions or so forth, and wisdom where wisdom is the total absence of the superimposition of essences, the total absence of the superimposition of independence and an engagement with things as interdependent, as selfless, as impermanent, a spontaneous kind of engagement that allows the kind of virtuoso manifestation of compassionate action. This is what leads us to stop seeing ourselves as the centers of the universe to recognizing the kind of selflessness that allows us to understand ourselves as constantly an interaction and an interdependence with others.

It's a rejection of our specialness, a rejection of the idea that the first person pronoun I marks something different, something special in the universe. If you honestly believe that of the entire universe you are the one thing whose interests determine attention then you can't possibly do anything to advance those interests, let alone the interests of anybody else, and your life will be a meaningless blip in the history of the cosmos. But if you can understand, and not only understand but engage with the wisdom that you are part and parcel of an entire universe with which you are interdependent, you can make a difference; that's the idea.

With Śāntideva in this beautiful text, *Bodhicāryāvatāra*, we find a really distinctively Mahāyāna Buddhist account of the meaningful life, this great vehicle animated by this understanding of the emptiness of essence and the centrality of the value of compassion that emerges from a real understanding of the fundamental nature of reality. This is a vision of a meaningful life, as a life that is permeated by and founded in compassion and awareness of the real nature of the universe. It's an account that is grounded in an understanding of vice as having its foundation in fear. So that when we cultivate compassion, when we cultivate an understanding of interdependence, we banish fear. That's the only way to banish fear because to the degree to which we think that we are independent and we are the only thing that matters, awareness of the fact that we are going to end our lives can only mean that the only thing that matters will come to an end, and that's what generates the fear of death that animates in turn our vice.

This is a vision that says that the only way we can eradicate that fear and hence eradicate vice is through the cultivation of virtue. Those virtues involve both intellectual virtues, of understanding, meditation, wisdom, philosophical analysis, and the moral virtues of compassion and generosity. Śāntideva's vision is that this kind of cultivation—the bodhisattva path—leads us to an entirely new way of experiencing ourselves. To experience ourselves as selfless, to experience ourselves as interdependent, to experience ourselves as those who can benefit the world, and it gives us an entirely different way of experiencing the world. Then we can experience others in the world as intimately bound up with us, whose benefits and burdens are our benefits and burdens. Whose pain, whose suffering is our pain and suffering and whose pain and suffering we can alleviate in the process of alleviating our own, hence the possibility of a life that can truly make a difference.

We've seen tremendous parallels here to other people we've examined, to the work of Aristotle, to the work of Marcus Aurelius, in some ways to the work of Laozi, and even if you think about Zhuangzi. This is all happening in India of course, but it's all going to move to China because Buddhism moves to China, and when Buddhism moves to China we're going to see that it interacts with Daoism and a whole new thing is born. That new this is Zen, and that's where we're going to go in our next lecture.

Zen—The Moon in a Dewdrop and Impermanence
Lecture 20

The Zen (Chinese: Chan) tradition sees its own beginning in a special moment of wordless communication between the Buddha and one monk, Maha Kasyapa. Since that moment, the Buddha's realization about the nature of reality, gained from contemplation of a single flower, has been passed from one Zen master to another in an unbroken line of transmission.

Zen came to China in the late 5th or early 6th century C.E. with the monk Bodhidharma, regarded as the first Chinese patriarch in a succession of six. The story of the sixth patriarch, Hui Neng, brings to life some of what is pregnant in Zen. Hui Neng, an illiterate woodcutter, was living at the temple when the fifth patriarch held a poetry contest to choose his successor. The patriarch's principal disciple, Senxiu, came up with this verse: "The body is the Bodhi tree; the mind is a clear mirror. Always strive to polish it. Let no dust alight." The physical practice of Buddhism is like the tree under which the Buddha gained awakening; it's the physical prop that makes awakening possible. The mind, like a mirror, is naturally luminous and reflects the nature of reality. We see echoes of Confucianism in the emphasis on polishing and cultivating that mirror. Finally, "Let no dust alight" tells us to keep our minds clear of emotions and delusions.

Hui Neng's response was this poem: "Bodhi originally has no tree. The mirror has no stand. Buddha nature is primordially clean and pure. Where could dust even alight?" Here, awakening doesn't depend on physical being; it depends on the primordial nature of the mind—the mirror—which has no stand. In other words, don't worry about the ordinary physical world; pay attention to experience. Further, our ability to attain awakening "is primordially clean and pure." The attractions and aversions highlighted by Senxiu's poem aren't even part of our primordial nature.

The second verse reads: "The mind is the Bodhi tree. The body is a mirror stand. The mirror is primordially clean and pure. How could it ever be dusty?" Here, the mind is the support for awakening, while the body merely holds up the mind. And given that the mind is "primordially clean," what we need to eliminate is the idea of cultivation. In doing so, we'll find that we are already fully awakened, already, effectively, a Buddha.

Zen Buddhism is suspicious of language and conceptuality and emphasizes direct experience and meditation as opposed to study.

Zen Buddhism is suspicious of language and conceptuality and emphasizes direct experience and meditation as opposed to study. If you understand your own nature, you attain Buddhahood. Much of Zen training hinges on puzzles called *coagons*: What is the sound of one hand clapping? These puzzles are meant to make us realize that rational and discursive thought doesn't work; solutions come with sudden insight. Understanding this inner process leads us to understand our own minds.

In the Zen tradition, each of us has a primordial capacity to understand ourselves and the world completely, to live in a fully awakened, spontaneous way. Practice is a matter of recovering or uncovering that Buddha nature. Zen also emphasizes the idea that beauty *is* the world, and seeing beauty is part of what it is to understand the world.

The notion of impermanence plays a much more central role in Zen than it does in other Buddhist traditions. While Indian Buddhism makes a distinction between gross and subtle impermanence, Zen also distinguishes metaphysical impermanence, an impermanence in the nature of things. The idea here is this: Zen focuses on our own mind and experience, and the mind is subtly impermanent; our thoughts change from moment to moment. Because of this, we are constantly experiencing subtle impermanence. Our own mental states provide us with the foundation for a constant experience of constant change. But because of our fear of death, we reinterpret the experience of impermanence as an experience of constancy, thus creating a layer between ourselves and reality and between ourselves and genuine experience. As a result, we live in a meaningless dream world even though we have the constant reality of a beautiful, impermanent world before our perception all the time.

We close with a poem from Dōgen: "Being in the world: To what might it be compared? Dwelling in a dewdrop fallen from a waterfowl's beak, the image of the moon." Dōgen compares "being in the world"—our experience—to a dewdrop from a bird's beak—something delicate, impermanent, and unbelievably beautiful. Further, the moon is contained in this tiny dewdrop, just as being in the world entails containing the vastness of reality within us—but only momentarily. The deepest kind of beauty is that which reveals impermanence because in doing so, it reveals the nature of our minds and reality. We can experience reality only if we grasp and celebrate impermanence. ∎

Suggested Reading

Kasulis, *Zen Action, Zen Person.*

Suzuki, *Zen Buddhism.*

Study Questions

1. How is Zen a continuation of Indian Buddhist ideas? What does it draw from Daoism?

2. Why is impermanence such an important part of the Zen understanding of the nature of reality?

Zen—The Moon in a Dewdrop and Impermanence
Lecture 20—Transcript

Welcome back. It's good to see you again. In our last couple of lectures we've been spending our time back in India, but today we're returning to China and then moving slowly to Japan. We're going to be exploring the Chan or Zen tradition. I'm going to ask you to bear with me because sometimes things will get a little bit abstract and a little bit complex, and you might begin to lose the sense that we're really talking about the meaning of life, but we are. I promise you that if we really focus on some of these abstract details, all will become clear.

Zen is notoriously a bit obscure, but my hope is that by moving methodically and clearly we can actually make this transparent and revealing, because to my mind, the Zen tradition is one of the more profound and beautiful developments of philosophy in the history of humankind.

So far we've examined two main strands of thought about the meaningful life that are going to come together in Chan as it's called in Chinese, or Zen as it's called Japanese. The first is the Daoist tradition from China and the second is the Indian Mahāyāna Buddhist tradition. We've already seen that the Daoist tradition, which is indigenously Chinese, places a great deal of emphasis on nature, on our own human nature, and on the dangers imposed by cultivation, the accretion of social forms, language, conceptuality and so forth, and emphasizes the need in order to lead a life worth living to pare down rather than to build up, to eliminate all of those accretions, and a real emphasis on the development of spontaneity. We've also seen in Daoism a real suspicion of rational thought, of reason, of rules, and of discipline in favor again of a spontaneous perceptual engagement with reality.

In the Indian Mahāyāna Buddhist tradition we've seen some very different things, some of which we might expect to be in tension with some of these Daoist ideas, and indeed there will be some creative tension. In the Indian tradition we have an emphasis on the interdependence of phenomenon, on the fact that everything arises in dependence on countless causes and conditions. That each of our actions, each of our perceptions, each of our thoughts, and every moment of our experience is interdependent on countless many causes and conditions some of which are within us, some of which are outside.

We saw an emphasis on the development of compassion, and we saw the thesis developed that compassion is a natural outgrowth of rational analysis. In the Indian Buddhist tradition, rather than a suspicion of reason and rational analysis, we had a valorization of reason, of reason as our guide to understanding our fundamental nature of reality, and a conviction that once we understand the fundamental nature of reality, compassion emerges quite naturally. We saw that compassion and reason were proposed jointly as the solutions to the problem of suffering, because suffering on this view, the meaningless life, is grounded in this primal confusion about the nature of reality that gives rise to attraction and aversion. Reason eliminates that confusion, when attraction and aversion drop off, compassion arises with the awareness of interdependence.

Buddhism was always a missionary tradition. It was a tradition in which Buddhist monks and later nuns went out to spread the Buddhist word first all over India and then into Sri Lanka and Southeast Asia, then up into China, later into Tibet, off into east Asia, and of course in our own day all over the world.

Often times when Buddhism entered a culture it entered a culture that was not a fully scholastic literary culture, and Buddhism could work its magic on that culture. That's the case, for instance, in Tibet where there was no literacy, very little scholastic tradition at all, a very primitive religious tradition, and when Buddhism came in it really resulted in a wholesale import of the high medieval boost culture of India.

When Buddhism entered China, things were very, very different because China, of course, was already a very old civilization with well-developed philosophical and religious traditions in Daoism and Confucianism. When Buddhism entered it was always interpreted through the lenses of Daoism and Confucianism. When Buddhism was translated into Chinese, it was translated into a language that was already rich with philosophical resonance.

When we see Buddhism coming into China, we see not only Chinese civilization transformed by Buddhism, but more importantly Buddhism sinified, made Chinese and partly through this kind of interfusion with ideas that we will recognize as Daoist and sometimes Confucian ideas. That will be the project.

Our program for today is going to run roughly as follows: I'm going to begin with a brief history of the Chan, or Zen, tradition. Once again Chan is the Chinese pronunciation, Zen is the Japanese. By the way, Chan is the Chinese pronunciation of a Sanskrit word, prajna, awareness or meditation, and so it's the meditation tradition.

Then we'll talk about some of the distinctive features of Zen within the Buddhist world. We'll talk a little bit about the nature of impermanence and the way that that is reconceived in Zen. Then we'll talk about the relationship between impermanence and our experience of ourselves, and we're going to finish with our really pretty Zen poem by the great Zen philosopher, Dogen.

So as we begin to do a bit of history of the Zen tradition we're going to talk about that history both from a kind of internal perspective discussing how the Zen tradition tells its own story, but also we're going to talk about how contemporary scholars of Zen see the tradition from the outside.

Let's begin with the inside. Where does Zen actually see itself beginning? It sees itself beginning in a wonderful, beautiful episode in the early history of Buddhism that is recorded in the Pali Canon, in the early discourses of the Buddha. It's the story of a brief interaction between the Buddha and one of his principal disciples, Maha Kasyapa, and it goes like this: The Buddha was sitting before a huge assembly of monks who were waiting, expecting to hear a teaching from the Buddha, because that's what he did a lot. Instead of beginning to speak the Buddha picked up a single flower and just held it up. Everybody stared, but one monk, Maha Kasyapa smiled and the story is that at that moment the Buddha realized that Maha Kasyapa understood what he was—well I can't say talking about—understood what he was communicating, and in the Zen internal tradition, this is the first transmission of Zen because Zen sees itself as a special transmission that runs through an unbroken lineage of wordless mind-to-mind transmission.

From the Zen point of view what happened was, the Buddha had a realization, a realization about the nature of reality, and the Buddha recognized that that realization could be communicated to somebody who would understand it by merely contemplating that flower. Kasyapa contemplated the flower in the right way and came to understand. Kasyapa passed that realization to his disciples and so on and so on and so on, and each Zen master now, who is authoritative with respect to teaching, traces his or her own transmission lineage back to that initial episode, whether that transmission is actually authenticatable is a different story, but every Zen master would take it for granted that his or her transmission lineage goes back to that event and is unbroken.

Zen came to China with the great monk Bodhidharma late in the 5th or early in the 6th CE, and as I said, it came into a kind of already rich cultural milieu. It's important to note that by that time not only do we have an already-established Confucian and Daoist tradition which began in China, but we've also got earlier transmissions of Buddhism because Buddhism began to come into China around the 2nd century, and so for a few hundred years other Buddhist schools are there. Zen is a kind of latecomer into China. Zen had to kind of fight its way in.

Bodhidharma emphasized serious long term sitting meditation called Zazen, just sitting and meditating, and introduced a new sutra into the Chinese milieu, the Lankavatara or decent into Lanka sutra which became very important. Bodhidharma established a lineage with a succession of patriarchs. He's regarded as the first Chinese patriarch. Then there's a succession of five patriarchs in a unified lineage. Then we come to the sixth patriarch, Hui Neng. With Hui Neng we're going to tell a story. It's a really good Zen story and it will really bring to life some of what's pregnant in Zen.

Hui Neng, as the story has it, was a kind of rustic country bumpkin woodcutter. One day he was in the market and he heard a monk reciting a particular sutra, the diamond sutra, and he had a sudden realization. He suddenly understood something he hadn't understood before. We don't know the content of the realization, but he asked, where can you go to study this? He was told to go to the temple of the fifth patriarch where you could study this. He went and asked for admission, and he was an illiterate country bumpkin, so he was basically put to work in the kitchen pounding rice. He pounded rice in the kitchen for a number of years.

Then the fifth patriarch was getting old and needed to organize his succession. He organized his succession in the following creative way. He held a poetry contest, we'd now call it a poetry slam, and challenged monks in the monastery to write a poem on a particular wall in the monastery demonstrating their realization. All of the monks assumed that the vice abbot—the principal disciple over the fifth patriarch and Senxiu, was going to win the competition, so nobody even bothered writing a poem and the wall stayed blank and the wall stayed blank and the wall stayed blank.

Finally, Senxiu wrote this poem on the wall. He came up at night when everybody was sleeping, wrote the poem and it was found in the morning. Senxiu's poem goes like this: "The body is the Bodhi tree, the mind is a clear mirror. Always strive to polish it. Let no dust alight." What does this mean? It's a very straight forward poem. It's a very straight forward poem. When he says, the body is the Bodhi tree, he's saying look, our own physical practice is like the tree under which the Buddha himself gained awakening. That is, it's the physical prop that makes it possible for us to gain awakening. That's fair enough. The mind is a clear mirror. Our mind is naturally luminous and it reflects the nature of reality if only we pay attention to it. So far so good, nothing is mysterious.

Then he says, and we can see the echoes of say Confucianism here, "Always strive to polish it." Keep it really clean. Really work on cultivating it. Remember that Confucian line, cut, ground, polished. "Let no dust alight." That is, don't let the afflictions, emotions, delusions, confusion, attraction, and aversion land in your mind; keep it clean. That's a pretty good poem. That's a pretty good poem. You'd be happy if you wrote that poem for your Zen master I'll bet. Of course the fifth patriarch was happy. He said that's pretty good.

The next day, all of the monks came and saw this poem on the wall and they were all impressed and amazed and poor old Hui Neng, who was illiterate, had to ask somebody to read it to him. Another monk read it to him, and he thought and he thought, and the next night Hui Neng came up to the wall and he had to bring somebody with him, but he gave dictation and had the following two verses written on the wall right next to Senxiu's poem. The first verse he wrote was—now let me recall the original poem first. The original poem was: "The body is the Bodhi tree, the mind is a clear mirror. Always strive to polish it. Let no dust alight." What did Hui Neng write? He wrote, "Bodhi"—that is awakening—"originally has no tree. The mirror has no stand. Buddha-nature"—that is our primordial nature as potentially awakened—"is primordially clean and pure. Where could dust even alight?"

Let's pause on that verse for a minute. When he says, Bodhi originally has no tree, he's talking about that body that was supposed to be the Bodhi tree. He's saying, look, awakening doesn't necessarily depend on our physical being. Awakening depends upon something that's well beyond our ordinary physical nature, the primordial nature of our mind. The mirror—the mind—has no stand. That is, don't worry about the ordinary physical world. Be paying attention to experience.

Then he says, "Buddha nature"—that is our ability to attain awakening—"is primordially clean and pure. Where could dust alight?" What's he saying? He's saying, look, Senxiu is focused on all of this defilement, on all of these attractions and aversions and all of the things we need to get rid of. Those aren't even part of our primordial nature. If we're trying to understand ourselves, then don't pay attention to all of these adventitious things that really aren't so important.

Then comes the second verse which is a wonderful clincher. He says, "The mind is the Bodhi tree." That is, the support for an awakening is the mind itself. "The body is a mirror stand." All it's doing is holding up the thing you care about. "The mirror"—that is the mind—"is primordially clean and pure. How could it ever be dusty?" So Hui Neng is asking the question, where do you even find all of these things you want to get rid of? Stop this notion of cultivation. If you simply pay attention to your fundamental nature, you'll understand that you already are fully awakened, already fully, effectively a Buddha. That's a very, very dramatic line.

Now what happens? The fifth patriarch looks at Hui Neng's poems and says, you've got it, hands him the robe and bulb, and disappears, and Hui Neng becomes the sixth patriarch, and this school becomes very dominant in Tang and Song Dynasty China. Zen flourishes after this, develops very powerful monasteries that become politically important as well, and produces an enormous literature of philosophical writing, religious writing, poetry, inspires tons of painting, and becomes a tradition that we've come to know and love, and flourishes tremendously in China.

In the 12th century the Japanese monk, Esai, comes to China to study, because Japanese and Korean monks all came to China at this point to study Buddhism, and he brought one of the Zen lineages, the so-called Linji lineage, back to Japan where it became established as what we now know as the Rinzai lineages in Japan. The other main lineage in Japan is Soto, and we're going to be talking a lot about that in a little bit. The Soto lineage, which in Chinese was the Caogon lineage, was brought to Japan in the 14th century by the monk, scholar and poet, Dogen. We'll be talking about Dogen a bit later on.

Zen flourished in Japan, flourished in Korea, and has become a very important tradition there generating again wonderful literature, profound philosophy, and a lot of very important, powerful temples, and beautiful art. In the 20th century Zen started coming to the west, first with Suzuki Roshi and then a series of other great Roshis, great Japanese teachers who have flourished and produced many disciples in the west where Zen is now very, very well established. That's a brief history.

How does Zen see itself? As we said, Zen sees itself as being this kind of special transmission of insight outside of scriptures. As the Zen teachers say, no dependence on word and letters, a direct pointing to the human mind, seeing into one's own nature and attaining Buddhahood, that's a quote from Bodhidharma. Bodhidharma says, don't depend on words and letters, Zen is just a pointing to the mind. If you understand your own nature, you attain Buddhahood.

This is the idea that a really fully-awakened life, a life worth leading, is a life in which you understand exactly one thing, that is your own nature, the nature of your own mind. Zen always sees itself as this kind of non-discursive, non-conceptual tradition using non-verbal means like that flower, like slaps and hits and art and poetry to get people to transform directly, to get people to have a direct insight into their own minds and hence into all of reality. It's handed from mind-to-mind not text-to-text. In Zen we also have the tremendous emphasis on teacher/disciple lineages and anybody who is a serious Zen practitioner can refer to their teacher, tell you who their teacher's teacher was and so forth. These lineages are carefully mapped back to the Buddha himself and the initial moment with Kasyapa. So we're going to see that the roots of Zen are Indian and explicitly Indian but also has this tremendous Daoist infusion.

I want to mention before we go further into details some distinctive features of the Chan and Zen tradition. First we've already mentioned it has this kind of antinomian character. Zen is suspicious of words, conceptuality, analysis, and logic, and emphasizes direct experience and meditation as opposed to study. In Zen monasteries you often see very little philosophical and textual study but a lot of meditation aimed immediately at self transformation and the tremendous focus on the nature of mind.

There's a paradox here of course, because while Zen explicitly in its own self description as choose textuality and discursivity, it has also produced probably the largest body of texts, literature, poems, of any Buddhist tradition. This paradox is one that's worth keeping in mind. There are a lot of paradoxical things about Zen. It's one of the things that makes it most famous in the west.

A lot of Zen training, especially in Rinzai tradition, hinges upon these puzzles called koans you've probably heard, what is the sound of one hand clapping? Does a dog have Buddha nature? These are meant to be puzzles that are meant to occupy your mind, get you to try to think about them rationally, until you realize the rational and discursive thought can't work, leaving you with a sudden insight into the solution of the puzzle that comes from somewhere within you. And understanding the inner process allows you to understand, not the answer to the puzzle but your own mind, how it works and how it sees things. So its kind of use of paradox, non-discursivity, and koan is all central to Zen.

Also central to Zen is this idea that we saw in Hui Neng's poem of primordial awakening and Buddha nature, the idea that each of us has, as our fundamental character this Buddha nature, this primordial capacity to understand ourselves and the world completely, to live in a fully awakened, spontaneous way, and that practice is a matter of recovering or uncovering that Buddha nature, notice the influence of Daoism here. Recovering an original nature rather than creating something else.

Finally, in all of Zen there's a beautifully aesthetic dimension. We're going to encounter that in a short while, and the use of art, painting, calligraphy, poetry, music, and Zen has always been part of the tradition. Because Zen emphasizes that beauty is the world and the value of seeing beauty as part of what it is to understand the world as you take up with life meaningfully.

I said earlier and we're now coming to that issue, Zen also focuses deeply on the notion of impermanence or momentariness. This idea plays a central role in Zen. much more central than it does even in other Buddhist traditions that emphasize the importance of impermanence. In India we've already encountered this distinction between gross and subtle impermanence. I'll remind you of that briefly. Things are grossly impermanent and we notice that they change from day-to-day-to-day. Our hair gets greyer and we lose some of our hair. The weather changes from sunny to rainy, back to sunny again. Our children get older, leaves fall from trees. We're aware of this kind of impermanence all the time.

The second kind of impermanence we encountered is what we call subtle impermanence. That is the momentary change from moment-to-moment-to-moment that is so quick that it escapes our notice but is the necessary condition of even gross impermanence that nothing remains the same from moment-to-moment, atoms are exchanged, things get a second older every second, things wear down and so forth. We've already encountered those.

In Zen we get this slightly more detailed analysis because we distinguish this kind of metaphysical impermanence, an impermanence in the nature of things with a phenomenological impermanence. The idea is this: Zen focuses on our own mind, on our own experience, on the way we take up with the world. The point is that not only is our own mind impermanent, subtly, that is our conscious states, our thoughts are changing from moment-to-moment-to-moment-to-moment, never lasting for more than a second. But if we pay attention to our own experience, because our mental states are changing from moment-to-moment-to moment, we are constantly experiencing subtle impermanence. Our own mental states provide us with the foundation for a constant experience of constant change. Every perception we have is constantly changing, as you move your head at every second, at every microsecond the field of vision in front of your eyes is changing. The field of sound that you're experiencing changes from moment-to-moment, and we were experiencing that. But of course we're not always conscious that we're experiencing it.

The Zen analysis of primal confusion, this root of suffering, is this. That while we are constantly experiencing our minds in the world as they are, that is as subtly and permanent and we have this phenomenology of impermanence, we ignore the fact that we're experiencing it. We ignore our own experience masking it with conception. Masking it with logic, with discursive thought, with language, and with conceptuality, and take this constant experience of impermanence and reinterpret it as an experience of constancy and permanence, thus creating a layer between us and not only reality but between ourselves and our own genuine experience.

Our primordial awakening is constituted by the fact that we are in fact already experiencing reality as it is, which is the foundation of compassion, the foundation of joy, the foundation of understanding ourselves. But we're constantly suppressing that understanding with a layer of conceptuality. Doing that of course also suppresses our awareness of death and the significance of that impermanence. For Zen that's part of the reason that we do this. Remember the wheel of life that we saw, all in the jaws of death.

Because we're afraid of dying, because we're afraid of our impermanence, we tend to suppress that awareness and even though we are constantly perceiving impermanence, we conceive permanence in order to forestall that terror. What that enables us to do by forestalling that is to live in a kind of dream world, a world that's really quite meaningless, a world that's really quite trivial, even though we have the constant reality of a beautiful impermanent world before our perception all the time.

Similarly, our own personal continuum, that is the continuum of our mental states, it's constantly dependently originated, constantly impermanent. The Zen claim, the claim when Hui Neng says there is no mirror isn't to say that we don't exist, it's to say that there's nothing like a mirror that's constantly permanently there waiting for dust to come and go. Rather, the mirror itself is constantly changing, constantly transforming. It has no existence from moment-to-moment. We do exist but we exist as continuum, though we grasp ourselves as continuums instead of as continua. We take ourselves to be continuing things, not these sequences.

What happens is that we perceive our own impermanence and hence our own mortality. It terrifies us, so we reconceive ourselves as permanent and substantial to hold down that fear of death, and in doing that Zen practitioners think we then alienate ourselves, not only from the world, not only from others, but from ourselves as well. It's only relinquishing this kind of grasping and therefore relinquishing conceptuality, thought and textuality that we're able to return to that primordial state that gives our lives meaning.

We see both Indian, Buddhist, and Daoist residences here and they're just fraught throughout. Now I promised you a poem right? I promised you a poem, and it's my favorite Zen poem. I get to share it with you now. It's a Zen poem from Dogen, this great Japanese scholar who lost his parents very early in his life and became very obsessed with the notion of impermanence, traveled from Japan to China to learn Chan, and ended up bringing the lineage back to Japan which became the great Soto lineage.

What does Dogen write in this beautiful poem? He writes,

> Being in the world:
> To what might it be compared?
> Dwelling in a dewdrop
> Fallen from a waterfowl's beak,
> The image of the moon.

Dogen is comparing being in the world, not the world, but our experience, what life is like, the way we lead our lives. Really, what is he comparing it to? He's comparing it to the image of the moon in a dewdrop that has just fallen from a waterfowl's beak. It's delicate. It's impermanent. It's unbelievably beautiful though.

This idea of the connection between impermanence and beauty is so important. Dogen is pointing out not that the moon and the dewdrop is beautiful despite being impermanent. He's emphasizing that it's beautiful precisely because it's impermanent, and he's also emphasizing that this entire moon, this vast celestial body, is contained in this tiny dewdrop, and what being in the world is like is containing this vastness of reality, in perfection and beauty, perfect and beautiful because it's contained within us but only momentarily. It's that emphasis on momentariness and beauty that really marks Dogen's thought.

On this view, impermanence is no tragedy. Impermanence is reality. Death is no tragedy, not a catastrophe; it's part of reality. Impermanence is exactly what makes our existence possible. It's the very nature of our existence. No impermanence, no reality, no existence; If you want a world, you take impermanence. You put it in a dewdrop, drop it from the waterfowl's beak. It also grounds a very special kind of beauty. In Japanese there's a lovely term for this, awarē, which means the beauty of passing things, the way that cherry blossoms are especially beautiful because they last for such a short time. The way that a flower is especially beautiful just before it fades, and in the Japanese Zen context this is meant to be the deepest kind of beauty because it's the beauty that reveals impermanence; therefore the beauty that reveals the nature of our minds, therefore the beauty that reveals reality.

We can only experience this reality if we grasp and celebrate impermanence. That's what gives our lives meaning, that's what gives them aesthetic meaning. That's what gives them value because we actually care about those moments, noticing how few they are. That's what gives them contact with the reality that we live in because it doesn't superimpose a false conception of permanence on this, but interacts with the world and ourselves just as we are.

This of course deepens a lot of ideas that we've already encountered both through India and from China but also you'll notice in Stoicism, and it aestheticises them in a wonderful way. The aesteticisation should remind you, by the way, of Marcus Aurelius, his lion's brow, his figs. In our next lecture we're going to continue to discuss Zen and talk about the Zen account of awakening and what a realized life, a meaningful life, looks like from this Zen perspective. Stay tuned.

Zen—Being-Time and Primordial Awakening
Lecture 21

If you really apprehend emptiness—this notion of voidness of essence—then all you apprehend is the ordinary nature of ordinary things.

The Indian philosopher Nagarjuna distinguished between two truths that are distinct in one sense but constitute a fundamental unity. Conventional or everyday truth posits entity, while ultimate truth sees phenomena as empty of essence, empty of independence, and empty of permanence. The unity between these two truths arises as follows: One way to characterize the ultimate truth of emptiness is to say that conventional phenomena are no more than conventional; their identities are posited by us, but they do not inherently have identities. The two truths are distinct in our awareness but are ontologically unified, that is, unified in being.

The emptiness of phenomena is itself empty. For my hand to be empty is for it to have the property of emptiness, but the emptiness of my hand depends on my hand. If I don't have a hand, I don't have any emptiness of my hand. The notion of emptiness here is not a deeper reality behind ordinary things but the actual reality of ordinary things—itself empty of essence, empty of independence, and empty of permanence. We don't say that ordinary things are empty; there is just emptiness. Even emptiness is empty.

The Heart sutra helps us understand this idea of the emptiness of emptiness and the nonduality of ultimate and conventional truth. In this sutra, the question is asked: How does one become truly wise? The answer is that anyone who wants to understand the nature of reality should contemplate its components and see that each of them is empty of essence. The sutra then gives us the fourfold profundity: Form is empty, but emptiness is form. Form isn't different from emptiness; emptiness isn't different from form. The point here is that form—physical reality—is empty. But to be empty is just to be the emptiness of ordinary things; there is no deeper reality behind that idea. The fact that emptiness and form are different from each other means that if you truly understand both conventional phenomena and emptiness, you understand the ordinary world around us, which is nothing but empty phenomena. Thus, these two truths, even though they involve two different apprehensions of the world, are actually nondually related—they're the same thing.

In this sense, for Zen, **phenomenology**—the nature of our experience—joins with **metaphysics**. Metaphysically, we understand that there's no difference between ordinary reality and its ultimate nature. But phenomenologically, we understand that to experience ordinary reality is to see things as they are, not to see beyond them. This ties to the distinction between perception and conception, two modes of awareness with different objects: the particular and the universal. Universals are permanent, independent, and unreal. Perception can reveal reality to us, but conception, because it always involves engagement with abstract concepts, is deceptive. If we superimpose conception over perception, we fail to see actual momentary phenomena and, thus, fail to see the ultimate nature of reality. But if we can strip away that superimposition, we realize the absence of duality between the conventional and the ultimate.

Perception can reveal reality to us, but conception, because it always involves engagement with abstract concepts, is deceptive.

This stripping away also allows us to see the absence of duality between subject and object. In ordinary experience, we distinguish ourselves as the subjects and everything else around us, including people, as objects; thus, we're the center of the world. But once we drop the notion that we exist as substantial phenomena and see that we are interdependent, constantly changing processes, then that pole of subject and object disappears. This is what enables spontaneity and allows us to enter into the experience that Dōgen called **being-time**, real presence in the world.

Dōgen emphasizes that existence itself is temporal. Time is the nature of our world, not an abstract container in which the world occurs. Time is change; thus, it's constituted by things that are changing. Things don't happen in time;

time exists because things happen. Time has two aspects: It is experienced as flowing, and it is arrayed simultaneously, like Dōgen's mountain range. We may experience only the present right now, but the present exists and is significant only in its relationship to the past and the future. To ignore the moment that we live in is to lose reality, because all that is real is that moment, but to ignore the past and the future is to lose the meaning of reality.

The goal of Zen practice is full awakening, which is not to suddenly see beyond reality but to see reality as it is. Dōgen tells us that we are constantly perceiving things as impermanent, interdependent, and essenceless, but we then superimpose conception on them. That primordial perception, however, is the ground of our Buddha nature, what makes it possible for us to be awakened. We are always, in every moment, primordially awakened, and our task is to recover that state through mindfulness and meditation. ∎

Important Terms

being-time: The intimate union of existence and temporality; the fact that to exist is to be impermanent yet to have a past and a future to which one is essentially connected and the fact that human existence is always experienced in relation to past, present, and future.

metaphysics: The study of the fundamental nature of reality.

phenomenology: Inner experience, or the theory of inner experience.

Suggested Reading

Kasulis, *Zen Action, Zen Person.*

Stambaugh, *Impermanence Is Buddha Nature.*

1. In what sense are the two truths different? In what sense are they identical? Why is a nondual understanding of their relation so central to Zen?

2. What does it mean to say that we are primordially awakened? Why is practice necessary at all if this is true?

Zen—Being-Time and Primordial Awakening
Lecture 21—Transcript

Let's continue our exploration of the Zen tradition and of the Zen account of what a truly meaningful life looks like. In our last lecture we introduced many of the fundamental ideas in Zen and especially the emphasis that Zen places on understanding our own mind, the nature of our own experience, and understanding the world through this focus on impermanence and momentariness, and the emphasis on the notion of a kind of primordial awakening that requires recovery.

Today we're going to go deeper into the Zen analysis. Things will get a bit more abstract, but I'm hoping that by the end we'll make complete sense of this idea of our own Buddha nature and primordial awakening as the foundation for the meaning of our lives.

We're going to talk first about the complex idea of dualism and non-dualism, duality and non-duality in Zen. Many people who are familiar even a little bit with Zen rhetoric and Zen literature understand this idea of non-duality or subject/object unity, so we'll talk about that a bit. We'll talk further about the complex relationship between perception and conception and the need to focus on perception as a mode for taking up with the world to reduce conception, and that idea of course comes in from Daoism.

Then we're going to come back into Dogen himself and really focus on the idea that Dogen develops of being time in Japanese, uji, this word being-time, one word, and a primordial presence in the world. That will lead us to a discussion of the concept of Buddha-nature, to understand the notion of primordial awakening, and then we'll be able to conclude with a Zen account of mindfulness and what it is to find the meaning of life by living in each moment fully present. That's the plan for today.

Let's begin by talking about this idea of duality and non-duality. This is going to take us back to India, and we're going to be moving back to the Indian roots of Zen. The Zen tradition regards the great 2nd and 3rd century Indian philosopher Nāgārjuna—that's the guy who went down to the naggas, the sea serpents, to recover the Prajnaparamita sutras if you remember our discussion of the rise of Mahāyāna. This guy, Nāgārjuna, the snake guy, they all see him as an important patriarch for Zen, and they all pay a great deal of attention to Nāgārjuna's philosophical work. The particular philosophical work of Nāgārjuna that will be important for this tradition is the one called *Mūlamadhyamakakārikā*, which means fundamental verses on the middle way. The reason that's important is because it is in that text specifically in the 24th chapter that Nāgārjuna distinguishes what he calls the two truths or two realities and explains that even though they're distinct in one sense, they constitute a fundamental unity.

When Nāgārjuna does this he distinguishes conventional or every day mundane truth from ultimate truth. Conventional, mundane truth is the way the world appears to our ordinary consciousness. The fact that grass is green and snow is white, that we are interdependent, that water is made out of H_2O, all of this is part of everyday, mundane conventional truth, and it's very important to grasp mundane truth because if you don't you get into big trouble.

This mundane truth or conventional truth, Nāgārjuna thought, is not the ultimate story about things. The ultimate story about things is that mundane phenomenon are empty of essence, empty of independence, empty of permanence. They are in fact impermanent, interdependent, essenceless phenomenon, and our ordinary mode of taking up with the world as we've said, and we've talked about the danger of that, is to superimpose permanence, essence, independence, on these things which themselves are empty of all of that.

We can see that two truths as distinct and that one of them posited entity which we naively take up as permanent, independent phenomenon including ourselves by the way, including our own minds. The other one says these things are empty of being the way that we actually normally take them to be. But when we see them that way, we also see that there's a deep unity between the two truths, because one way to characterize the ultimate truth of emptiness is that conventional phenomenon are just conventional, they're no more than that. Their identities are posited by us conventionally through names, through language, through conceptuality and they're posited on things that do not inherently have those identities. The two truths are distinct in our awareness but are ontologically unified, are unified in being.

This gives rise to the idea that not only are phenomenon empty but their emptiness, that is the fact that they are empty, is also itself empty. Because for a thing, like a table or like my hand to be empty, is for it to have this property of emptiness, but the emptiness of my hand depends upon my hand. If I don't have a hand I don't have any emptiness of my hand. For that reason this notion of emptiness itself is not understood in Majjhimā Buddhism, in this middle way Buddhism, should be a deeper reality behind ordinary things, but to be just the reality of ordinary things, so itself to be empty of essence, empty of independence, empty of permanence. For that reason we don't say that ordinary things are empty; there's just emptiness. We say that even emptiness is empty, it's emptiness all the way down.

You'll recall that when we talked about the Mahāyāna we said that there was this new sutra foundation for the Mahāyāna that constituted in these sutras that might have been left with the sea serpents or might have been written about 500 years after the Buddha's death being discovered. The word sutra, let's remember, refers to a discourse that is attributed to the Buddha, either as the Buddha's own speech or as something said in the presence of the Buddha that the Buddha approved.

One of the really important sutras for the foundation of Zen is the so-called Heart Sūtra or heart of wisdom sutra. A sutra which by the way contemporary scholars now believe may well have been or probably was composed in China and then sent back to India, retranslated into Sanskrit, and now has this kind of faux Indian ancestry. I want to talk to you a little bit about the beginning of the heart sutra to understand this idea of the emptiness of emptiness and of the non duality of the ultimate and the conventional truth.

The story of the Heart Sūtra, it's a very short sutra, and it's a text that almost every Buddhist in any Buddhist country memorizes in the way that Christians memorize the Lord's Prayer and Jews memorize the Shammah— it's a very short text, about a page long. But it begins roughly like this: The Buddha is hanging out on this small mountain near Rajgir that you can visit today called Vulture Peak. He's up there with a big assembly of monks and bodhisattvas and deities and all kinds of celestial beings. With him are a number of his close disciples. The Buddha is up there in meditation and he's meditating on this kind of contemplation that's called the enumeration of phenomenon, that is a contemplation of the mammoth old nature of reality, the complexity of reality and how things are interdependent.

While he's doing that, his chief disciple in the poly tradition, Shariputra, who was regarded in shravakana, the disciples Buddhism, as the foremost of the wise, the wisest of all of the disciples, asks if bodhisattva, who's hanging out there, Avalokiteshvara, who is the embodiment of compassion in the Mahāyāna tradition. So Shariputra asks Avalokiteshvara, hey, how does a person who's in a noble lineage—somebody who wants to be noble—practice the profound perfection of wisdom? That is, how does one become truly wise? The answer to that question is really interesting. There's one nice little footnote on this, Avalokiteshvara answers him, it actually goes like this, Shariputra says, how does a son of noble lineage practice the perfection of wisdom, and Avalokiteshvara replies, a son or daughter of noble lineage who wants to practice the perfection of wisdom—one of the earliest feminist moments in Buddhism—I kind of love that.

But anyway, here's what he says. He says that somebody who wants to really understand the nature of reality should contemplate the components of reality, the aggregates as they're called, the heaps, the piles, and should see that each of them is empty of essence. Then we get to this important line, often called the four-fold profundity. He says, form is empty but emptiness is form. Form isn't different from emptiness, emptiness isn't different from form. What does that mean? It's very obscure and there are many different commentaries to try to explain this but the point is actually pretty simple. The point is just that form, that is physical reality—that's what the word form means, physical reality—physical reality is empty of essence, empty of permanence, empty of independence. But emptiness is form, that is to be empty is just to be the emptiness of ordinary things. It's not a deeper reality behind that.

When we say emptiness and form are different from one another, we mean that if you really understand what it is to be an ordinary conventional phenomenon, if you really understand it, you understand that it's empty, impermanent, interdependent; and if you really understand emptiness, you just understand the ordinary world around us which is nothing but empty phenomenon.

In this sense, these two truths, these two realities, even though they involve two different kinds of apprehension of the world, one in terms of just ordinary stuff and the other in terms of its deep nature, are actually non-dually related, they're the same thing, and if you really apprehend things fully, conventionally, you apprehend their ultimate nature. If you really apprehend emptiness this notion of voidness, of essence, then all you apprehend is the ordinary nature of ordinary things.

In this sense, for Zen, phenomenology, the nature of our own experience, joins with metaphysics. Metaphysically we understand that there's no difference between ordinary reality and its ultimate nature. But phenomenologically, that is in terms of our own experience, we understand that to really experience ordinary reality the way it is, is to understand—to experience it as it is ultimately: impermanent, constantly changing without essence. And to experience that is just to see things as they are, not to see behind them. Not to see beyond them. Not to see reality that's hidden from ordinary consciousness, but to see the reality that is there in front of ordinary consciousness all the time. That is to see the reality of who we are as we in fact are, to understand ourselves as we experience ourselves and not as we project that experience of ourselves.

All of this ties deeply to the distinction so important to the Zen tradition between perception and conception. From a Zen perspective, when we distinguish between perception and conception we're distinguishing between two modes of awareness, one by our six senses. Remember in a Buddhist tradition we have our five ordinary senses and then the introspective sense by which we examine our own minds and our own consciousness. When you look inside and see how you're feeling, you're using that sixth sense, it's not ESP, inference, when they go beyond what's sensorally available to us and to draw conclusions from it.

From a Buddhist point of view these two kinds of awareness have two different objects. The awareness of our senses are particular things. When I see an apple I see a particular apple. When I see a tree I see a particular tree. I don't see applehood in general. When I see red I see a particular patch of red, not redness. But conception, inference, takes as its object universalism, abstract qualities. So when I think about apples, I'm not thinking necessarily about a particular apple, I'm thinking about apples in general. When I think about red I'm thinking about the color, not a particular patch.

The importance of this is that if you think about universals, that is these abstract concepts, they've got an important property. They're permanent, that is you don't say red could go out of existence sometime, and they're independent of their particular instantiations. Even if I went around the world with a white paintbrush and painted everything that was red, white, I wouldn't eliminate redness. I would just eliminate all of the instances of redness. Redness would still be there waiting for the next strawberry to ripen.

Because they're independent and because they're permanent, Buddhists argue and to go through these arguments would take us far afield, but take my word for it, that they're actually unreal, that universals are the wrong kinds of things to be real, because to be real is to be impermanent, interdependent and so forth. For this reason, Buddhists of all stripes think that even though perception, including intraspection, can reveal reality to us, conception because it always involves engagement with abstract concepts, and those abstract concepts have unreal objects is always deceptive.

For this reason, when we think about ourselves or other things as permanent, that is as having identity over time, when I imagine that I am the same person who delivered the first lecture on Zen or who will deliver the next lecture, or who is even delivering this lecture at the very beginning when I greeted you, that I am imputing to myself an identity over time that results from my employing a concept, the concept of moments of J. Garfield's existence, and engaging with that concept instead of engaging with each moment of my existence.

That concept isn't real, it's purely deceptive, and so our experience of permanence, like our experience of independence, results from this super imposition of conception over perception. By superimposing conception over perception, we fail to see actual momentary phenomenon. We see these illusory, permanent phenomenon, these illusory independent phenomenon, and we've superimposed them over what's real. It's as though we've put a film between ourselves and reality and all we see is the weird film.

Of course in doing that, we fail to see the ultimate nature of reality. We fail to see the interdependence and the impermanence of things, including the interdependence and the impermanence of ourselves and our own state and our own experience. That is, we fail to see that our being in the world is like the moon and the dew drops falling from the waterfowl's beak. Instead we think, hey, we're here for a while. Things are cool. We don't need to worry about anything at all, and death isn't really going to happen. It happens to other people.

If we can strip away that superimposition, then and only then do we get to see conventional reality as it is, actual interdependent, impermanent, constantly changing phenomenon. Therefore, by seeing them as impermanent, as interdependent, as constantly changing, as essenceless, to see the ultimate nature of reality, when we do that we see the absence of the duality between the conventional and the ultimate, that texts like the Heart Sūtra or like Nāgārjuna's *Mūlamadhyamakakārikā* are teaching.

Also in doing that another duality disappears. This is a profound and important duality. The duality that disappears and the duality that so often structures ordinary, diluted, meaningless lives is subject/object duality. Why is it so important and why does it disappear? It's important for precisely the following reason: In ordinary experience, we distinguish ourselves as the subjects and everything else around us as objects, including you. Including the people we know and love, all just kind of sit there as objects, and they sit there as distinct from and independent of us, and that allows us to experience reality in what I call the polar coordinate way. Where I am at the center of the universe and everything else is experienced in relation to me, my tree, my mother, my child, my dog, my friend, my enemy, my students, people who aren't my students, and so forth. So I think that the nature of things is given by their relationship to me, a subject, and therefore I become the most important thing in the world, since everything literally revolves around me.

Thinking about that for even a moment we see it's a pretty stupid idea. It's a stupid idea, but from a Zen perspective it's the idea that underlies all of our ordinary engagements. Once we drop the notion that we exist as substantial phenomena, and we are interdependent constantly changing processes engaged with everything else, then that pole of subject and object disappears because there no longer is the permanent subject experience to be the subject of its objects.

Therefore, by obtaining this kind of non-dual awareness we are finally able to engage with reality as it is, not reality as we conceptually project it. That's what allows us to have an openness to others, to take others seriously, not just as our object for things related to us, but as non-different from us, others. To see ourselves as just a continuum of processes engaged with them, and it allows us to also be open to experience our own experience and not to repackage it through conceptual thought and words.

As Daoists would have emphasized and the Zen practitioners also emphasize, that is what enables our spontaneity. That's what enables us to just act instead of to calculate and deliberate. That allows us to be truly effective.

Finally in this whole package we can see that by doing that it decreases the attachment and the aversion that are those secondary roots of suffering that emerge from the primal confusion of seeing ourselves at the center pole— as the center of the universe. When you've got that, you become attached to things as yours and you become attached to yourself. You can drop that attachment, drop that aversion, and so drop the suffering by dropping the non-dual awareness.

Dropping that non-dual awareness allows us to enter into a kind of experience, this kind of experience that Dogen thinks is central to the meaningful life, what we're really after, which Dogen calls being-time or presence, real presence in the world. The term again in Japanese is Uji—it's just as a compound of being and time. He develops this in his wonderful and very large and very obscure, I promise you, text called *Shobogenzo*. If you get really interested in Dogen, this is the text you'll read. But I warn you it's a text that requires a great deal of patience. It's complex, obscure, but it rewards close reading. We're not going to be reading the text closely, but we are going to be talking about the ideas.

Dogen emphasizes that existence itself is temporal. It's saturated with time. As Dogen would put it, time is the nature of our world not the kind of abstract container in which the world occurs. If you think for instance about Isaac Newton and the Newtonian view about space and time that so characterized a lot of our ordinary modern conception and reflects our kind of ordinary consciousness, we think of time as this big container that's got the past in it, it's got the future in it, it's got the present, and we kind of move through time. Dogen points out that that actually doesn't make any sense. It's not that there's time and stuff happening in time. Time is change and so it's constituted by things that are changing. Things don't happen in time; time exists because things happen.

Dogen emphasizes that time, thought about this way, which is so central to our being and which we so rarely really allow ourselves to experience, has two fundamental aspects, and these aspects are what really are at the heart of understanding the nature of our lives and why our lives are worth living.

The first aspect for Dogen is that time is experienced as moving, we experience it as a succession. One event follows another, one generation follows another. One season follows another. We think of time as kind of flowing from the past to the future, past the present, and we experience it in this modest of change. In that sense we think of time as something that's just kind of current. We saw that vision of time in the words of Marcus Aurelius as well as in the words of Lucretius.

But Dogen points out that there's a second aspect of time beyond time as motion and change, and he refers to this as time arrayed or ranging, and the simile he uses is it's like a mountain range. When you survey a mountain range, the mountains over there and the mountains over there both exist at the same time. If we pan our eyes from left to right, we see the mountains in succession but the mountains are arrayed simultaneously with one another.

Just so says Dogen, when we imagine the past, the present, and the future, they're set out arrayed like a mountain range. We may only right now be experiencing the present, but the present only exists and only is significant in its relationship to the past and its relationship to the future.

Like a mountain range, no matter how good a climber you are, you can only be on one peak at a time. In that sense an individual living in time can only be living at one moment and not in multiple moments simultaneously. When we talk about time being arrayed, we don't mean that we are living in the past, present, and future simultaneously; we're only on one peak in that array. That peak gets its location, gets its significance because it is after a past, before a future, causally connected to those, and that we won't stay on that peak, we'll move to the next peak, the next peak, the next peak.

For Dogen, given that the real nature of reality and of our own experience is time, and given that time has these two dimensions, flowing and ranged out, to live in actual presence, to actually live in the moment of time in which I am now talking and you are now listening is to live precisely in a single moment which vanishes just as quickly as it arises. It's that impermanent. However, that moment is a moment which is only a moment in the context of a past and a future that give it meaning. The moment that you are experiencing right now has its significance, has its meaning, and has its own reality only because of everything that came before it including for instance all of this lecture that has come before this present moment now, only is important because it precedes what comes after it, including all of the things perhaps that I'm going to say after this, and whatever you're going to do after you stop listening or stop watching this lecture.

To ignore the moment that we live in is to lose reality, because all that's real is that moment in which we exist. But to ignore the past and the future is to lose the very meaning of that reality. For Dogen, the point about temporality is that our reality, where we live is right here, right now, at this moment. But to only pay attention to the moment in which we live is to lose its significance. Not to live in the moment is to lose reality completely. To live only in that moment without awareness of its interconnection is to make our life completely meaningless.

The goal of all Zen practice, Zen study, Zen meditation, sitting, just like the goal of all Buddhist practice, is full awakening. Buddhism is called

Buddhism because it's about Buddhahood. It's about leading an awakened life, as we saw Śāntideva's concern to help us do. It's to lead a life that is lived in awareness of who we are, what we're doing, who's around us, and to be maximally effective for our lives to be fully, fully meaningful.

That requires a complete understanding of existence, of our own existence and of the existence of all that's around us. To awaken is therefore not to suddenly see beyond reality, it's not to suddenly live somewhere else. It's not for everything around us to disappear. It's to see reality as it is. That's what's so important about the Zen insight, is there's nothing behind reality that's realer than it. There isn't something beyond us that gives our lives meaning, beyond our lives that gives our lives meaning, beyond the world that gives our lives meaning. What gives our lives meaning on this view is to fully understand, to fully engage with the world in which we find ourselves, because the ultimate reality of that world, as we saw a few moments ago, is identical with its conventional reality. Waking up is just to see reality as it is and that is to drop conceptual superimposition, to drop all of this kind of thought and cultivation, to drop all of this linguistic and dispersive engagement just to perceive, to actually look, to actually listen, to actually introspect, and to perceive the impermanent, interdependent phenomenon around us and in us and that we are as impermanent, interdependent phenomenon which eliminates the self grasping that generates the selfishness, subject/object duality, and all of the suffering that falls in train.

Dogen's deep insight is we do that all the time. We are constantly perceiving, and what we're perceiving is always something impermanent, interdependent and essenceless. We do that for a moment and then we superimpose conception and labels and ideas and thoughts, and mist it up almost as soon as we see it clearly. That phenomenological ground, that primordial perception is the ground of our Buddha-nature. That is what makes it possible for us to be awakened. Buddha-nature is just the potentiality for living a fully awakened life. We are in this sense primordially awakened, always in every moment perceiving reality just as it is. Our task is to recover that state. Notice how Daoist that is. To recover our actual nature and to get rid of the conceptual accretions that hide us.

That's why in this tradition, mindfulness is so important. You remember we emphasized mindfulness when we talked about Śāntideva, that need to kind of guard practice. Zen practice is all about mindfulness, the constant awareness of the nature of our own thought and our own being in every moment. The point is, it's necessary because that's what stops the conceptual superimposition. We can become aware of what we're perceiving. We can become aware of what we're feeling and of what's around us, and in that awareness not be tempted to make the next move and to occlude it from ourselves.

This is hard. It's hard to live with that kind of constant, momentary awareness and that's why Zen recommends and requires such constant meditation and practice. It's a meditation and practice to become aware of reality just as it is. According to Dogen the result of that is the perception of the impermanence of the world, the beauty of the world and the perfection of the world that we already live in, perfection of the mundane world, and that can generate a kind of happiness and an understanding of the meaning of life without a quest for an illusory transcendence.

Awareness therefore has always been available to us. It's always available. A meaningful life, the happy life from the Zen perspective, only requires a transformation of our mind. It only requires the recovery of the perfect mind with which we were born. The echoes of Daoism are tremendous here. But there's also this wonderful synthesis with these deep Buddhist ideas about impermanence and interdependence and the two truths that gives these ideas a deeper conceptual grounding and a more profound grip on our own phenomenology and awareness.

Taking Stock of the Classical World
Lecture 22

Each of these distinctions, each of these debates, finds itself echoed in Asia and in the West, and I'm hoping that's one of the things that's worth learning from comparing all of these texts and putting them together: When human beings ask about the meaning of life, all of the range of alternatives seems to crop up in almost every culture we imagine.

So far in the course, we've examined the classical worlds of India, China, the Hebrews, and Greece. Before we turn to the modern world, we'll take stock of where we are and see what questions remain. Of course, we shouldn't expect a single answer to our central question: What is the meaning of life?

The Bhagavad-Gītā and the book of Job were clearly oriented to finding the meaning of life in our relationship to the divine. Marcus Aurelius, though he didn't focus on divinity, was working in a Stoic tradition, which posits a divine creator, Zeus. Other texts we've looked at, such as those of Aristotle, Confucius, Daoism, and Buddhism, try to find the meaning of life in a mundane context, although Aristotle and Confucius were more concerned with the manifest nature of reality, while Daoism and Buddhism focused on a deeper, fundamental nature of reality.

Some of the texts we've examined, again, the Bhagavad-Gītā, Job, and the texts of Confucius, see the meaning of life as concerned with what is permanent and stable, while other texts find it in connection to the universality and beauty of the ephemeral. Marcus Aurelius directed our attention to the beauty of the aged lion and overripe figs. The Buddha, Śāntideva, and Dōgen also emphasized that everything around us, including ourselves, is conditioned by impermanence and is, in the end, ephemeral.

We saw an emphasis on careful cultivation and socialization in the texts of Aristotle and Confucius. We might also say this of Śāntideva in his exposition of the bodhisattva path and the cultivation of the six perfections. Others have argued that cultivation is precisely the problem and that the meaning of life is to be found in paring away cultivation and returning to our natural selves. We've seen that idea articulated forcefully in the Daodejing, the *Zhuangzi*, and the work of Zen philosophers.

These answers offer us enormous plurality but also a cluster of common dimensions. They all address the central question of the meaning of life in terms of our relationship to some much larger context; they recognize that the question itself is initially posed by our finitude; and they all emphasize the importance of achieving some kind of spontaneity. Let's examine each of these unanimities in turn.

Some of the texts we've examined, again, the Bhagavad-Gītā, Job, and the texts of Confucius, see the meaning of life as concerned with what is permanent and stable, while other texts find it in connection to the universality and beauty of the ephemeral.

In some texts, such as the Bhagavad-Gītā, we find that life gets its meaning through our comprehension of the divinity of the cosmos and ourselves and through our union with the divine cosmos. Job suggests that we understand our lives as meaningful when we accept the incomprehensibility and the transcendence of the divine. Both the Daoists and Confucians argue that the meaningful life is one that is led in harmony with a cosmic order properly understood. The Stoics, too, argue that it's our rationality that enables us to harmonize with the rational divine. But the Stoics share with Aristotle a sense that the social dimension is the larger context, and for the Confucians, of course, social role is everything. The Buddhist context offers a complicated dialectic between the social and the cosmic.

The second area of unanimity is the emphasis on finitude. In the Bhagavad-Gītā, we saw that our finite nature generates attachment to things and makes our lives trivial. Transcending our own suffering requires us to recognize our finitude as the source of the problem. In Job, we saw that coming to grips with our finitude in the context of an infinite universe permits us to lead meaningful lives in a universe that's fundamentally incomprehensible. The Stoics and Epicureans also urged us to come to terms with the fact that we are very small parts in a complex whole. For Buddhism, it's the recognition of our causal and temporal finitude in the context of a vast array of conditioned existence that causes suffering; again, understanding ourselves and our resulting responsibilities as part of a larger whole gives us the possibility of leading a meaningful life.

Finally, we've seen that all these texts emphasize spontaneity, the idea of the good life as the virtuoso life. The Gītā valorizes nonattached action, action that is made possible by recognition of our union with the divine. Aristotle, as we saw, distinguished virtuous action from action that is simply in accordance with virtue. The Confucians emphasized a kind of cultivated spontaneity, while the Daoists valued a natural spontaneity. The Buddhists focus on nonconceptual engagement with the world, as opposed to conceptual engagement.

Thus far, we've seen that the achievement of a virtuoso life requires a confrontation with our own finitude in relation to the vastness of the universe in which we live. It's also notable that the virtuoso life isn't that of a soloist on stage but of an ensemble player, because virtuosity is manifested in the joyful discharge of our social responsibilities. ∎

Study Questions

1. Why is the problem of finitude and death so central to human questions about the meaning of life?

2. What are the reasons for preferring a transcendent to a mundane context or a permanent to an impermanent context for human meaning, or vice versa?

Taking Stock of the Classical World
Lecture 22—Transcript

Hi, nice to be back with you. So far in this course we've been spending most of our time in the classical world. I call it the classical world though it's actually been several classical worlds. We've examined the world of classical India, classical China, the classical Semitic world and the classical Greek world. What comes up next after this lecture will be inhabiting modernity, primarily but not exclusively, European modernity.

As we hit this nice juncture point where we're moving from the classical to the modern, it's probably a good time to take stock and see where we are so far, see what questions remain, and anticipate some of the differences between the texts and the ideas that we've been examining thus far and those that we're going to be examining in the remainder of the course.

The one thing that I want to point out at this point, and this is probably obvious to you, while we promised to ask the question, what is the meaning of life, and to show that it could be asked in a serious, deep, thoughtful, and well-reasoned way, and while I promise that we will see answers—plural—to the question what is it to lead a meaningful life, I never promised you a kind of unanimity or a clear, single answer to that question. Though we've seen many answers, we have not seen a single answer. We have found that so far we have encountered no real unanimity in an approach to understanding the meaning of life.

Some of the texts that we have read have been clearly oriented to finding the meaning of life in our relationship to the divine. Examples of those would be the *Bhagavad-Gīta* where the meaningful life was a life literally lived in union with Krishna, where Krishna was the embodiment of divinity.

Another example of course would be Job where it's our orientation to God and in fact our release of an expectation that God is somehow organizing the universe around us that leads to the possibility of finding meaning in a life which might otherwise be meaningless.

Marcus Aurelius, though he didn't spend a lot of time thinking about divinity, was clearly working in a Stoic tradition, and that's a tradition in which the entire universe is permeated by this kind of divine rationality that comes from its divine creator, Zeus, and where we need to think about the meaning of our lives partly in terms of cultivating the rationality that we share with the divinity and putting aside the passions that would never afflict the divinity.

Even though you might say there's nothing at all in common with the vision of union that we see in the *Bhagavad-Gīta*, the vision of kind of solitude and distance that we find in Job, and the idea of careful emulation that we find in Stoic philosophy, all three of these are unified by thinking that finding the meaning of life requires understanding our orientation with respect to divinity.

Others that we've looked at try to find the meaning of life in a very mundane context. Again, even though we're going to see a difference in orientation here to those that I've just mentioned, we're not going to find unanimity among them. For instance Aristotle argued that a meaningful life, a life of happiness, is a life lived in this kind of careful cultivation of individual virtues in a social context and indeed requires things like friendship, material goods, moral strength, and all of the other kinds of dimensions of eudemonia, of flourishing.

Confucius we saw, in a very different Chinese context, shares with Aristotle the idea that the meaning of life is effectively a mundane idea but focuses primarily on things like ritual and filial piety, propriety, virtue, and our very particular social context, the roles that we play in our societies.

Daoists and Buddhists alike strive to find the meaning of life in a very mundane world, but in each of those cases, that mundane world is understood as interfused with a kind of ultimate reality, the Dao in the case of the Daoists and emptiness—this kind of interdependence in the case of the Buddhists. In each of those cases our orientation is very much to the way ordinary things are, not to some divinity who controls them but rather to a deeper fundamental nature of reality, unlike what we might call the manifest nature of reality that played such an important role for Aristotle and Confucius.

Some of the people who we've examined and the text we've examined see the meaning of life as fundamentally concerned with what is permanent, what is stable, as opposed to what is ephemeral. The *Bhagavad-Gītā* is really clear about that. When Arjuna is admonished by Krishna not to pay attention to things that come and go, not to pay attention to the temporal, but to pay attention to what's permanent, to what's essential in the universe., the divinity is important primarily because of its stability and permanence as opposed to warriors who are born and die and pass away and so forth.

Job advises us to pay attention to what's permanent as well, in this case a very different kind of permanence. But still to let go of what's temporary, to notice that life itself isn't such an important thing, that the important things are the world, the structure of reality in the context of which we lead our lives. Confucius, though you might not have noticed it so much, places a great emphasis on this idea of charm, of heaven, and the respects in which our ordinary social lives, and hence our individual lives, gain their order by being in harmony with this overarching order of the heavens, this overarching order of the universe.

Of course for the Daoists, this whole idea of the way the universe is as opposed to individual ways that we might take up with it plays a very deep and important role. On the other hand, some of the texts that we've examined find the meaning of life not in connection to the permanent but rather specifically in connection to the ephemeral and in an acceptance of the importance of the ephemeral, the universality of ephemerality, and beauty in the context of the ephemeral.

Of course the most obvious examples of that would be Marcus Aurelius who directs our attention to the beauty in the aged lion, the beauty in flowers that are about to fall, the beauty in figs that are overripe, and so forth, but also the Buddhists. We saw that the Buddha himself, Śāntideva, but also Dogen really emphasized that everything around us, everything without exception including ourselves is conditioned by impermanence and is in the end ephemeral. Not just over a long period of time, as say Marcus Aurelius was emphasizing, but moment-to-moment ephemorality that we are constantly changing and that if we are to find meaning in our lives it's to find meaning not in something permanent beyond the impermanent, but to find meaning in the impermanent itself and in its impermanence.

Some of the people who we've read have emphasized careful cultivation and socialization, that we need to work on ourselves, that we are, at best, raw material, raw material that needs to be cultivated, cut, polished, ground, built up, perfected. We see this in Aristotle, who of course sees children as fairly rough material who need to be brought up properly, who need friends and who need parents to cultivate virtue in them, more with practical wisdom, moral strength and so forth.

We certainly see this in Confucius of course, the metaphors are all Confucian. It's social cultivation, the development of propriety, the development of an appreciation for the classics, the development of an understanding of our social roles that makes our lives worth living in the first place. Of course Śāntideva, in his exposition of the bodhisattva path and the cultivation of the six bodhisattva perfections, each of which requires strenuous, arduous work in self perfection with an enormous amount of mindfulness to that, is another example of somebody who believes that finding the meaning of life amounts to a careful construction and cultivation of a higher self.

Others have argued that cultivation is precisely the problem and that the meaning of life is to be found in getting rid of all that cultivation, getting past it, shedding it, paring it away, and returning to nature, to returning to our natural selves. We've seen that articulated very forcefully in the *Daodejing* and in the Zhuangzi, but also in the work of Zen philosophers, particularly Dogen, each of whom argues that it's our social and conceptual accretions that get in the way of our leading a meaningful life. They don't facilitate it.

All of these are dimensions of divergence that we've encountered, and it's also worth recognizing that these dimensions cross cut. There are some people who, for instance, might orient to the divine and the permanent, others to the impermanent. Some might orient to the social and to the transcendent and so forth. These all cross cut but more importantly and more interestingly—and this might have been a surprise to you—there's no clean east/west divide here. It's not as though we say, ah the wisdom traditions of Asia direct us to the transcendent and the permanent, and the kind of pragmatic traditions of the west and focus on the ephemeral and the mundane.

Each of these distinctions, each of these debates, finds itself echoed in Asia and in the west, and I'm hoping that's one of the things that's worth learning from comparing all of these texts and putting them together. When human beings ask about the meaning of life, all of the range of alternatives seem to crop up in almost every culture we imagine. The first thing we notice is this enormous plurality and that it's a messy plurality, there's a lot of thought that is preceded on this question, a lot of answers, and so far at least in the classical world, nothing that could count as unanimity, though plenty of insight to be gleaned.

On the other hand, there are a cluster of common dimensions to the answers that we've seen, and it's worth paying attention not only to the diversity but also to places where we find some consensus. For one thing, as I anticipated at the very beginning of this course, everybody we've encountered who addresses the question what is the meaning of life or how can I lead a meaningful life, addresses that question in terms of our own relationship to some much larger context. That's not surprising. Remember when we talked at the very beginning about the various meanings of the word meaning we saw that what each of the three of them had in common was a reference to something beyond, and so there's no surprise there.

Almost everybody we've examined emphasizes a social dimension to a meaningful life, that somehow, what makes our life meaningful are our relationships to others and our roles in society and our fulfillment of those roles and contributing to the welfare of others, certainly most of them.

Everybody we've examined recognizes that the problem of the meaning of life is initially posed by our finitude. Almost everybody we've examined pays attention to the fact that we are born and die a very short time later. We've seen that in the Gītā with Krishna admonishing Arjuna that the people he confronts and who he's worried about killing are born and they die regardless of what we do, and that lives have to be thought of as meaningful even though finite.

Job reminds us that a human being is born up and cut down and forgotten and this all happens in a flash. Śāntideva really emphasizes this constant life in the jaws of death. All of these people are emphasizing our own finitude and the problem of death. You might not have thought about it before reading these texts, but everybody who worries about finding our lives meaningful and what it is to find a life meaningful argues that you first have to take the problem of death seriously. That we can't understand our lives as meaningful unless we face death and understand the centrality of death to our lives without coming to terms with that reality. There's no way that we can lead an authentic life, no way that we can lead a meaningful life. Some of the folks we've read, especially the Buddhists, argue that it's the very suppression of a taking seriously of our death that leads to the shallowness and the meaninglessness of inauthentic lives.

The other thing that might have been surprising is that almost everybody we've examined, almost every text we've read, has emphasized the importance of achieving spontaneity in some sense. This I've put before as the idea that the good life is the virtuoso life, a life in which we lead a spontaneous, effortless kind of existence, not a studied, calculated existence.

Let's begin with this idea that the larger context is always important. In some texts, like say the *Bhagavad-Gītā*, we find the idea that our life gets its meaning precisely through our comprehension of the divinity of the cosmos, our comprehension of our own divinity and of our union with that kind of divine cosmos. This is a context that's a kind of cosmic context. Job suggests that we understand our lives as meaningful when we accept the incomprehensibility and the transcendence of the divine and the fact that we lead our lives as finite beings in the context of this incomprehensible cosmos.

The Daoists and Confucians also adopt this cosmic sense of context in very different ways, one through positive cultivation, one through pairing away. Each argues that the meaningful life is one that is led in harmony with a cosmic order properly understood. The stoics too argued that it's our rationality that enables us to harmonize with the rational divine, with the rational cosmic order. In all of these traditions we find a kind of cosmic dimension as essential to making sense of our lives.

Other traditions also emphasize a social dimension as the larger context that's important to the meaning of life. Aristotle argued that the virtuous life is the life of a citizen, and when Aristotle examines his virtues they are virtues like generosity, friendliness, courage, magnanimity and so forth that are all virtues that are manifested in a social context, virtues that are cultivated in social context, virtues of friendship that involve connection to those who share our social context.

For Aristotle the context that makes life meaningful, that makes happiness possible, the context that makes it possible for a human being to flourish in the full sense, it's not a cosmic context, it's a social context. It's the context of the Polis. The Stoics of course shared this sense of the social role as the important role in determining the meaning of life. We saw so much emphasis in Seneca and in Marcus Aurelius on the development of kindness, patience, good interpersonal relations, and a sense of what we owe to others as what makes our lives meaningful, and Marcus Aurelius in his meditations is so eloquent about that.

For the Confucians of course, social role is everything. I mean the mandate of heaven is important and we've stressed that, but when we pay attention to the details it's the family, it's filial piety, it's warm heartedness and humanness, these two twin virtues of ren and li, of warm heartedness and propriety, each of which is manifested in concrete social relations. Each of which is particular to the social relations in which a particular individual follows. For all of these it's the social context that provides the larger context.

Buddhism gives us a slightly different vision of course. For Buddhism the context in which our lives become meaningful is the context of samsāra, a world that we share of suffering and a world that's constituted by these three levels of suffering, the suffering of ordinary pain, the suffering of change, and the suffering of pervasive conditioning. That is both social and cosmic. The problem is set by this ubiquity of suffering and it's both set further by the fact that we're so totally interdependent. The solution is found in the problem itself. The insight into interdependence gives us the possibility of the development of compassion, and that forces us to think of ourselves as having a role and a commitment and a responsibility to the universe as a whole. So we get this very complicated dialectic between the social and the cosmic in Buddhism.

The second big area of unanimity that we examine, which again has its diversity within it is this emphasis on the importance of finitude. In the *Bhagavad-Gītā* we saw that it's our finite nature, it's our limitedness that generates the kinds of attachment on the kinds of relationship to things that come and go to not killing our relatives, for instance, if you want a nice example, that makes our lives trivial.

The desires and the aversions that we need to transcend in order to achieve unity with the divine, transcending these sources of our own suffering and confusion requires us to recognize our finitude as the source of the problem and to transcend it in a kind of an infinite unity with the cosmos itself.

In Job we saw that it's our inability to understand the universe that causes this kind of experience of the world as simply awful, but a coming to grips with our finitude in the context of an infinite universe that allows us the kind of acceptance that permits us to lead a meaningful life in a universe that's fundamentally incomprehensible. In either case the problem is set by the recognition of our finitude in the context of an infinite reality, in this case an infinite divinity, and in fact an infinitively incomprehensible divinity.

The Stoics and the Epicureans saw the whole problem with the meaning of life as faced by our recognition of the fact that when we examine the universe it is temporally infinite in the past, temporally infinite in the future, spatially infinite, at least for all practical purposes, and that we constitute such a tiny piece of the whole. The solution to the question of the meaning of life for the Stoics and the Epicureans alike consists in coming to terms with that fact. With the fact that we are really very small in the whole, and the coming to terms involves understanding the relationship that even a very small part has to a very complex whole.

Finally Buddhism frames the whole problem of suffering in terms of our own impermanence and subject to external causes and conditions and the inevitability of our death with all of the anxiety that that brings in train. For Buddhism it's the recognition of our causal and temporal finitude in the context of this vast array of conditioned existence that causes suffering and an understanding of why that involves us as being a part of a larger whole and the responsibilities that implicates that gives us the possibility of leading a meaningful life in that context.

Spontaneity, this may have been the surprise that there's so much emphasis on spontaneity in these texts. The Gītā as we've seen, valorizes non-attached action, action that is made possible by recognition of our union with the divine. As Krishna says to Arjuna, don't worry about the consequences, don't think, just act. Pick up that bow and fight. This is a kind of spontaneity that arises as a consequence in the Gītā of the cultivation of these three yogas. It's an achieved spontaneity. We don't get the spontaneity without cultivating the yoga of action, Karma yoga, the yoga of knowledge, jñana yoga, and the yoga of devotion, Bhakti yoga. The whole point of that assiduous cultivation is to free ourselves from the immediate impact of desires, attractions and aversions and to allow us to act freely, that is spontaneously, with no attachment to the consequences of our actions. So spontaneity emerges in the Gītā very quickly.

Spontaneity also plays a big role in Aristotle because as we saw for Aristotle, when we want to distinguish virtuous action from action which may be simply in accordance with virtue, the distinction is drawn on the basis of this fact, virtuous action is chosen for its own sake out of our character, something that gives us pleasure, something we just want to do.

The Confucians really emphasized the importance of the cultivation of spontaneity. We saw all of the Aristotelian affinities, but with a lot more emphasis than Aristotle on the cultivation of spontaneity in this kind of very refined, polished, eloquent propriety and etiquette. The Daoists also valued spontaneity for all that they disagreed with the Confucians. It's just that they valued a natural spontaneity, not a cultivated spontaneity. They were deeply suspicious of the Confucian view of what spontaneity amounted to. But they agreed with the Confucians completely that the meaningful life is a spontaneous virtuoso life.

Though we didn't emphasize this as much, for the Buddhists there's an important sense of spontaneity as well, and that comes from the emphasis on non-conceptual engagement with the world as opposed to conceptual engagement. As we saw, especially in the Zen tradition, conceptuality is distrusted, distrusted for some of the same reasons that the Daoists distrust it, but also because conceptuality always involves engagement with what's not real, whereas perception brings us into contact with reality, including the reality of our own nature.

When we stop superimposing all of the conceptual stuff, all the linguistic stuff, we are able to act in response to perception. To simply react as it were naturally as opposed to studiedly. We have an element of spontaneity that's important in the meaningful life as well; so much for these kinds of general, broad kinds of agreement.

There's something else that I hope that you've learned as we've taken this tour through the classical world and that is something about literary style and reading. Not every lecture that we've had together has been a textual lecture, but many of them have been, and in those textural lectures I've been very concerned to read with you, as I read in my office with my students on the campuses where I teach. In doing that, what we've been doing together is examining texts and talking about how to extract meaning from it. We've seen texts of various kinds. We've seen epic poetry as in the Gītā. We've seen philosophical poetry as in Job and in Śāntideva's *Bodhicāryāvatāra*. We've seen this intensely first-person meditational journal writing of Marcus Aurelius, amusing parables in *Zhuangzi* and very careful analytical writing that really sets out the arguments in ferocious gory detail in Aristotle, then in a very different, slightly metaphorical way in the *Daodejing*.

What I've been trying to emphasize with you is that each of these styles of writing requires its own style of reading and reflection. Sometimes our task is to get beyond the metaphor, to get beyond the clever story, to get beyond the image, and to reconstruct the argument that lies behind the text but is not articulated in the text. Sometimes the task is to read the carefully-articulated argument that focuses so much on detail and then to extrapolate the big picture that makes sense of that argument and that makes it important.

If you keep reading philosophically in the future, it's really important to develop these skills. It's really important to know what kind of text one is picking up, how to read it, and to not be satisfied with the ink marks on the page but to really pay attention to the interpretative task that we are called upon to perform when we engage with a text of somebody who is long dead and communicating to us only through these marks on a page.

I hope that this is a useful phenomenon for you because we're going to continue doing it as we approach modernity in the next few lectures. There is a broad unity in this diversity. There's a broad consensus among all of the people that we've read, however much there is disagreement. If the meaningful life is the virtuoso life and that is a life that is to be achieved through both contemplation and practice, that achievement in turn requires a confrontation with our own finitude and limitation, our own smallness and the vastness of the universe in which we live.

If we are able to take our finitude seriously and to really get a grasp of the fundamental nature of the universe and to settle that in through cultivation, through meditation, through contemplation, even though it may take effort, that effortless virtuosity of action is a possibility, is a goal, is what makes our lives worth living. It's also worth seeing that we have this kind of agreement—at least a broad agreement that this virtuoso life to which we aspire as human beings isn't the life of a soloists on stage, but it's the life of an ensemble player, because the virtuosity we aim to cultivate is a virtuosity in interaction, in social roles, and it's manifested in the effortless and joyful discharge of our social responsibilities.

What follows? We are going to be turning from the ancient to the modern world. One of the things that you may not have noticed so much in the ancient world, but to which I now want to call your attention, is that we've often been looking at ancient traditions, the Aristotelian tradition, the Buddhist tradition, the Daoist tradition, the Confucian tradition, the Hindu tradition, and so forth. So we've been thinking in terms of these very large, social and philosophical movements even though we've been choosing individual representatives and texts.

When we hit modernity things are going to be different. We're going to see much more of an emphasis on individuality, free thinking, breaking free of tradition as opposed to following tradition. Modernity is going to involve a systematic engagement of thought with the new sciences that arise beginning in the 16th and 17th centuries and with the democratic political ideals, the respect for individual rights, for individual obligations, and for the need for individuals to develop their own potential in the context of societies. We're going to see a lot of these ideas of democracy, rationality, science, and a rejection of tradition developed in modernity. But at the same time we are going to see all of these rejections, all of these emphases on individuality manifested by taking up in creative new ways and transforming the ideas that emerge from the classical world, both Asian and western.

In our next lecture we're going to begin to look at the modernist ideas of David Hume, and we're going to see Aristotelian ideas and sometimes stoic and skeptic ideas brought into dialogue with science and democracy. Please join me for this tremendous revolution in our thinking that's about to begin.

Hume's Skepticism and the Place of God
Lecture 23

Like Job, Hume is saying, God may not be accessible to reason, but the fact that he's not accessible to reason need not matter to us. We can choose to have a theological life and a relationship to religion if we want. We can choose not to if we want, but we don't need to provide arguments or reasons, like Job's friends, in order to make our religious lives make sense.

As we move from the classical world to the modern European world, we note a major transition in modes of thought. In Europe in the 17th and 18th centuries, the rise of science and the scientific method led to skepticism about the value of tradition, an emphasis on individuality and free thinking, and the gradual evolution of secularism.

European modernity is grounded in a divide between science and religion that can be traced to the Catholic Church's persecution of Galileo after his establishment of the heliocentric model of the universe. As a result, philosophy and political science began to push the church aside as either irrelevant or hostile to the progress of social, scientific, and political thinking. The break between reason and faith also forced an emphasis on the primacy of the individual and the rise of rights. The doctrine of **foundationalism** emerged, the idea that we know things because of our observations in the laboratory or by reasoning, not through scripture. Classical Greek skepticism also played an important role in the emergence of the scientific method and the critique of religion that animated early European modernity.

God found himself in a precarious spot with the development of European modernity and its rejection of theology as a foundation for knowledge. In persecuting Galileo, the church realized that science was asserting its own authority as the measure of reality, which meant that it was undermining the authority of the church. With the new skeptical approach of science, the existence of God required proof.

David Hume was one of the thinkers who was most instrumental in reviving classical skepticism. Like the classical skeptics, he used reason to attack the pretensions of reason, to show that reason itself is self-undermining. Hume also introduced the idea of naturalism to philosophy, arguing that if we want to know what human life is about, we need to subject ourselves to the methods of science. Hume further recognized that we are not entirely rational beings; just as important as our reason are our emotions and our imagination.

Among the proofs put forth for the existence of God was the argument from design, which Hume refuted decisively. According to this argument, the fact that the universe is replete with complex, perfectly functioning phenomena means that it must have been created by an intelligent designer. If you find a working watch on a beach, you don't assume that it developed organically out of the sand; you assume that it was the work of an intelligent designer.

In the 17th and 18th centuries, Europe began focusing more on the individual than on the context in which individuals led their lives; individualism emerged as an important hallmark of European modernity.

Hume pointed out that this argument is nonprobative; that is, it doesn't prove its conclusion. For one thing, most artifacts are small, while universes are huge, and when there are significant differences between phenomena, arguments from analogy do not work. Moreover, arguments from analogy gain strength from many instances, but the design of the universe is a unique case. According to Hume, we also know that certain complex things in our world, such as animals and plants, grow naturally through biological reproduction. If we want to argue that the world must be created in the same way that these complex organisms are, we should expect that the world grows by organic biological development, not through intelligent design.

Hume further argued that if the world was designed, it wasn't, in fact, all that well designed. Think of all the things that go wrong in nature—floods, earthquakes—and with the human body. Finally, the assumption of design leads to an assumption that the design was carried out by designers with which we are familiar: architects, engineers, and other mortal, finite human beings. If the world was designed, we can conclude that it was probably designed by a committee of rather unintelligent mortals.

Hume also pointed out that the proponents of the design argument seem to agree with atheists that belief in the existence of God should be based on reason. Hume argued that many of our most important beliefs, such as beliefs in the external world or the regularity of nature, aren't rational but instinctual and emotional. In other words, our instincts and our passions lead us to beliefs and practices that are reasonable. It is, thus, part of our nature to trust our senses and to trust reason. Theism may not be susceptible to proof either, but it doesn't follow that theism is unreasonable; it might not even demand proof. If that's the case, then faith should be relegated to the realm of the private sphere, while we leave what is rationally judicable in the public sphere. ■

Name to Know

Hume, David (1711–1776): David Hume was a philosophical prodigy and a central figure of the Scottish Enlightenment.

Important Term

foundationalism: The doctrine that knowledge must rest on a basis. Examples of foundations of knowledge are perception and reason.

Suggested Reading

Coventry, *Hume: A Guide for the Perplexed.*

Hume, *Dialogues Concerning Natural Religion.*

Study Questions

1. What are the central pillars of European modernity? How are they related to one another?

2. Why is the argument from design such a modern argument for the existence of God? How does Hume show it to be a failure? What are the consequences of his critique for Christianity?

Hume's Skepticism and the Place of God
Lecture 23—Transcript

It is my great pleasure to welcome you to the modern world. We ordinarily date the onset of European modernity some time around the 17th century. We'll in fact be picking up with modernity in the 18th century with the work of David Hume.

When we make this transition from the classical world to the modern world we're not just making a transition in time, it's not just that the text that we'll be reading and the people whose views we'll be discussing are nearer to us in time than those we've been heretofore considering. Rather we're going to be looking at a major transition in modes of thought. As we saw in the classical world, we tended to be thinking about the meaning of life in terms of these big, social contexts, and the texts themselves seem to be arrayed in terms of schools of thought.

In modernity things are going to be different. For one thing modernity—especially European modernity—is very much conditioned by the rise of science. The rise of science and the scientific method leads to a skepticism about the importance and the value of tradition. That's going to be important because we'll see an emphasis on individuality and free thinking in modernity that we didn't encounter so much in the classical tradition. Even though some of the skeptical arguments that will animate modernity come from a classical tradition, they will be deployed in very different ways. I emphasize again because we sometimes get that confused in this area of globalization that modernity is a culturally-specific phenomenon. European modernity, Asian modernity, African modernities—may be very different kinds of modernity. We are going to be focusing specifically on European modernity right now which emerges as science develops on the European continent in the 17th and 18th centuries and as movements for liberal democracy take route.

In the classical world we saw an emphasis when we talked about human life and the meaning of human life on the social and transcendent dimensions of our lives. That is, the dimensions of our lives that are led in relationship to our cultures and societies or to some transcendent god or to the universe. In modernity that emphasis is going to change and we'll be focusing instead very much on immanent issues but more importantly focusing more on the individual than on the context in which individuals lead their lives, and individualism will emerge as an important hallmark of European modernity.

We're picking our discussion up with the work of David Hume, and we're going to track development of modern ideas from David Hume to Immanuel Kant to John Stuart Mill. As we do that we are going to see a gradual evolution of an idea that underlies most contemporary forms of liberal democracy in Europe, the United States, and many other parts of the world. That is a secularism. The conviction that there's a separation between religious views and public views, and that the public order should not be responsive to a religious order.

We'll be watching the evolution of individualism, the idea that the individual is the fundamental unit of analysis, and that individual rights, individual liberties and individual obligations are paramount duties of a society to respect and to foster. We will be examining the evolution of the strong public private distinction that, for instance, animates much of contemporary American culture and political life. The idea that there's a rigid divide between what is in the public domain and available to others and what happens behind closed doors in private.

We're going to see that public/private distinction introduced by David Hume, but we're going to see that in Hume's thought the understanding of our nature as individuals is still developed in terms of our social contexts. What Hume does do that gets this discussion of publicity and privacy going is that he tosses out this emphasis on the transcendent dimensions of human life in favor of understanding our lives exclusively in terms of our relationships to immanent phenomenon.

Kant is going to reinforce this public/private distinction, and in Kant we're going to get the introduction of the importance of the liberty of thought and the liberty of speech. Kant will really emphasize for the first time in European thought and in human thought really, the importance of autonomy and reason as hallmarks of humanity, and it's the Kantian emphasis on autonomy and reason that become the hallmarks of modernity from a political perspective, those people recognized very much as underpinnings of a lot of our contemporary society.

John Stuart Mill, as we will see, follows Kant in this emphasis on individual liberty and individual freedom. But Mill develops a far more articulated expression and a far more nuanced expression of the view that our lives and the lives of all of those around us are only meaningful to the extent that we are self expressive, creative, free individuals, and that the only good society is a society which not only permits this kind of self expression and freedom, but which encourages it and really draws a clear distinction between the public and the private.

In modernity, as we're going to see, the meaningful life is still a life connected to a social order. But the social order is very different from any social order imagined in any of the antiquities that we've imagined. It's a liberal social order, an individualistic social order. A social order in which the society is constituted by the mutual interaction of individually free distinct individuals who come together to form a society rather than a preexisting society that creates and constructs its individuals.

Today we're going to begin by characterizing in a bit more detail the nature of European modernity. Because without understanding the nature of that modernity and the ideological and social forces that drive it, it's very hard to understand how we conceptualize meaningful life in the modern context.

We'll talk a little bit about the role of skepticism in the underpinnings of European modernity and what happens to the role of God in human life as modernity takes hold. We will emphasize Hume's very unique position in the European enlightenment and in particular Hume's attack on the traditional role of God as playing a place in the domain of reason and in the public sphere. And Hume's introduction of the idea that belief might be reasonable even if it's not rational, which offers us the beginnings of the underpinning of the private sphere.

We begin by talking about the structure of European modernity itself. European modernity is grounded in a divide between science and religion that we can trace very specifically to the Galileo affair. When Galileo really established the heliocentric model of the universe, the idea that the planets revolve around the sun instead of the sun and the planets and the fixed stars revolving around the Earth, he was of course persecuted by the Catholic church for a view that was contrary to church dogma.

When Galileo was persecuted, it was clear to philosophy as a field that it had to make a choice. Philosophy could cast its lot with science and Galileo, or with the church. Fortunately, philosophy made the right choice and threw its lot in with science and Galileo. So philosophical thinking and political thinking, starting with the Galileo affair, pretty much pushed the church aside as either irrelevant or hostile to the progress of social, scientific, and political thinking. That divorce shapes the relationship between philosophy and religion, and the public and the private spheres ever since Galileo.

What that does is it constructs reason and faith, not as supporting one another as they did in the middle ages and in antiquity, but rather as opposing forces, that faith runs contrary to reason and reason often takes itself in directions that faith can never countenance.

The other piece of this is that it forced an emphasis on the primacy of the individual and the rise of rights. Galileo thought individually. Galileo thought freely, and Galileo and others like him developed the new science that made prosperity, commerce, and politics possible in the modern era. For that reason this kind of emphasis on individuality became a very important aspect in European modernity. Another less often appreciated feature of European modernity is this emphasis on the self, the individual who's now going to become this free locus of value as a unified subject and transparent to itself, that we actually know ourselves and our views. We don't need to be told what we think from outside, or what we ought to think, but that we are autonomous in that sense.

Furthermore, a kind of foundationalism. The foundationalism is a theory about knowledge. The idea here is that what we know we know because of our observations in the laboratory or by reasoning. In particular it is not a foundationalism in scripture. What we know is under our own control. All of this allows for us to valorize an ideal of progress as opposed to a return to the source. Classically we think of knowledge as the exegesis of sacred or otherwise authoritative classical texts, and we think of knowledge as developing by a successively better understanding of those original ideas. In modernity we think of knowledge as arising through progress. Through leaving old ideas behind and developing new ideas as research takes us.

One surprising thing though about the history of European modernity is that it owes a certain amount of its genesis to the revival of a very classical idea, and that was the Greek idea of skepticism, especially the Peronian skepticism that was articulated so completely by the 1st or 2nd century philosopher, Sextus Empiricus. What the Greek skeptics emphasized in their critique of earlier Greek ideas was a rejection of authority as a basis of knowledge, a commitment to reason and to questioning receive knowledge, to the primacy of our own experience in our cognitive lives, and always attempt to undermine or to demand justification for claims that are made, not taking anything on faith.

This skepticism played an important methodological role in the scientific method and in the critique of religion that animated early European modernity. Skepticism in science required questioning received dogma, worrying about data, repeating experiments, demanding justification, and skepticism in the critique of religion required asking do we really have reasons to believe the truth of these scriptures or the truth of these teachings, and if not, what do we do about them? This revival of skeptical skepticism, while it appeared to be the revival of one more ancient tradition, in fact was one of the sparks that generated the success of science and the attack on religion that allowed modernity to get a foothold in Europe.

God hence, found himself in a precarious spot as European modernity developed. Modernism rejects the theological as a foundation for knowledge and rejects the bible and religious scripture as authority. For that reason the very existence of God or at least the importance of God was held to be threatened by science. The church in one sense was right to persecute Galileo, because while you might not think that it's such a big thing to have an alternative model of the solar system, what hangs on that for religion? Why is it so important that we have a heliocentric versus a geocentric model of a solar system? That doesn't seem to be deep theology.

What's deep theology is who gets to say though. What the church realized in Galileo's work was that science was asserting its own authority as the measure of reality, and the assertion of authority by science meant the undermining of the authority of the church as a measure of reality. For that reason, as I said, God is now somehow problematic, no longer something that could be taken for granted, because in this new skeptical approach nothing can be taken for granted. For that reason, God becomes an object who needs proof. His existence requires proof. Reason is getting an upper hand here but this atheism—the possibility of atheism, raises anxiety. It raises anxiety in the church and it raises anxiety in the public.

For that reason, in the early modern period a kind of small cottage industry develops of articulating proofs for the existence of God. Among the proofs for the existence of God that were developed during this period, or that actually we should say that became popular during this period because they have much older roots. The argument from design became the most popular, and the argument from design was the most popular because it looked like a scientific argument. It looks like an argument that begins by marshalling evidence, arguing from analogy, and giving us a kind of argument to the best explanation. The arguments from design move to a kind of center stage, among those who wanted to defend the existence and importance of God in the modern period.

Hume is the person who effectively demolishes that argument. Hume was born in about 1711 and died in 1776. He was a skeptic and was one of the people who was most instrumental in reviving classical skepticism. He was also an atheist even though he did not publish any of his explicitly atheistic texts during his lifetime. Because of suspicion of his atheism, he was always a kind of outsider to academia. He attempted to secure a university post but was ruled ineligible because his faith was not sufficiently secure. Nonetheless, Hume had a very active public life. He was a diplomat, a representative of the Court of St. James in Paris. He was a very influential historian, and his history of the kings of England was a definitive history for years and years after his death.

Hume, like the classical skeptics, liked to use reason to attack the pretensions of reason, to show that reason itself was self-undermining and forces us to ask very hard questions. Most importantly, I think, it was Hume who introduced the idea of naturalism to philosophy. This is really important for us who are thinking about the meaning of life. It was Hume who argued that if we want to know what human life is about, if we want to know what we are, we really need to subject ourselves to the methods of science, and that the problem of understanding life and the importance of life is a subpart of the science of human nature. If we understand what kind of beings we are, Hume argued, then we can understand what's good for us. Hume devoted most of his life to understanding what he called human nature, a kind of proto-psychologist.

In part of this enterprise, Hume recognized that we are not entirely rational beings. However much we might pretend, say as an Aristotelian would think, that what's distinctive about us is our reason. Hume argued that every bit as important as our reason, maybe more important, are our passions—that is our emotional lives—and our imagination. It's central to Hume's thinking that a meaningful and a good human life is a life in which the passions and the imagination have a central role as well as reason.

The question is now how did Hume succeed so dramatically in vanishing God from the domain of reason and making this massive move to distinguish the private sphere of religion from the public sphere of political life and rational debate? He did it, as I said, by refuting the argument from design and refuting it decisively.

How does the argument from design go? Well in brief it's like this: We look at the universe and it's full of very complex phenomenon that just seem designed perfectly to fulfill their functions. For instance, if we look at our eyes, they're so well designed for seeing things. Our ears are so well designed for hearing things, our legs are really good at walking, and if you look around the universe you see all these things that fulfill their functions really well—remember we're long before Darwin right now.

Normally, the proponent of the argument of design continues, when we see a complex object designed perfectly to fulfill a function, we assume that it was created by an intelligent designer. The classic arguments that you always see and that Hume quotes in his own dialogues on natural religion, if you're walking down a beach and you run across a watch and you pick it up and it's ticking and it's working and it tells time beautifully and it tells the day of the week and so forth, you don't assume that the watch developed naturally as an organic object out of sand. You assume that because it's so intricate and so well-designed for a particular function that it was designed by an intelligent designer. So, the argument concludes, since so many things in the universe, and indeed if we get rhapsodic enough, we say the universe as a whole seems so intricate, its parts fit so well together it must have been designed by an intelligent designer.

Notice that this argument becomes really important in the context of modernity. It looks like the last bull work against atheism. It keeps God in the picture, and if you thought that what makes a human life significant and important is a relationship to God and you also think that science is a really good thing and you don't want to go the way of a church and persecute Galileo, you want to allow science to continue, then you want some way of using science to defend the existence of God and the argument from design looks tailor-made for the purpose.

Hume, nonetheless, demolishes it. Hume points out several things. First, he says, it is seriously non-probative. That is it does not get its conclusion. For one thing, he points out, there are big disanalogies between universes and artifacts. We've noticed that. Most artifacts we've seen them get designed, they're relatively small. They're relatively temporary. Worlds are big. We've never seen them get designed and, Hume points out, that when you get big differences between phenomena, arguments from analogy no longer work. His analogy is very nice. He says, look if I see a sheep and I notice that its heart pumps its blood, and I look at a dog and notice that its blood is circulating, I infer that there must be a heart because dogs and sheep are relatively similar.

But if I were to look at a tree and see that its sap circulates and conclude on the analogy of the mammal that the tree must have a heart, then I argue fallaciously, because the disanalogies between animals and trees are sufficient that an argument from analogy won't go through. Similarly Hume points out there's an even greater disanalogy between the artifacts we observe and whole universes, so that argument doesn't get any purchase.

Moreover, Hume says, when you get arguments by analogy like this, inductive arguments going, they gain their strength from many instances. It's not just that sheep and dogs have hearts, but cats have hearts and cows have hearts and wolves have hearts and so forth. So you need many instances to make the arguments look good. But, Hume asks the proponent of the arguments from design, how many worlds have you seen created? How many worlds have you seen designed? It's not as though we have a kind of inductive argument that says, oh that world was designed, that world was designed, that world was designed, so this world must be designed. We have a unique case and arguments for analogy don't work in such cases.

Moreover Hume points out, if we like the analogy, it's really not a very good one for the argument from design. Because if we look at really complex things that we know and love in our world, the most complex things, the things we can't even create like animals or vegetables or plants or flowers, they grow naturally through biological reproduction. If the argument is that the world as a whole must be created in the same way that these complex organs and animals are, we should expect that the world is not designed by an intelligent creator, but that it grows by organic biological development; and that doesn't prove that there is a god, that seems to prove that there isn't one.

That's a problem. So for these reasons, Hume argued, the argument from design doesn't get its conclusion, but he went further. He argued that the argument from design if it proves anything proves way too much. Why is that? Well, if you look at the world, maybe it's designed but it's not all that well designed. Think about how many people you know who have needed knee replacements or hip replacements or who have been born with disabilities. Think about all of the floods and earthquakes and things that go wrong. If the world was designed, Hume points out, it seems to have been designed maybe as a rough draft, maybe the rude essay of an infant deity. It seems to have been designed by an amateur god, not a god we'd actually want to worship or care about.

Moreover, Hume points out, suppose it is design. What do we know about really complex things that are designed: bridges, airplanes, cities—Hume of course didn't mention airplanes, I'm mentioning airplanes they weren't around yet. Most of them aren't designed by a single designer, but by a committee. So if the world is really as complex as the proponent of the argument suggests, we ought to conclude that it was designed not by a single, dumb god, but by a committee of dumb gods, which is not what the theist wants after all.

Finally, Hume points out, if we also think that it was designed, then if we think that the world was designed because it's similar to other artifacts we've seen designed, then we ought to think that its designer is similar to the designers with which we are familiar. But who are the designers with which you're familiar: architects, engineers, landscape designers and so forth. They are all mortal, finite, deficient human beings. We should conclude that if there's somebody who designed the universe, A, there's a bunch of them working together, B, they are mortal, finite and deficient, and C they're rather dumb.

It doesn't appear, Hume thinks, that the argument from design is anything we can rest on. Of course that's problematic because if we thought that in the context of science the only argument that was going to convince us that there really is a god is this argument from design—that is a scientific argument, we seem to be bereft. Notice this isn't peculiar to the 17th and 18th century because right now when we examine people who still try to prove that God exists in the context of science, the so-called fine tuning argument which is just a rehash of the argument from design is the most common argument charted out to try to prove the existence of God, always, we think, we don't want to go outside of science. We, as modernists, accept the authority of science and hope that it itself will give us God, and what Hume showed was there's not much of a possibility.

But, Hume pointed out, there's a twist. There is something very deep that we can learn from the argument from design and from its failure and from the drive to prove the existence of God. It's this twist that really forms the foundation for so much of our ideology of modernity, even though many people don't notice this. Hume points out that the proponent of the argument from design, as I've said several times, supposes that reason is the only reasonable basis for belief. That is, the proponent of the argument seems to agree with the atheist that we should only believe that God exists if we've got good reason to do so. The only difference is the atheist thinks there isn't any and the proponent of the argument from design falsely thinks there is.

Hume argues that many of our most important beliefs, the beliefs that really animate our lives and make it possible for us to lead lives in the first place, and as we'll see next time he includes among these beliefs in the external world, beliefs in the regularity of nature, even the belief in the utility of reason itself, aren't rational themselves. They're not based on reason. Let's think about that for a moment. If somebody actually questioned the existence of the external world and it was your job to convince this mad person that the world outside of themselves really does exist, how could you do it? You couldn't do it using reason. Why is that? You'd have to marshal some evidence, and any evidence you provided for the existence of the external world is going to be denied by the person you're trying to convince because she doesn't believe that there is any evidence in the first place.

Suppose you were trying to prove to somebody that reason is a rational thing to use. Remember, she is denying that reason is rational. What kind of reasons could you possibly mobilize to convince her? There would be none at all because any would simply beg the question. Hume points out that wherever our faith comes from, and it's a real faith and you notice it every time that you reach out for something, every time you take a step, every time you speak to somebody else, our faith in the existence of the world beyond ourselves, our faith in the regularity of nature that the sun is going to rise in the east and set in the west tomorrow just like it always has, rather than reverse those two. Again what's your reason for believing that?

He argues that all of these are based in our instincts, in our passions, in our emotional life, and in our conventions. For that reason, he argues, they're not unreasonable. That it is simply reasonable for us to pay attention to and to heed our own nature. It's part of our own nature to trust our senses. It's part of our own nature to trust reason. It's part of our own nature to interact with each other. So Hume argues that our passions and our conventions may lead us to beliefs and to practices that are totally reasonable. These are important parts of ourselves, even if not rational.

Maybe like that for theism Hume pointed out. Theism, Hume argued, may not be susceptible of proof—that's right—the argument from design doesn't work, but it doesn't follow from that that it's unreasonable because theism, he argued, might not even demand proof. Theism might be one of those things that's an option for you. I mean for instance, suppose you tell me that you love chocolate ice cream and I love vanilla ice cream. You don't need to prove to me that chocolate ice cream is good in order to eat it. I don't need to prove to you that vanilla ice cream is good in order to eat it. Such things aren't demanding of proof, which is good because they're not susceptible of proof. It's still reasonable for you to eat chocolate ice cream, reasonable for me to eat vanilla ice cream, even though neither of us can provide arguments justifying our taste to the other.

So, Hume pointed out, theism might be reasonable, but not rational. If theism is reasonable and not rational, then religion, faith and maybe a whole host of other things can be relegated to the realm of the private sphere, areas of private choice, things about which reasonable people might disagree, but about which they don't need to argue. Whereas we can leave what is rationally judicable in the public's sphere, things that we can actually talk about, reason about, and that way we can begin to construct our public lives in a way that allows us to find one kind of meaning in one sphere and a different kind of meaning in another.

Notice that this is a kind of curious, Jobian twist on modernity. This is one of the reasons I love Hume so much. He's always slightly different from everybody else. That is, like Job, Hume is saying, God may not be accessible to reason, but the fact that he's not accessible to reason need not matter to us. We can choose to have a theological life and a relationship to religion if we want. We can choose not to if we want, but we don't need to provide arguments or reasons like Job's friends in order to make our religious live make sense.

Here we begin to introduce this fundamental idea that animates so much of our lives today and so much of how we think about what it is to lead a good life, this distinction between the public and the private. Of course if we lead a life without God, and a life where reason isn't self-justifying, we still need to ask a question. How does that life make sense? What's significant about it? How can we make our lives appear meaningful after faith in God ceases to be the object of reason? That's the big project for European Modernity. That's the project that Hume begins to take up and that Kant and Mill inherit from him, and it's that project to which we're going to turn in our next lecture, examining where Hume goes from here, and there we're going to get textual again looking at Hume's own words. Please join me for that discussion.

Hume's Careless and Compassionate Vision
Lecture 24

> **Hume is pointing out that we are justified in our beliefs, even if we can't provide reasons for them, because we are the kinds of beings who participate in those kinds of lives.**

In the last lecture, we saw Hume argue that neither reason nor the senses can possibly be justified on their own or give us confidence in the things we take most for granted—the existence of the external world, causal connections, or the probative character of reason itself. But Hume points out that behavior, thinking, and discourse can be reasonable even if they are not rationally justified. In fact, it's not our reason or our sensory experiences that ground most of human life but certain biological and psychological dispositions—dispositions to believe in the external world, in causal connections, and so on. In *The Treatise of Human Nature*, Hume writes, "Nature, by an obstinate and uncontrollable necessity, has determin'd us to judge as well as to breathe and feel." We don't need reasons to believe in reason, the external world, or even God; these are things that simply emerge from the kind of animals that we are.

For Hume, our social relations and our social context are important to who we are because genuine happiness comes from our relationships to others and because a functioning society provides us with the external goods we need. At the same time, many of our deepest values and important traits are social in nature. Everything that gives our lives meaning, according to Hume's secular account, is social or socially constructed.

Both original nature and second nature are important to Hume in understanding who we are and how we live. We're equipped from birth with natural passions, such as a natural affection for our parents. Hume had the idea that natural affection, like Isaac Newton's gravitation, is a force of attraction and obeys a sort of inverse-square law; that is, the closer a person is to us, the more we naturally tend to like that person. However, Hume believed that if human society was governed completely by natural attraction, the result would be tightly knit bands of people devoted to each other and hostile or indifferent to everyone else. Obviously, this is no way to create a flourishing society.

Fortunately, Hume thinks that we are also born with a propensity to use our imagination. This allows us to see distinct things as similar to one another, and it is from this ability that justice and charity arise, the passions we need to stitch society together. Justice and charity are artificial in one sense—we construct them—but they're natural in that it is part of human nature to act in such a way as to cultivate them. In this sense, they constitute a second nature. Our primary nature can be found in our innate emotions and imagination, but the product of the imagination is the construction of the second nature, the emotions that hold society together.

Our primary nature can be found in our innate emotions and imagination, but the product of the imagination is the construction of the second nature, the emotions that hold society together.

According to Hume, even an injustice that doesn't affect us displeases us because "we consider it prejudicial to human society ... [and] we naturally *sympathize* with others in the sentiments they entertain of us. Thus self-interest is the original motive for the establishment of justice, but a sympathy with public interest is the source of the moral approbation which attends that virtue." It's in our own interests to extend our natural sympathies in order to construct stable societies that afford us goods. The moral approbation comes from the fact that we sympathize with public interest, because public interest is our own interest. These natural sentiments are extended into the public sphere, "but still nature must furnish the materials. ..." Parents, too, play a role in inculcating these kinds of sensibilities in their children.

On the question of naturalness, Hume says, "When I deny justice to be a natural virtue, I make use of the word *natural* only as oppos'd to *artificial* ... Mankind is an inventive species; and where an invention is obvious and absolutely necessary, it may properly be said to be natural as any thing ...." Although it sounds as if Hume is talking about an elaborate kind of Confucian cultivation, he is also, like the Daoists, asking us to realize our own original nature, which is seen to include the propensity for social artifice. It's through artifice that society makes us who we are and that society is made valuable. ■

In addition to our moral and social lives, the social context is also important to our cognitive lives. Knowledge, justification, judgment, and discourse are primarily social, discursive practices, things that we cannot engage in without a social context that makes language and the practices of science possible. Science is a social activity with standards that are socially constructed; even mathematical knowledge is a public phenomenon. Knowledge requires our passions and our imagination because it requires participation in public life that is made possible only by our emotional, passionate nature. ■

Suggested Reading

Hume, *A Treatise of Human Nature*.

Norton and Taylor, eds., *The Cambridge Companion to Hume*.

Study Questions

1. In what ways does Hume's skepticism underpin modernity? In what ways does it undermine it?

2. How does Hume's account of our social nature and the role of compassion compare with those of Aristotle and Śāntideva? In what ways is it different?

Hume's Careless and Compassionate Vision
Lecture 24—Transcript

Greetings. It's nice to be back with you. In our previous lecture we introduced European modernity emphasizing the important themes such as the rise of science and the rise of science and the emphasis on science as a source of knowledge, the gulf that opened up between science and religion, and the need for philosophy and public theory in general to follow science.

We looked at Hume's particular role in this whole adventure. Hume, as we saw, stands kind of on the cusp of a classical and a modern period. While he shares with a classical period an emphasis on the social nature of humanity, he's very much modernist in his emphasis on science and of his mobilization of science to push religion out of the public sphere.

Nonetheless, even in doing that we saw that he uses classical, skeptical arguments as the basis for drawing this distinction between the public and the private. In that discussion we focused on Hume's text, dialogues concerning natural religion, which in fact Hume had published posthumously because he was very worried about the tinge of atheism that animated that text and what that might do for his reputation.

Today we'll be turning to Hume's best known and probably his best philosophical text which was written at the other end of his life. He wrote *The Treatise of Human Nature* when he was in his early 20s. It was really the work of a prodigy. It was a text which unfortunately, and to Hume's great sadness, was largely ignored during his life and when it wasn't ignored it was unfortunately ridiculed. But it stood the test of time and now is regarded as one of the great classics of modern philosophy. In my own view, the language in the Treatise is especially gorgeous. I think Hume is one of the greatest of the Elizabethan writers of English. Nonetheless the arguments are often fairly abstract and a bit complex, so we'll sometimes be moving through some difficult territory today, so bear with me.

Today what we're going to do is look at how Hume's naturalism and his emphasis on science generates a very different view of human life from that we've been used to and of what it is to lead a human life and how Hume's naturalism underlies his account of what the meaning of human life is. We'll begin with a discussion of Hume's skepticism and naturalism, how those play together, including a discussion of the distinction Hume inherits from Aristotle between nature and second nature.

We'll continue to talk about why the social dimension is for Hume so very important to our social lives, but also our cognitive lives, emphasizing Hume's distinctive view of the role of the passions and the imagination and convention not only in our social intercourse but also in our cognitive lives.

This will lead us to an understanding of why for Hume even though he arrives at these conclusions through a naturalistic understanding of human beings and human nature, the social dimension is so important to who we are and what gives our lives meaning. For Hume we're going to have a very unique account of artificial virtues and how those artificial virtues tie to natural virtues.

Let's begin by a brief review of Hume's skepticism. Even in our discussion of Buddhism, but also in many of the discussions we've had throughout this course, we've seen that the obvious places to look for foundations of human knowledge are reason or the senses, particularly ones with Hume we push scriptural authority out of the arena. What's left to us? Well what we learn from our senses and what we can infer using reason. We saw, for instance, in our discussion of Buddhist philosophy how important it was to distinguish those two things. They were taken for granted as the two sources of knowledge.

Hume, however, argues that neither reason nor the senses can possibly be justified on their own and can give us confidence even in the things that we take most for granted; that is, the existence of the external world, causal connections or the probative character of reason itself. Hume argues that if we think carefully about, for instance, the existence of the external world, something we all have to take for granted, the idea that the trees that grow in our garden are actually real, that the chair that I sit on actually will support me, that if I take one step forward the ground will not disappear before me, that when I speak to somebody else they actually exist. In short, the fact that I'm not just dreaming, that reality around me is a concrete object. Hume says where could that idea come from? If you think that it comes from your senses, you're deluding yourself because what do our senses give us if we simply focus on the senses themselves? They give us sensations, visual sensations, auditory sensations.

Those sensations would seem just as real to us if we were asleep, if we were dreaming. There's no reason in the sensations themselves to think that they're actually caused by external objects. To figure that out we would need an argument. We would need to know that sensations are always caused by external things. Our senses can't tell us that because they rest with the sensations, and reason can't tell us that either. Reason can't tell us that because all that reason has to work with is what the senses delivered, namely sensations. There is never any contact directly with anything outside of ourselves.

Moreover, reason cannot even justify its own operations. After all, suppose you gave me a rational argument to believe that my sensations are caused by something external to me. I might still ask you, why should a rational argument convince me? How would I then justify that? The senses of course can't justify reason, but reason can't do it either or we'd be arguing in a circle. So Hume concludes, even for the most obvious fact that we take for granted that there is a world beyond us, we have no justification in senses or in reason. Hume makes exactly the same moves regarding causation and very, very famous arguments.

The question then Hume asks is, should we therefore give up our belief that there's an external world? Should we give up all of our discussion with other people? Should we decide that we never have any reason for anything at all? Hume says, no, no, no. Just as in the case of religious belief that we examined yesterday, Hume points out, behavior, thinking, convictions, discourse can be reasonable even if it's not rationally justified. Hume argues that we are set up biologically to believe in the external world. We are set up biologically, psychologically, to believe that causal connections are real even if we never perceive them. We are set up biologically, cognitively, to take arguments as convincing.

Hume argues that if you pay attention to human nature, you see that it's not our reason, not even our sensory experience that grounds most of our lives, but it's actually these kinds of biological dispositions that Hume refers to as imagination. Our imagination and our passions, the things that we're naturally forced to do that we're passive in that rely on connecting things in an automatic psychological way, not a calculating way, that underlie who we are.

You might think that this is profoundly negative, that Hume is arguing that all we are these kinds of creatures buffeted about and forced to believe unreasonable things. It's actually in Hume's hands very constructive, very affirming. Hume is pointing out that we are justified in our beliefs, even if we can't provide reasons for them, because we are the kinds of beings who participate in those kinds of lives. If we want to understand human knowledge and human life, Hume argues, first we have to understand who we are.

Now I want to read you a lovely passage in *The Treatise* where Hume discusses this. "Nature, by an obstinate and uncontrollable necessity, has determin'd us to judge as well as to breathe and feel." Notice that point. That it's not that we have good reasons to judge that things are true, it's that nature has just made it part of us. That just as we breathe and we feel without attempting to, without calculating, we judge that there's an external world, that reasons are good reasons just naturally. "Nor can we ever forbear viewing certain objects in a stronger and fuller light ... than we can hinder ourselves from thinking as long as we are awake, or seeing surrounding bodies, when we turn our eyes to them in the broad sunshine."

Hume's point is this: You don't need reasons to believe in reason. You don't need reasons to believe in the external world, just as you don't need reasons to believe in God. These are things that simply well up out of what kinds of animals we are. But so far we're just focusing on our internal nature. Distinctive in Hume's account of who we are and what life is like is emphasis on the social dimension. Hume argues that our social relations and our social context are important to who we are for several reasons. One is it's the source of all of our genuine happiness, that our real happiness in life comes from our relationships to one another. Hume led a very happy life by the way, and when he died in Paris, his obituary referred to him as la bonne David—the good David—and argued that he was just the model for a humane, social life. He led a happy life in social relations, and his parties were famous both in Scotland and in France.

Secondly, Hume points out, if we don't have a functioning society—if our society falls apart, we just don't have the external goods that we need. Remember Hume is an Edinburgh man. He was growing up in a city devoted to commerce at the peak of its financial power, and he noticed that things like fleets of ships, banks, commercial institutions, shops, all depended on complex networks of associations that relied upon trust and good will to function, and that if you had that trust in good will you had a society in which people prospered and where you had smiles on people's faces.

Moreover, Hume points out, many of our deepest values and many of our important traits are social traits. In this sense Hume is a more classical guy, not an individualist. He's a modernist very much in his emphasis on science and naturalism and on his public private distinction. For Hume a society isn't composed of independent individuals, as we'll see that it will be for Kant and Mill very soon. Instead, for Hume as for Aristotle or for Confucius, individuals are constituted by society.

Here's Hume on the topic. Hume writes, "In man alone, [the] unnatural conjunction of infirmity, and of necessity, may be observed in its greatest perfection." It's a lovely piece of irony where he says unnatural because of course what he means is natural, but he means surprising that we are weak physically. We are not capable of taking care of ourselves individually but we need a whole lot. "Not only the food, which is required for is sustenance, flies his search … or at least requires his labor to be produced, but he must be possessed of cloaths and lodging, to defend him against the injuries of the weather." So we're the kinds of beings who have a hard time catching our food, a hard time raising our food. We have to clothe ourselves, we need houses. We are very needy kinds of creatures and if you think about the challenge of meeting all of those needs on your own, it's kind of daunting.

Hume continues, "Tis by society alone he is able to supply his defects, and raise himself up. … By society all his infirmities are compensated, and tho' in that situation his wants multiply every moment." Hume is noticing that the more you've got the more you want and that many of our needs and desires are socially constructed. "Yet his abilities are still more augmented, and leave him in every respect more happy, than 'tis possible for him, in his savage and solitary situation, ever to become." No matter what the problems are with society, Hume points out, we are a lot better socially. Even though many of our needs are socially constructed, society even gives us the power to satisfy those.

Everything that gives our lives meaning, Hume thinks, is social or socially constructed. That is this participation in this rich social context. This is a very secular account of the meaning of life, a social, secular account with echoes of Aristotle and with echoes of Confucius. Still there's going to be a deep modernity to it when we talk about Hume's account of how we realize this and what it does to us.

Hume follows Aristotle but deepens the account in distinguishing between what we might call nature or original nature and second nature. Both are very important to Hume in understanding who we are and how we live. We come equipped from birth, biologically Hume thinks, with a bunch of natural passions, the tendency to get angry when we're injured, but also natural affection and Hume thinks this is a really important feature of our lives. We grow up, we're born with a natural affection for our parents, for those who are very close to us, and a natural tendency as parents to develop affection for our children. Hume is enough of a scientist to recognize that these kinds of natural endowments are essential if the species is going to survive biologically.

But Hume is deeply influenced by Newton. Hume is a contemporary of Newton, he's paying attention to what Newton is doing, and Hume had the idea that natural affection, like gravitation, is a force of attraction. Like gravitation, Hume thought, natural affection obeys a sort of inverse square law. That is, the closer somebody is to us, the more we naturally tend to like them. We like our parents most of all and our siblings. Our uncles and aunts we're a little bit less attached to and our cousins a little less, second cousins it's getting a little bit indifferent, and the further people are out from us the less this natural affection connects us to them.

Now Hume thinks, this is actually a potential problem. If you think about what happens to forces, or what forces do that obey inverse square laws, they clump things together with big spaces between them. Think about the physical universe, gravitation gives us planets and suns and solar systems, but vast spaces between the bodies and vast spaces between the stars and solar systems.

Similarly Hume thinks, if you just allow human society to be governed by natural affection, what you're going to get are tightly-knit bands of people passionately devoted to each other and hostile to, or at least indifferent to, everybody else. In one place Hume compares this to what he imagines, the state is for nomadic tribes in the desert, fiercely loyal to each other but indifferent to or hostile to the welfare of others. Hume thinks this is no way to create a flourishing society. You're not going to get prosperous Edinburgh. You're not going to get Europe out of these competing kinds of bands. You're going to get gang warfare or something like this.

Hume thinks if we want to have a flourishing society, which is necessary condition of our own flourishing, of human flourishing, we need to somehow extend the force of these natural attractions. We can't sit tight with this inverse square law. Fortunately Hume thinks, we are also born with another natural faculty, an innate cognitive propensity to use our imagination, and our imagination allows us to see distinct things as similar to one another. As when, for instance, we see distinct shades of red and group them all under red. Or we see distinct breeds of dogs and imaginatively recognize them as all of a kind of a kind of dog. That's what our imagination does. It kind of instinctively puts similar things together and allows us to treat them alike. Again, Hume doesn't think that there's a good reason to do that, it's not reason or sense perception that justifies this but rather a natural, cognitive propensity with say biological roots.

Hume thinks the imagination will allow us to see those who are more distant to us as akin to those who are very close to us, and that will give rise, as we'll see in a few moments to a sense of justice, to a sense of charity, and to other passions directed to those who are farther from us. These passions are what we need to stitch a whole society together. They're artificial in one sense. We're not born with these attitudes, we do these things to ourselves, we construct them in ourselves individually and collectively.

In another sense, Hume points out, they are very natural. They're natural in the sense that even though they're not innate, it is part of human nature to act so as to cultivate them. That's where they constitute a second nature. The raw material, the primary nature are our innate human emotions, and the product of this kind of imaginative work and discursive work and social work is the construction of the second nature, the emotions that actually stitch society together. Here's what Hume says, "A man naturally loves his children better than his nephews, his nephews better than his cousins, his cousins better than strangers." This is that inverse square law at work. "Tis certain that no affection of the human mind has both a sufficient force and a proper direction to counter-balance the love of gain and render men fit members of society, by making them abstain from the possessions of others. Benevolence to strangers is too weak for this purpose." That is, when we come to strangers or people who are distant from us, greed or outward hostility will overwhelm any affection that is innate in us.

> [W]hen injustice is so distant from us, as no way to affect our interest, it still displeases us, as we consider it prejudicial to human society ... [and] we naturally sympathize with others in the sentiments they entertain of us. Thus self-interest is the original motive for the establishment of justice, but a sympathy with public interest is the source of the moral approbation which attends that virtue.

That's a really important point to focus on. Hume says it's in our own interests to extend our natural sympathies so as to construct stable societies that afford to us all of the goods that societies afford. That's one thing, but notice that that by itself doesn't make it something that we would regard as good, only something as useful. Where does the moral approbation come from? The moral approbation comes from the fact that we really have a sympathy with public interest, because public interest is our own interest.

Now the mechanism, "Politicians ... extend the natural sentiments beyond their original bounds, but still nature must furnish the materials." So this is the point, politicians, that is—by this he doesn't mean candidates for public office, but people who operate in the public sphere, operate to use rhetoric, to use advertising, to use language, to use persuasion, to get us to extend our sentiments. So, Hume says,

> As public praise and blame increases our esteem for justice [literature, speeches, public discussion in coffee houses] so private education and instruction contribute to the same effect. For as parents easily observe that a man is more useful both to himself and others ... the greater a degree of probity and honor he is endow'd with. ... For these reasons they are induced to inculcate on their children, from their earliest infancy, the principles of probity, and teach them to regard the observance of these rules ... as worthy and honorable.

Note the wonderful echo here both of Aristotle and Confucius of the importance of childrearing for inculcating these kinds of sensibilities and character that are good for us individually and good for us collectively, good for us individually because of what they do for our reputation and because they enable us to live in a society that affords us happiness and meaningful lives, and good for us collectively because when we are each better people we are all better people.

Now on this question about naturalness, Hume is very eloquent, he says, "[W]hen I deny justice to be a natural virtue, I make use of the word *natural* only as oppos'd to *artificial*. ... Mankind is an inventive species; and where an invention is obvious and absolutely necessary, it may properly be said to be natural as any thing." That's the point about second nature, that because it is natural for us to construct artificial things, artifices are natural for human beings.

Again now, Hume while it sounds like he's talking about an elaborate kind of cultivation is also asking us to realize our own nature. It's a kind of paradoxical synthesis of Confucianism and Daoism if you want. With the Confucians, he's urging this careful, social cultivation of who we are and a transformation of us from our innate state. But with the Daoists, he's urging what we really want to do is to recover our original nature, a nature now seen in a more sophisticated way to include the propensity to social artifice.

It's through these artifices, these extensions of our passions, these extensions of our concerns and the construction of networks of relationship, that society makes us who we are Hume thinks. Our sense of justice, our concern for others, our sympathy for the downtrodden, these are the things that make us valuable. Those are the kinds of people we want to be. The construction of us as that kind of person requires these social processes, these collective processes, and also the workings of our own imaginations and natural passions. Note that reason, that perception plays almost no role in this.

These are also the things that make our societies valuable, and notice that for Hume, all of these virtues, all of these characteristics are socially constituted. They make society possible, society in turn makes them possible, so there's a reciprocal feedback here. This is the dimension that Hume very much shares with classical theorists such as Aristotle and Confucius, the idea that the social and the individual are deeply interpenetrating. Hume argues—and this is most dramatically—that it's not just to our moral lives and our social lives that the social context is important, but also to our cognitive lives, and this sets Hume apart from almost everybody else in Europe, the idea that even as thinkers we are not individuals, but as thinkers we're essentially embedded in social context.

The reason for this is that Hume thinks that knowledge, justification, judgment, and discourse are primarily social, discursive practices, things that we cannot even begin to conceive of engaging in without a social context that makes the language and the practices of justification and science possible. Hume is not enamored of the view that Robinson Caruso could become a great scientist or could justify his views to himself. He thinks that requires a seminar, a laboratory, a public discussion.

Hume is going to argue that the very edifice of modernity requires a kind of social context; because what modernity requires is reason, justification and science. Science, Hume thinks, is first and foremost a social activity that people do together and whose standards are socially constructed. Here's a really dramatic passage from Hume about this. It's absolutely fascinating.

Hume writes, "There is no algebraist nor mathematician so expert in the science"—now notice that he's chosen mathematics here. The science that we tend to think of as the one more than any other that a person could prosecute individually in the privacy of her own study without relying on anybody else. Even that, Hume thinks is impossible. Let me start again. Sorry, I get carried away. "There is no algebraist nor mathematician so expert in the science, as to place entire confidence in any truth immediately upon his discovery of it." So you want to imagine now this mathematician is up in her study late at night. She proves the theorem she was after. Is she convinced now that she has actually proven it? Does she feel like she knows it? Hume answers, no. "Every time he runs over his proofs, his confidence increases." So what happens? The mathematician checks the proof, checks them again and again. "But still more by the approbation of his friends;" What do you do next when you wake up the next morning with these proofs that your pretty confident of? You take them into the department, show them to your colleagues. Ask them to check them because you might have made a mistake. "And is raised to the utmost perfection by the universal assent and approbation of the learned world."

Even after your friends in the department have checked them, you submit it to a journal, you ask referees to look at it, and only when the mathematical public has accepted it do you say, I know this to be true. For Hume, even knowledge, even mathematical knowledge, is a public phenomenon. Knowledge in this sense requires the kind of role of our passions and our imagination because it requires this participation in a public life and in a social life that's only made possible by our emotional, passionate nature. For Hume it's this individual, biological character together with our social character that's under girded by that biological character but extended by our social interactions and our social processes that makes it possible for us to have a cognitive life at all, for us to know anything at all.

Our passions and our emotions, our imagination and our social relations give rise to our actions. Those are the things that motivate us. They also give rise to our sense of who we are, to our sense of morality, to what's important. They motivate our ideologies, they motivate even our belief as we've seen that the world around us exists. Those, Hume points out, are purely biological and social processes, processes that require us, if we're going to understand who we are and what it is for us to lead a life, to take ourselves seriously as objects of scientific study, naturalistically but also to take ourselves seriously as social animals.

This is modernist in its naturalism. It's modernist in its skepticism. It's modernist in the way that it cleaves apart the study of what's public from the religious. It's still quite classical in its emphasis on the social character of human life and the fundamental role of the society informing us.

Our next stop in our very next lecture will be the work of the great German philosopher, Immanuel Kant, a philosopher who was deeply influenced by Hume, but who was also a severe critic of Hume. Kant was not a champion of the passions. Kant was not a champion of the social. He was a champion of reason and a champion of the individual, and it's Kant who really developed the thesis that reason, rationality, justification, and individual responsibility are essential to a meaningful human life and are the foundations of modernity.

Kant—Immaturity and the Challenge to Know
Lecture 25

For Kant, what makes our lives meaningful individually, what makes our lives meaningful as societies, is our ability to extend, to deepen, to correct what we know or to build on what is bequeathed to us from previous generations and to advance it. To abrogate that responsibility would be to abrogate genuine human life.

Immanuel Kant is the philosopher whose work set the bar, in a sense, for later philosophers. His writings are of such enormous importance that no one since his time can be considered a professional philosopher unless he or she has read and mastered the work of Kant.

The texts that give Kant this preeminence are *The Critique of Pure Reason*, on metaphysics and epistemology; *The Critique of Practical Reason*, on ethics; and *The Critique of Judgment*, on aesthetics. In these texts, Kant attempted to effect a Copernican revolution in metaphysics. Until Kant, philosophers had viewed thought, knowledge, morality, and aesthetic response as revolving around the objects of human experience—the structure of knowledge determined by considering external objects, the structure of morality determined by considering external acts, and so on. But Kant tried to understand how our knowledge, morality, and aesthetics work by putting the human mind, the human will, and human sensibility at the center. Like Hume, Kant also argued that religion should not intrude on the cognitive sphere.

The essay "What Is Enlightenment?" was written in the context of liberalization in the state of Prussia and a move to separate the faculties of theology and philosophy at the university where Kant taught. In it, Kant illustrates that the only meaningful life is one grounded in rational discourse in the public sphere. Here, we get Kant's famous motto for a meaningful life: *Sapere Aude!*, "Dare to know!"—an acknowledgment that knowledge and inquiry require not only intelligence but courage.

Kant argues that the European Enlightenment marked a separation between childhood and adulthood for humankind. In childhood, our actions are heteronomous, that is, determined by others, but to be an adult is to be autonomous and to reason for oneself. According to Kant, this autonomy is always inhibited by authority, particularly religious authority and ideological paternalism. Further, we are often complicit in our own juvenilization through cognitive or behavioral laziness. That's why it's important to dare to know: The Enlightenment doesn't simply liberate us, but it calls upon us to use that liberty to assert our own freedom of thought and speech and our willingness to participate in the public sphere.

Private discourse might be restricted for reasons of confidentiality or for contractual reasons, but public discourse must be free.

Kant begins by telling us, "Enlightenment is man's emergence from his self-imposed immaturity" and goes on to say that immaturity is much easier than maturity. He writes, "If I have a book to have understanding in place of me, a spiritual advisor to have conscience for me, a doctor to judge my diet for me, and so on, I need not make any efforts at all. I need not think, so long as I can pay; others will soon enough take over the tiresome job for me." This is Kant's vision of a meaningless life.

Kant argues that authority, whether political or ecclesiastical, uses the excuse of paternalism and our own terror of disorder in society, as well as our own laziness, to keep us immature and obedient. Thus, our immaturity has two sources: our own willingness to be guided and the willingness of authority to take advantage of our immaturity to reinforce its own power and keep us docile. Coercion isn't necessary here. To overcome our immaturity, what's needed is the freedom and the courage "to make public use of one's reason in all matters."

Kant makes a distinction between the public and the private sphere that is the forerunner of our contemporary separation of these two realms. He defines the public sphere as the arena of intellectual discourse in the domains of science, philosophy, and politics. We enter this sphere purely as citizens, not office holders. By "private" discourse, Kant means discourse carried out in the conduct of a particular office or duty, even if that office is public. Private discourse might be restricted for reasons of confidentiality or for contractual reasons, but public discourse must be free. Kant gives us a wonderful example here of a pastor hired by a particular congregation. He must preach the doctrine of the church from the pulpit, but if he disagrees with church doctrine, he is also obligated to speak out in public against it. In fact, Kant thinks that no one, not even a clergyman, can be bound to believe anything, because the freedom to believe is the essence of enlightenment.

Kant explicitly ties human nature and the good life to intellectual, moral, and political progress, all of which presuppose the free use of reason. To refuse to think freely or refuse to engage in public discourse violates the human rights of all, because we all have rights to one another's ideas. This model of the good life, which takes for granted the importance of progress, freedom, rationality, and secularism, is one we've inherited in our own society. ■

Name to Know

Kant, Immanuel (1724–1804): Immanuel Kant is almost universally regarded as the greatest of all European philosophers.

Important Term

Sapere Aude!: Kant's motto of enlightenment: "Dare to know!"

Suggested Reading

Kant, *An Answer to the Question: 'What Is Enlightenment?'*

Schmidt, ed., *What Is Enlightenment? Eighteenth-Century Answers and Twentieth-Century Questions.*

1. How does Kant draw the distinction between the public and the private spheres? How is that different from the way we draw the same distinction in contemporary discourse and jurisprudence?

2. Why, on Kant's view, do we have not only a *right* but a *duty* to participate in the public sphere by exercising free speech and thought?

Kant—Immaturity and the Challenge to Know
Lecture 25—Transcript

Welcome back to our exploration of how modernity influences our thinking about the meaning of life. In our last few lectures we were talking about the contributions of David Hume, who as we said stood kind of at the cusp between a classical kind of thinking and modern thinking about life and about the meaning of life.

Today we're going to focus on the great Prussian philosopher, Immanuel Kant. In Kant we really see that the modern viewpoint of the renaissance, the enlightenment is in full swing, and we're going to recognize these ideas as very much ideas that are the foundations of our own viewpoints.

Kant is an interesting figure for many reasons. The great American philosopher, Richard Rorty once said that Kant was the person who professionalized philosophy, and that's true in at least two senses. In one sense it's true because Kant was the first truly great philosopher in the history of the Western tradition since the fall of Aristotle's academy to also be actually a professor of philosophy.

Hume, for instance, was a diplomat and all of the other philosophers in between the fall of the academy and Kant had day jobs doing something else—they were scientists, they were diplomats, they were lawyers—but philosophy was a kind of gentle person's hobby. Kant however was a professor of philosophy, was a professor of philosophy at the University of Konigsberg, and we're going to see that the talk that Kant gave that we'll be addressing today fits very much within that context.

The second sense though in which Kant professionalized philosophy—and this again is due to Rorty—is that Kant wrote books that were of such enormous importance that nobody since then could be considered a professional philosopher unless they read and mastered them; sort of providing the kind of bar that you have to cross to be considered a respectable philosopher, and that's really important too. In our profession, the philosophical profession, we often for instance distinguished philosophers as pre-Kantian philosophers or post-Kantian philosophers. Nobody talks about a pre-Humean or post-Humean philosopher, or a pre-Marcus Aurelius and post-Marcus Aurelius philosopher, or a pre-Niche or post-Niche philosopher. But pre-Kantian and post-Kantian, those terms just roll off the tongue. Kant is this real watershed in our profession.

The texts that give Kant this preeminence are this trio of critical texts that he wrote late in his life called *The Critique of Pure Reason* which was a text on metaphysics and epistemology, *The Critique of Practical Reason* which was a text on ethics, and *The Critique of Judgment* which was a text on aesthetics. In these texts, Kant attempted and many would say succeeded in affecting what he called in the preface to the first critique, the critique of pure reason, a Copernican revolution in metaphysics. That Copernican revolution isn't only important in understanding the structure of the critical philosophy, but also understanding the entire vision that animates Kant's philosophy and his role in modernity.

Copernicus remember, recognized that by following a Ptolemaic model of the nature of the universe in which the Earth was at the center of the universe and the sun and planets and stars revolved around the Earth. Some that couldn't make any sense at all of the motion of the heavenly bodies or sticking the Earth at the center. Instead, he said, if you put the sun at the center of the solar system and have the Earth revolve around the sun and the planets revolve around the sun, all of a sudden everything makes sense.

Similarly Kant thought, if you try to understand human thought, human knowledge, human morality, and human aesthetic response, by arguing that it all revolves around the objects we experience, that the structure of our knowledge is determined by external objects that we consider, that the structure of our morality is determined by regarding external acts and finding moral value in those acts themselves or moral disvalue, or that our aesthetic judgment is determined by the nature of the object, you won't make any sense of it at all.

Instead, he thought, if we think instead that objects of our knowledge are determined in their structure and their epistemic access by the nature of our own cognitive faculties, that morality has to do with our faculty of will, our faculty of judgment, our faculty of assessment, and that beauty has to do with the nature of human aesthetic response, then we can understand why we call some things beautiful, some actions good, and why we credit ourselves with knowing certain things about objects and why we find certain things unknowable.

What Kant did was to put the human mind, the human will, and human sensibility at the center of the universe, the individual person, and then try to understand how our knowledge, how our morality, how our aesthetics work by focusing on the mind. He put the individual at the center, and by putting the individual at the center we end up constructing one of these foundations of the idea of the modern that individuals are primary, individual rights, individual thought, individual knowledge.

Kant also followed Hume in arguing that his project was to circumscribe reason so as to make room for faith. Kant argued that there's no way that religion could possibly intrude in this sphere in which we think, reason, discuss, make moral judgments, or understand beauty. That religion belongs outside of the entire sphere of what we do cognitively together. Kant wanted to establish a very firm foundation for the sciences and for public activity, for collective action, and for politics that was independent of faith, and in that respect he very much is following Hume.

The address that we're going to talk about today has the title *What is Called Enlightenment,* and it's Kant's thinking about the European enlightenment so explicitly about modernity itself. Kant is thematizing the modern explicitly in a way that for instance Hume never did. Kant is aware that some big transformation has happened and is trying to understand it. There's no need to explain it.

What Kant is going to be doing is to explain the nature of enlightenment and why—this is important—that the only meaningful human life, what makes our lives worth living, is a particular kind of public life, but it's a public life of reason, a life grounded in rational discourse in a public sphere.

The context for this is complex. On the one hand we have Frederick the Great who is then King of Prussia where Kant is living, advancing this great liberalization in which State control is relaxed, more commerce is allowed, more free press is allowed, more free discussion is allowed, the universities are set free, and so it's in the context of this public relaxation of constraints on discourse and constraints on action, and in the context of the explicit decision to make the universities autonomous in order to allow them to freely pursue knowledge and to innovate that Kant is writing.

He's also writing, by the way, in the context of an interesting development within his own university, and that is that before this, philosophy and theology had always been part of the same faculty. This was true in Europe from the Middle Ages where philosophy was thought of as a part of theology. But as Kant is writing, Kant is leading the philosophy faculty into a separation from theology so that philosophy is explicitly again aligning itself with science and divorcing itself from discussions of God, and that also forms the context for Kant's address, the text that we're going to read together today.

Kant argues very famously in this address that the motto of the enlightenment, the motto of awakening, the motto of the meaningful life for human beings is, as he puts it, *Sapere Aude!* In Latin, it's "dare to know." Kant is arguing that knowledge and inquiry requires not only intelligence, it requires courage, and that awakening and the activity of leading our lives meaningfully in the context of awakening is an act of great courage.

Let's first outline Kant's argument and then we'll move into the text and see how he realizes it. Kant argues that what's important about the European enlightenment, what's important about this kind of dawning of modernity, is very much that it allows people to—as he really puts it—to grow up, to become for the first time in human history he thinks, real adults. That is, to realize our natures as actual, fully-formed human beings. Kant thematizes this entire issue in terms of the relationship between juvenility, between being just children and childlike, and being adult. He argues that if you're going to realize your potential it means that you grow up.

For Kant the big difference between childhood and adulthood and this deep sense, that is what we might say, a life of trivial childishness and a life of meaningful adult participation is rational autonomy, that children are heteronomous, their actions, their views are determined by others, their teachers, their parents, whatever. But to be an adult is to be autonomous and to reason for one's self. Kant will argue that this autonomy that is still essential to leading a real human life, a meaningful human adult life, is always inhibited by authority and he especially identifies religious authority—here he's really following Hume—and ideological paternalism, even if it's secular as the juvenilizing influences from which we seek to emancipate ourselves in modernity.

Kant argues that we can't always blame those from outside of us, our pastors or ideologs, for our own maturity. Central to Kant's argument is that we are often complicit in our own juvenilization, and that we are complicit in that through our own cognitive or behavioral laziness. That's why he thinks it's so important to dare to know. He argues that the enlightenment doesn't simply liberate us but it calls upon ourselves to take that liberty and to assert our own absolute freedom of thought and speech and our willingness to participate in the public sphere, and that calling upon us to assert these rights is complementary to the demand on the State to respect them.

The guiding theme, as I've said, in Kant's entire discussion is this theme of maturity versus immaturity. Let's see how Kant puts the point. Kant writes, "Enlightenment is man's emergence from his self-imposed immaturity." Note that, self-imposed immaturity, Kant is not arguing that somebody else is forcing us to be juvenile but that we tend to allow ourselves to be juvenilized. "Immaturity," Kant says, "is the inability to use one's own understanding without the guidance of another. This immaturity is self-incurred if its cause is not lack of understanding, but lack of resolution and courage to use it without the guidance of another." Again Kant is arguing that we often impose this upon ourselves. "The motto of the enlightenment is thus *Sapere aude!* Have the courage to use your own understanding."

Kant argues that immaturity is actually a lot easier than maturity; it's much easier to be a child. He writes, "Laziness and cowardice are the reasons why such a large proportion of men … gladly remain immature for life." Laziness and cowardice. Now listen to this lovely prose, "

> It is so convenient to be immature! If I have a book to have understanding in place of me, a spiritual advisor to have conscience for me, a doctor to judge my diet for me, and so on, I need not make

any efforts at all. I need not think, so long as I can pay, others will soon enough take over the tiresome job for me.

This is really central to Kant's vision of what it is to lead a meaningless life. To lead a life where we simply give over the responsibility for our own thinking, for our own lifestyle, for our own religious beliefs to somebody else and simply allow ourselves to be led by the views of others.

Kant then argues that what authority does, whether it's political authority or ecclesiastical authority, is to use the excuse of paternalism and our own terror of disorder in society as well as our own willingness to avoid hard work, to keep us immature and obedient. Now, Kant began with the complicity end, now he talks about how social structures take advantage of that complicity to enforce immaturity. Again it's kind of fun prose. Kant writes, "Having first infatuated their domesticated animals,"—that's us by the way—"And carefully prevented the docile creatures from daring to take a single step without the leading-strings to which they are tied, they next show them the danger which threatens them if they try to walk unaided."

Kant thinks that what happens is you begin by a bit of laziness, and then those who are involved in education or involved in religious life begin to warn you that that's the right way to behave, that's the right way to be. Because if you try to think for yourself, you might make mistakes, if you try to act for yourself you might do something wrong. The world is a dangerous place and authority keeps you safe. Kant advises, "For enlightenment … all that is needed is freedom. And the freedom in question is the most innocuous form of all: freedom to make public use of one's reason in all matters." That's it. For Kant, the foundation of all of this is the freedom to reason, to think, and to talk publicly in a public sphere to our fellows, to participate as citizens. "But I hear on all sides the cry: Don't argue! The officer says: Don't argue, get on parade! The tax-official: Don't argue, pay! The clergyman: Don't argue, believe! I reply: The public use of man's reason must always be free, and it alone can bring about enlightenment among men."

Kant is pointing out that there's this dual source of immaturity, of meaninglessness in modern life that we need to overcome. The first source is our own laziness and willingness to be guided, willingness to accept paternalism. That immaturity on our own, Kant argues, is aided and abetted by authority. Authority is always willing to take advantage of that immaturity in order to reinforce power and to keep us docile. Immaturity then is simply constituted for Kant by the abdication of the responsibility to think. That abdication, once affected, is enforced and maintained by laziness and fear. Coercion isn't even necessary. We don't need thought police coming around to our houses to tell us what to believe or what not to believe. We don't need to be told we're going to be excommunicated for this, or beaten for that.

Fear and laziness will do the trick, Kant thinks, without the police. That's why we need a certain amount of real courage. But, Kant points out, even though the freedom that we're talking about is the freedom to think and to speak in public, not all thought and speech is protected like this. Not all thought and speech ought to be free. This is where Kant introduces, really for the first time in philosophical thought, the clear distinction between the public and the private, a distinction that we saw Hume beginning to work towards in his discussion of the relationship between religion and reasonable belief.

For Kant there is a very clear distinction between the public and the private sphere, and it's the public sphere in which reason and maturity are realized, not the private sphere. On the other hand, Kant's distinction between the public and the private, even though it's the kind of foundation of our contemporary distinction that's so important to us and enshrined in the US constitution in places like the first amendment, the second amendment and the fourth amendment and the fifth amendment, so much the foundation of a lot of our own thinking. Kant's distinction is not our distinction. It's the forerunner of our distinction. Kant is going to define the public as this sphere of intellectual discourse in which we discuss ideas and policies only with regard to whether they're true or false, appropriate or inappropriate. For Kant, the public sphere is this sphere of science, philosophy and politics.

In short, the public sphere is this sphere we enter purely as citizens but importantly not as office holders. For Kant, when I speak as an officer of a university or when somebody speaks as a police officer, or when somebody speaks as a lawyer or as a pastor, that is in a particular role that they've been chosen for in a particular institution, even if that institution was public, then they're speaking privately, speaking in a way that may be constrained. Let's see how Kant works this out. He says, "By the public use of one's own reason I mean that use which anyone may make of it as a man of learning addressing the entire reading public." So again, the public use of reason here is identified with scholarship—of course Kant is a professor—but in general identified with public discourse about ideas that matter to all of us. "What I term the private use of reason is that which a person may make of it in a particular civil post or office with which he is entrusted."

Note that this is just not the familiar public/private distinction that we inherit from people like Locke and Mill that's enshrined in American Constitutional law. By "pubic" here, Kant is really clear that he means the discourse in which we engage qua citizens, with other citizens, the discourse that's involved in active, collective participation in discussing ideas and policies. When Kant thinks about private discourse he means discourse that's carried out in the conduct of a particular office or a particular duty, even if that office is public. That is, discourse that's part of our jobs.

For instance, private discourse might be restricted for all kinds of reasons. I'm a teacher. I'm bound to confidentiality with regard to my students. So I can't discuss my student's work or my grades with you even if I wanted to. If you're hired as somebody's lawyer, you are bound by client/lawyer privilege. There are all kinds of things that you can't talk about. That's private discourse. Moreover, if I hire you as a lawyer, I hire you to represent my case, not to represent the other guy's case.

If a student hires me as a teacher, they hire me to work with them, not to work with somebody else. We can be contractually obligated to engage in certain kinds of speech or to refrain from certain kinds of speech because of posts that we have as individuals agreed to undertake. Sometimes we just plain have a job to do. Even if it might be a public job, it might very much require us to do as we are told, even where we disagree with a policy.

Imagine another kind of case, you're hired by the federal government and you're hired as a civil servant in an agency that is now forced to execute a policy determined by an administration with which you may not agree. Your job as a civil servant isn't to obstruct the policy, it's to execute the policy and to defend the policy, even if privately you disagree with it. Now publicly, as a citizen in a town meeting you might argue against it, and Kant is arguing your public speech may not be restricted, but your private speech as an officer may indeed be constrained. So this is how Kant is distinguishing public from private.

He argues that all of these restrictions on private speech and action are legitimate because they're freely undertaken. We agree to take the job; I agree to be a teacher and to maintain confidentiality. You may agree to be an attorney or to take the job with the federal government. If you don't want your speech restricted in those ways, you don't take the job, Kant thinks, but public discourse must be free. Kant puts it this way, "But insofar as this or that individual who acts as part of the machine"—isn't that wonderful language Kant is already talking about the government or corporations as machine, way before his time. "But insofar as this or that individual who acts as part of the machine also considers himself part of a complete commonwealth"—that is insofar as we also think of ourselves as citizens of public society—"Who may … address a public in the truest sense of the word, he may indeed argue without harming the affairs in which he is employed … in a passive capacity."

That's the point. You might be compelled to execute a particular policy or to say certain things as a matter of your duty or as a matter of contract if you're a military officer, a lawyer, a tax collector, a teacher, even a pastor. But despite the restrictions on your speech and the restrictions on your behavior in the private execution of your voluntarily- undertaken duties Kant emphasizes, you still have not only the right but even the obligation to speak out against even those policies you're forced to execute so long as you do it in the public sphere.

As a lawyer for instance, perhaps you're defending an energy company in some matter but you actually think the law that is on their favor is a bad law. You could still publicly campaign for the repeal of the law, nothing wrong with that. Kant even gives us this wonderful example in the domain of religion—for Kant, religion is really important in all of this, for the very reasons that it was important for Hume. Kant sees religion as maybe the most dangerous enemy of maturity. So he gives us this great example of a clergyman who has accepted the job as pastor of a particular church. If he has accepted this job, and Kant very much thinks of it as a job, as pastor of a church, he's bound to teach the doctrines of the church. He has signed a contract. I'm going to be a pastor of this congregational church or this Methodist church. I'll teach cannon law, I'll teach the doctrine.

In the pulpit or even in Ecclesiastical counseling, he's got to advance the church doctrine. Kant said, let's imagine that he's actually a free-thinking kind of guy and he actually disagrees with some church doctrine that he's bound to teach. Then, Kant says, he is not only free to but even obligated to speak in public against those doctrines, maybe to publish articles in learned journals or to give speeches to secular audiences about this. So Kant thinks, even though as a pastor he may have to say certain things, as a public citizen he is not only permitted to but required to criticize the very doctrines he teaches from the pulpit. This is very stern stuff, this is very stern stuff.

Kant thinks, in fact, more deeply, that nobody can ever be bound to believe anything, not even a clergyman, not even a devout member of a religious community can ever give up the freedom to believe, because the freedom to believe, for Kant, is the essence of enlightenment, the essence of what it is to lead a genuinely human life. Can we be bound to believe? Not even a church or other religious community can obligate its members and future members to believe, nor can a society.

"One age cannot enter into an alliance … to put the next age in a position where it would be impossible for it to extend and correct its knowledge." Let's stop there for a minute. Impossible for it to extend or correct its knowledge, for Kant, what makes our lives meaningful individually, what makes our lives meaningful as societies, is our ability to extend, to deepen, to correct what we know, or to build on what is bequeathed to us from previous generations and to advance it. To abrogate that responsibility would be to abrogate genuine human life. So he says,

> One age cannot enter into an alliance … to put the next age in a position where it would be impossible for it to extend and correct its knowledge … or make any progress … in enlightenment. This

would be a crime against human nature, whose original destiny lies precisely in such progress.

Here Kant is explicitly tying human nature, human destiny and the good life to progress, intellectual progress, moral progress, political progress.

That progress presupposes the free use of reason. For that reason the abrogation of the free use of reason is the worst thing you can do to somebody. But that abrogation can be accomplished both by external authority and by self-imposed immaturity, and for Kant it's the self-imposed immaturity that's always the most dangerous. Because the mission of a human being for Kant is progress, that includes intellectual progress and that requires the kind of freedom of thought that he is demanding here. Freedom of thought and speech are what are essential to leading a truly human life.

Kant's conclusion is quite dramatic. He writes, "[To] renounce ... enlightenment completely, whether for his own person, or even more so, for later generations, means violating and trampling underfoot the sacred rights of mankind." That's really powerful stuff. That means to refuse to think freely. To refuse to engage in public discourse isn't just to give up your own prerogative. It is in doing that to violate everybody else's human rights because we have rights to each other's ideas, because it's our ideas that allow goods to be obtained for others. "But something which a people may not even impose on itself can still less be imposed upon it by a monarch." So Kant points out that we can't individually or collectively step back from the obligation to think freely, to speak freely, and to participate freely in public life. This is a very characteristically modern European model of what the human good is. This is the model of human good and of human life and of society that we've inherited in our own society. And a model that takes for granted the importance of progress, the importance of freedom and the importance in the enterprise of progress and freedom of individuals, of rationality, and of liberty. It's an individualistic, rationalist, libertarian, democratic ideal of the human life.

Kant comes back to religion at the end in an important way. He says, "I have portrayed ... religion as the focal point of enlightenment ... first because [that is what our rulers use most often for ideological control] and secondly, because religious immaturity is the most pernicious and dishonorable variety of all." Why the most pernicious and dishonorable? It's because in religious immaturity we simply give up our right to think deeply for ourselves about the very most important values in our lives. We give up the right to do what we need to do in public, to engage in rational discourse.

This is the very final and most important pillar of European enlightenment. The meaningful life is not just civil life as it was for Hume. It's essentially secular life. It's a life led in the absence of religion. It's a life led with religion being something we do optionally behind closed doors, or in our temple or synagogue or church, not something that intrudes into the public. This secularism, this emphasis on freedom is what constitutes human life we are going to see blooming in the next lecture in the thought of John Stuart Mill. I hope you'll join me for that.

Mill's Call to Individuality and to Liberty
Lecture 26

Mill is not talking about the destiny of society, collective obligation, progress. He's talking only about the individual. This is a superbly individualist construction of privacy and liberty and a continued move, following Kant, away from any kind of paternalism, again, going much further than Kant did.

In our exploration of European modernity, we've moved from a social to an individualistic conception of the good life and from sentiment to reason. In **John Stuart Mill**, we will see an elaboration of Kant's public/private distinction and an extension of his focus on the individual into an even more individualistic model of civil society.

Mill was the son of James Mill, one of the founders of **utilitarianism** in England. From his father, he received an intense education in the classics of Greece and Rome, as well as mathematics, science, and political philosophy. In later life, he became an ardent social, economic, and political reformer.

Mill begins his work *On Liberty* with an articulation of what he calls the "harm principle": The only time it is permissible for a society or an individual to interfere with the freedom of others is for self-protection. Such interference is not even permitted to prevent others from harming themselves, although we may attempt to reason with those who are bent on self-destructive behavior. Echoing our American conception of individual freedom, Mill writes, "Over himself, over his own body and mind, the individual is sovereign." Thus, he creates a much stronger protection for Kant's sphere of privacy and moves farther away from paternalism: Everything that doesn't affect the welfare of others is private. Exceptions to the harm principle include parents protecting their children and colonial administrators governing "barbarians."

Mill, like Kant, was also concerned about the tyranny of the majority. Mill writes, "Society … practices a social tyranny more formidable than many kinds of political oppression, since… it leaves fewer means of escape, penetrating more deeply into the details of life and enslaving the soul itself." Social tyranny comes to us through advertising, through politics, and through the expectation that we must believe, think, or behave in certain ways. It constrains and cramps individual liberty, not just as explicit legal pressure or censorship might, but because there's nothing to challenge social tyranny and no escape from it.

Echoing our American conception of individual freedom, Mill writes, "Over himself, over his own body and mind, the individual is sovereign."

A society that enables us to lead truly meaningful lives must take measures to mitigate social tyranny. Conditions for individuality don't emerge by accident; they must be actively encouraged by government. Mill calls for an activist government that moves against monopoly of the public space by social tyrannies and the majority. This idea enters the American tradition in the work of John Dewey and his thinking about American education.

As part of his defense of absolute freedom of thought and expression, Mill gives us his famous dilemma argument, in which he claims that speech or thought should be defended and protected even if it is false or dangerous. Suppressing ideas, Mill argues, slows progress and carries with it the possibility that we might be proved wrong; again, the persecution of Galileo serves as an example. More importantly, even if an idea is harmful or false, suppressing it deprives us of the opportunity to refute it rationally by argument and bullies believers into ideological submission. Ideas may be driven underground, where they may cause more harm than if they had been openly debated and properly put to rest.

Another reason for absolute freedom of speech derives from the absolute value Mill accords to pluralism in society, a radical idea for his time. Mill points out that refuting rival ideas or perspectives often gives us a clearer idea of what we ourselves think and why. He also says that different views or traditions may be better for different people and that there's no reason to impose uniformity when variety brings wider benefits. Pluralism in a society brings to its citizens increased ideological ferment and offers opportunities to share new ideas and traditions, all of which are sources of happiness. Mill noted—and we note in our society today—that many people see diversity and individuality as factors that promote disunity, even conflict. But Mill showed that they promote progress and originality, making life better for all.

Mill's distinction between self-regarding acts—acts that don't affect others—and other-regarding acts—acts that affect others or may harm them—replaces Kant's distinction between public and private. In American society and jurisprudence today, we think of other-regarding acts as those in which the law has some say, but self-regarding acts remain in the zone of privacy. Still, critical speech should always be protected.

What we see in Mill is the final flowering of individualism and **libertarianism** that runs throughout the modern viewpoint. From Hume to Mill, we evolve much deeper secularism, a much deeper individualism, and a much stronger public/private distinction. In Mill's contemporary expression, our lives are meaningful only when we are self-expressive, free individuals, and they are meaningful for precisely that reason, not because of our social context. ∎

Name to Know

Mill, John Stuart (1806–1873): John Stuart Mill was the son of the historian James Mill, a close follower of the Utilitarian philosopher Jeremy Bentham.

Important Terms

libertarianism: The belief that individuals should have the maximum personal liberty consistent with the liberty of others; resistance of the intrusion of the law into the private sphere.

utilitarianism: A moral theory according to which actions are right to the degree to which they promote happiness or pleasure and wrong to the degree that they promote unhappiness or pain.

Mill, *On Liberty*.

————, *The Spirit of the Age, On Liberty, The Subjection of Women*, ed. Alan Ryan.

Study Questions

1. How are Mill's and Kant's conceptions of liberty, of publicity and privacy, and of the obligations of the state with regard to speech and opinion, similar? How are they different?

2. Why does Mill believe that the state must actively encourage, as opposed to merely tolerate, free speech and individual development? What does this say about the necessary social conditions of leading a meaningful life?

Mill's Call to Individuality and to Liberty
Lecture 26—Transcript

In this lecture we're going to conclude our development of a positive characterization of European Modernity, the kind of tradition that underlies a lot of our contemporary societies and the values with which we grow up.

We began by looking at the foundations of modernity and the views of David Hume where we saw the beginnings of the development of a distinction between scientific and religious knowledge and the development of a kind of skepticism and a kind of foundationalism in European thought.

In Kant we find this. We began to see the development of the clear public/private distinction and an emphasis on individual freedom of thought and freedom of speech, and of the responsibility of the individual to free thought and to free speech. In Kant that free thought and free speech was grounded in this notion of a kind of collective destiny and a collective responsibility of our societies to intellectual progress.

Things have been moving from a more social to a more individualistic conception from Hume to Kant. We've been moving from the sentiment to reason, and in Mill we are going to see a deep elaboration of the Kantian distinction between the public and the private into the distinction that we now take for granted, as well as an elaboration of Kant's idea that it's the individual who matters, an individual thought, individual speech, and individual freedom, into an even more individualistic model of what civil society looks like, and a theory of privacy and of individual liberty that we will all recognize as very much akin to that that under-girds American civil society.

John Stuart Mill is a fascinating human being as well as a fascinating philosopher. He was the son of an important philosopher, James Mill, who was one of the founders of the utilitarian movement in England along with his close friend, Jeremy Bentham. James Mill actually worked for the East India Company and wrote a very influential and very strange, I must say, history of British rule in India.

John Stuart Mill, whose work we'll be examining, had a very odd upbringing. You might say that his childhood was a kind of joint experiment conducted by James Mill and Jeremy Bentham to produce the ideally-educated individual. He was indeed a prodigy which helped, but James Mill and Bentham, in order to make sure that John Stuart Mill got this ideal education, kept him completely isolated from other children his age; he knew no other children when he was young, except his own younger brothers and sisters. He was taught Greek from a very early age. By the age three or four, his Greek apparently was really good. By age six he had mastered classical Greek, was reading Plato and Herodotus, and by age eight had read the complete works of Aristotle, at which point they began teaching him Latin.

By age ten he had read all of the Latin classics and was apparently as fluent in Latin and Greek as any classics professor you could find. He was also during this time being pumped full of mathematics and the science of the day and political philosophy, so that by the time John Stuart Mill entered early adolescence he had what we would regard as a spectacular university education. I'm not advising this though as a way to raise your children. By late adolescence, John Stuart Mill suffered a significant breakdown, was depressed, and had kind of precarious mental health through much of his life. Nonetheless, he accomplished an enormous amount. He was an ardent social reformer. He was one of the first major male philosophers—maybe the first—to really defend the rights of women. He was an ardent feminist. He was an advocate of democracy in England and of democracy outside. He read Toqueville's *Democracy in America* very closely and thought a lot both about the advantages of democracy and about its dangers. He was really interested in social reform, economic reform, and political reform.

His very best known work is called *Utilitarianism,* and it is a passionate defense of utilitarianism, this idea that an action is good in proportion to the amount of benefit that it does, bad in proportion to the amount of harm that it does. This work is one of the foundations of utilitarian theory. We're not going to look at utilitarianism. We're going to look at a work that I find much more interesting. That is his work *On Liberty*, a very powerfully-argued work that really defends a very clear, articulate sense of individual liberty and does so using extraordinarily lucid arguments.

Let me review with you what some of the central argument is going to be, and then we're going to actually move into the text. Mill will begin by defending what he calls the Harm Principle and the limits of the Harm Principle, and as we'll see, that is an idea that it's only harm to others that can limit individual freedom and liberty. He's then going to discuss, and here he's going to be following Kant but with some very interesting twists, the danger of the tyranny of the majority, and the consequent obligations of civil society not only to permit individuality ideological pluralism and cultural pluralism, but actually to encourage it. So it's going to go well beyond Kant in that respect.

We're not only going to get a requirement on the State not to suppress individuality, but to actively encourage it. Mill will defend an absolute freedom of thought and expression and defend it with great clarity. In part of that defense we're going to see his famous dilemma/argument in which he's going to argue that thought and expression should be defended and protected even if it's false, even if it's pernicious, even if it's dangerous. Finally we'll conclude with Mill's famous argument for the absolute value of plurality. That plurality in society, cultural plurality, aesthetic plurality, intellectual plurality, religious plurality, is valuable in itself. So we've got the kind of under-girdings not only of a literal political order, but of the kind of pluralism that often animates contemporary American political theory.

The conclusion that we're going to see Mill defend, and the conclusion that was very dramatic in the early 19th century was that human life and meaningful human life in particular requires a society that does not only permit freedom of thought, as Kant argued, but rather one that actively facilitates freedom of thought and speech, and a society that does not only tolerate or permit diversity but actually encourages and facilitates genuine diversity of ways of life and ways of thinking, so this is a really dramatic and refreshing, and for its time, radical manifesto. It's a manifesto that's going to suggest that a meaningful life is an individual life that involves this clear and deliberate exercise of freedom and thought in a society that actually encourages and facilitates it. Let's move to Mill's text now.

We're now going to find Mill articulating the Harm principle. This is a principle that has been influential not only in philosophy but very often in law and in jurisprudence. Mill writes, "The sole end for which mankind are warranted, individually or collectively, in interfering with the liberty of any of their number is self-protection." Let's pause on that for a moment. Mill is now talking about when and only when it's permissible for a society, for any individual, to interfere with anybody else's freedom of action or thought, and he says, only for self-protection, not for the good of another, let's follow it. "That the only purpose for which power can be rightfully exercised over any member of a civilized community, against his will, is to prevent harm to others. His own good, either physical or moral, is not a sufficient warrant." Let's again pause on that for a moment.

We often think okay, we have a right to prevent somebody from performing an action that might harm us or that might harm somebody else. But surely if somebody threatens to harm themselves, maybe to make themselves ill or to commit suicide or to damage their own financial prospects spectacularly, to do something that we regard as seriously self destructive, that we ought to be able to prevent them from doing that as well. Mill argues that we cannot. That the only purpose for which power can be rightfully exercised over any member of a civilized community against his will is to prevent harm to others. His own good, either physical or moral, Mill argues, is not a sufficient warrant.

Mill continues:

> He cannot rightfully be compelled either to do or forbear because it will be better for him to do so, because it would make him happier, because in the opinions of others, to do so would be wise, or even right. These are good reasons for remonstrating with him, or reasoning with him … but not for compelling him.

This is very, very powerful stuff and it's stuff that is extraordinarily rich. Mill is arguing that if we encounter somebody who is doing something that we think is stupid, self-destructive or conduced to his own misery it's right for us to argue with him. It's right for us to try to persuade him not to do so, but we have no justification on those grounds alone for compelling him to act or not to act. "To justify that"—Mill writes—"the conduct from which it is desired to deter him must be calculated to produce evil to someone else."

He emphasizes, "The only part of the conduct of anyone for which he is amenable to society is that which concerns others. ... Over himself, over his own body and mind, the individual is sovereign."

Let's repeat that. That sentence is kind of the hallmark of the final development of modernity, complete individualist libertarianism, "Over himself, over his own body and mind, the individual is sovereign." That's very deep, very powerful. Let's note a few things here. This Harm Principle which we're seeing in Mill is going to strike us as remarkably familiar. It's very close to our own, somewhat libertarian, American conception of individual freedom, that as long as I'm not infringing on anybody else's rights, I have the right to be let alone. It looks like our right to privacy. What it's doing, what Mill is doing is taking Kant's distinction between the public and private and creating a much stronger protection for the private and a much clearer and much larger zone of privacy. For Kant the public's fear was this fear in which we engaged collectively as citizens and everything else more or less was private. For Mill, everything is private that doesn't affect the welfare of others, and that's an enormous zone of our lives.

But also notice this—and I think this is a respect in which Mill is moving deeper into modernity than Kant did. For Kant, as we saw at the end of the last lecture, the reason for the strong protection of individual freedom and liberty, and of this public/private distinction was because of our collective, social obligation to make progress. But Mill is not talking about the destiny of society, collective obligation, progress. He's talking only about the individual. This is a superbly individualist construction of privacy and liberty and a continued move following Kant away from any kind of paternalism, again going much further than Kant did.

Mill does, as did Kant, limit the scope of this restriction. The Harm Principle is not unlimited. For instance, it doesn't imply, Mill argues to children or to the incompetent. As parents we can still keep our children from harming themselves, or if we find somebody who is genuinely mentally incompetent, crazy or whatever, then again the Harm Principle doesn't apply. We need to protect them from harm to self because they're not making reasoned choices, notice that reason is still at the center of here. If one is mature, if one is rational, the Harm Principle applies, and that of course we're deriving straight from Kant whose centered reason is what makes our lives worth living.

Mill is sometimes even more controversial about this. Remember, he was the son of a colonial administrator. This is a more controversial remark. He says, "Despotism"—that is dictatorship—"is a legitimate mode of government in dealing with barbarians, provided the end is their improvement and the means justified by actually effecting that end." So Mill is saying that if you're in a colonial administration over barbarians, and we can imagine who those were for Mill, that it's perfectly okay to be dictatorial so long as what you're doing is not acting in your own interest, but acting in theirs. "Liberty as a principle has no application … [until they] are capable of … free and open discussion. Until then there is nothing for them but implicit obedience to an Akbar or a Charlemagne." Of course in mentioning Akbar, the Mogul Emperor in India, Mill is very self-consciously defending British rule in India. This is certainly one of the more embarrassing parts of *On Liberty*, but there it is.

Mill, like Kant was worried about the tyranny of the majority. Mill articulates that worry in a much more focused way and makes much stronger stuff out of it. Let's follow Mill on this because he's really more worried about the tyranny of the majority than he is about the tyranny of individuals or the tyranny of the law, just as Kant was more worried about self-imposed immaturity than he was about externally imposed immaturity. Mill writes,

> [W]hen society itself is the tyrant … its means of tyrannizing are not restricted to the acts [of] political functionaries. Society … practices a social tyranny more formidable than many kinds of political oppression, since… it leaves fewer means of escape, penetrating more deeply into the details of life and enslaving the soul itself.

Mill might have been writing about junior high or high school. This notion of social tyranny and we get it through the advertising, we get it through politics, but we get it through this sense that there's a social expectation that we believe, think or behave in certain ways. Mill writes, "There is a limit to the legitimate interference of collective opinion with individual independence, and to find that limit, and maintain it … is as indispensable to a good condition of human affairs as protection against political despotism."

This is really strong because what Mill is recognizing is the insidiousness of social pressure. The fact that social pressure constrains and cramps individual liberty not just as explicit legal pressure or censorship might, but even more so it does it more to a greater degree because there's nothing to challenge, there's no escape, and it's not explicit so we don't have a way of arguing against it. It's an evil, a social evil that reduces our individual liberty in very subtle, but nonetheless coercive ways. So it suggests to Mill that a well-ordered society, a society that enables flourishing, a society that enables us to lead truly meaningful lives, must take measures to mitigate this kind of social tyranny or social pressure.

For that reason it's important that in order to assure flourishing lives for a citizenry, it's not enough to just let people alone. A government that just leaves people alone would be a government that leaves them to the mercy of social tyranny, of social pressure. For that reason, Mill thinks, conditions for individuality don't just emerge by accident. They have to be actively encouraged by government. This is not a call for a laissez faire libertarian government. It's a call for an activist government that moves against monopoly of the public space by social tyrannies and majority, so this is kind of radical.

Mill is arguing here that there's a kind of social obligation, a collective political obligation to generate individuality. The place where this really enters the American tradition is with the work of John Dewey and his thought about American education, arguing that the educational system has an obligation to generate free thinking individuals, not just people who know lots of stuff, and certainly not people who accept common wisdom. That idea in Dewey is coming straight out of John Stuart Mill. There's a lot of influence here in American society from Mill. Mill also defends an absolute freedom of speech and thought in the public sphere, and he gives it some very extended, very passionate defense. It's gorgeous, we don't have time to work through all of it here, but I really recommend that after you hear this lecture you pick up a copy of *On Liberty*. It's a stirring and beautiful text and you'll enjoy reading it.

What I want to do now is to articulate one of the central pieces of that argument and one that I think is extraordinarily profound and strikes some people as very surprising when they hear it. We call it the dilemma argument. Mill begins with an interesting dilemma. He points out that some speech is true and some speech is false. Sometimes we articulate things that we know to be true, might argue for instance that the Earth is round, but there are also flat Earthers out there who argue ferociously that the Earth is flat. Some people argue and defend evolutionary theory, some defend creationism, one of those positions is surely false, one of those positions may well be true.

Moreover he points out, some speech, some ideas, some thoughts or ideologies, are beneficial and some are in fact harmful. The question is should we be able to restrict any of it? Mill points out that many people think that while we would never want to suppress true speech, true ideas, or beneficial ideas, it would be okay to suppress ideas we know to be false or we know to be dangerous. Indeed many societies today restrict speech, publication, ideas because they don't want ideas that they regard as false, or ideas that they regard as dangerous or subversive to be expressed.

Mill argues that both of those are dangerous. He argues that of course ideas are either true or false. If they're true or beneficial—right, this kind of former end of the dilemma—then if we suppress them, believing that they're false or believing that they're harmful we are going to slow progress, we're going to prevent discovery, we're going to slow down science, and we're going to deprive people of access to the truth. Mill offers many examples of this. Of course the most famous one would be the persecution of Galileo. The church taking a belief which it believed to be false and believed to be harmful which ended up being true and beneficial, and suppressed it and we saw the horrible consequences. Mill offers a number of examples of these and with a little bit of imagination you can come up with quite a few.

The interesting piece is the other side of the dilemma. Why shouldn't we suppress speech which is false and harmful? Mill points two things out. One of course is, we might be wrong. That is, we might seriously believe— genuinely believe that a view is false or that it's harmful and it's not and we might suppress it in which case we ended up getting a Galileo situation. More importantly even if the view is harmful or false, by simply suppressing it we deprive ourselves of the opportunity to refute it rationally by argument. That is, people who may have believed it are kind of bullied politically or socially into not asserting it, not thinking about it, not articulating it, not defending it. But beating people into ideological submission, Mill pointed out, does not eliminate the belief. It does not get them not to believe it, it just gets them to be quiet about it. As he puts it, it drives these beliefs underground and when they're driven underground they're immune to refutation. We can't find them. We can't argue against them. We can't refute them. So Mill imagines we get this kind of underground economy of cancerous beliefs and views and arguments that build on themselves because people only hear that stuff. They never hear refutation, and the reason that they do not hear refutation is because the views have been suppressed. When that happens, Mill says, these views cause even more harm because if you kept them in the daylight, if you didn't persecute them, then in the clear light of day under rational examination, under open political discussion, the views would simply be refuted and they would die off on their own accord.

Mill says, when we confront this dilemma we should realize that whether we believe a view is true and beneficial or that we believe that the view is false and detrimental, there is no argument for suppression, only an argument for putting it out in the public domain for argument, discourse, defense or critique.

Mill also points out that there's another reason for absolute freedom of speech. That was the kind of dilemma argument. The second big argument though is his argument for the absolute value of pluralism and plurality in society. I think this was an argument that was way ahead of its time. We live in an era now where people are fond of talking about pluralistic, diverse societies, and the value of diversity. That wasn't true in the 19th century. It's worth remembering that we pick up this discourse about diversity very much from John Stuart Mill, so we're looking at the roots of a lot of our own ideology.

Mill points out that it's often hard to know of a bunch of rival ideas, rival perspectives, which one is true, which one is most beneficial. Even if we think we know which one is, he points out that our ideas, our thinking, our ideology, and our approaches are always approved through debate. By refuting somebody else we get a clearer idea of what we ourselves think and why. They get a clearer idea of why they're wrong and why our views might be right. Or of course we might find out, surprisingly, that we're wrong and improve our ideas by taking aboard ideas from others.

Many times Mill points out different views, different traditions. Especially he points out religious traditions or aesthetic traditions or traditions in food or lifestyle might be better for different people. There might be some parts of society who do really well as Catholics and some parts that do really well as Jews, some parts who do really well as Buddhists. Some parts who do really well not religious at all. Some people like modern art. Some people like classical art, and there's no reason to impose a uniformity when variety actually benefits more people.

Mill argues that society offers a lot more options to its citizens but also a lot more ideological ferment, hence a lot more stuff going on, a lot more **façon** if we've got pluralism. These are the things that generate happiness, the opportunity to lead your life and to engage in conversation over ideas that you want to have access to, also the opportunity to engage with people who are different from you, to eat food that's different from you, to observe art that you're not familiar with. These are all sources of happiness, and Mill argues if we're looking for human flourishing, even if I seriously and deeply believe that the music that I like best is best, that the literature that I like best is best, that the religious tradition to which I belong is best, to impose that on others does them no favors, does me no favors, and does my society no favors. The domain of individual liberty for Mill is vast because only by making it vast can we allow individuals to flourish.

In Mill's thought we see this tremendous importance of individuality, of individualism. It's not obvious if you just begin to think about it pre-reflectively. Why the cultivation of individuality and diversity is a good thing, it needs defense. That's a central insight of Mill's. That you can't just say, hey it's good to be individuals, it's good to be different. You need a reason for that. Indeed Mill noted and we can note in our present society that there are many people who see diversity and individuality as a bad thing. It promotes, some people think, disunity. It doesn't promote unity in society. It might promote conflict, and it also might allow people to choose lifestyles or views that we might think of as harmful to them or to society at large.

But Mill points out that this kind of individualism and pluralism, in fact, promotes progress. It's the rare individuals, it's the individuals whose creativity emerges from that, who are creative enough, progressive enough to break through social stagnation and to allow genuine social progress. Mill also argues that it makes for better citizens. He writes, "He who lets the world ... choose his plan of life"—note the echo of Kant here, right, very self conscious—"He who lets the world ... choose his plan of life ... [lives a life of] ape-like imitation." Worse than juvenile, ape-like, we're going down the phylo-genetic scale. "He who chooses a plan of life for himself uses all his faculties." So Mill argues, we're just plain better people; when we exercise that kind of choice we're more mature, we're more developed.

Moreover Mill points out, originality is what leads to material progress. Even if you just care about more goods and more material progress in society, you need originality, and originality only comes from pluralism and individuality. This is the plurality argument. We've seen that for Mill, coercion and criticism makes sense only when we're criticizing things that we believe to be wrong. That coercion and criticism is very different things. It's one thing to criticize of you. It's one thing to coerce somebody from holding that view. There's a difference between harm and offense. We might be offended by somebody's view, that's a reason to criticize. Only if that person is harming others can we coerce them to abandon the view or the behavior. Only harm or personal incompetence justifies coercion at all for Mill.

This distinction between self-regarding acts—that is acts that don't affect anybody else—and other regarding acts—acts that affect others and may harm them—ends up replacing Kant's distinction between public and private. Nowadays in American society and jurisprudence we think of other regarding acts as the ones where the law has got some say. But self-regarding acts as being within the zone of privacy that was recognized, for instance, in *Griswold vs. Connecticut*, the Supreme Court decision which decriminalized the use of contraceptives in Connecticut as a violation of individual behavior on the grounds that there was a zone of privacy that protected these things. That of course is also the basis of the *Roe vs. Wade* holding.

Note that for Mill this doesn't mean we can't criticize. Speech is always free, even critical speech, even speech we don't want to hear. For Mill offense is never a harm. Things I say may offend you, but offense doesn't harm you. You've got to be willing to be offended if you want to be part of a free society Mill thinks.

For this reason, Mill would be a real opponent of policies that prohibit so-called hate speech. He has a really nice example. It's the example of the corn merchant. We might say, in a public discourse, corn merchants are thieves, we need to control and to regulate the corn market; that's free speech. But we can't stand outside a corn merchant's house with an enraged mob with torches and say corn merchants are thieves, we've got to do something about corn merchants. That's inciting particular harm as opposed to public speech. Merely offensive speech, Mill argues, has to be protected.

Mill is defending the importance of individuality and liberty in modernity. What we see in Mill, as I said, is this kind of final flowering of this individualism and libertarianism that really runs through the modern viewpoint. From Hume to Mill we evolve much deeper secularism, a much deeper individualism, and a much stronger public/private distinction.

Mill is following Kant in developing that public/private distinction, but he's giving us the most modern, contemporary expression of the view, that our lives and the lives of our fellows are meaningful when and only when we are self-expressive free individuals and meaningful for precisely that reason, not because of our social context but because of who we are as individuals. This is the first purely individualistic doctrine of the meaning of life that we've seen. Mill provides us therefore with the strongest defense you could ever want of the connection between a meaningful life and a liberal social order.

This has been an articulation of what modernity is all about. If you join me in the next lecture we're going to begin looking at post modernity and looking at the kind of critiques of modernity that developed almost immediately in the 19th century, beginning with a kind of conservative critique in the work of Tolstoy, and getting more and more radical as we go; because what we're going to see is that this championing of the role of the individuality, the reliance on reason, gets questioned. The liberal social order is not something we can easily take for granted. It's an articulation that itself can be problematized. In the next lectures we're going to be examining a kind of critical take on the modernism we've developed over the last four. Please join me for those.

Tolstoy—Is Everyday Life the Real Thing?
Lecture 27

> Again, as we read the novel and experience all of this, there's a sense maybe of a kind of compassion or a sense of even contempt for [Ivan Ilych's] family and his friends, but there's more of a sense of embarrassment, I think. The sense of embarrassment comes from the fact that probably each of us at some point has reacted—even if we didn't like to admit it—to a death or an illness in exactly this way.

In addition to being a great novelist, **Lev (Leo) Tolstoy** was also an important social reformer and political activist in Russia. He believed that secularization and the mass society that results from secularization, coupled with capitalism, lead to a meaningless life. In *The Death of Ivan Ilych*, Tolstoy takes as his theme the importance of pre-modern spiritual values, including an awareness of death, the need to develop deep human relationships, and a connection to nature as opposed to an artificial society. He argues implicitly that a life led in a secular world—like Ivan Ilych's life and our own—is completely hopeless and, at death, leaves us feeling as though that life has been wasted.

The novel opens with a scene in which Ilych's friends and colleagues are discussing who will fill his position at work. Then Tolstoy writes, "The mere fact of the death of a near acquaintance aroused, as usual, in all who heard of it the complacent feeling that, 'It is he who is dead, not I.'" The sentiment is familiar to all of us; we push the thought of our own death away when we encounter the deaths of others. Ilych's wife tells us that his death was so painful that *she* could hardly bear it, focusing on her own grief. Another friend, Peter Ivanovich, denies that Ilych's death has any relationship to himself. This **depersonalization** of death is often how we deal with our own mortality and, for Tolstoy, is an inevitable consequence of secularism.

Tolstoy points out that Ilych is all of us: "Ivan Ilych's life had been most simple and most ordinary and therefore most terrible." When he falls ill, he at first denies the fact of his impending death. Like Ilych, we are all generally quite happy with an abstract understanding that death happens to everyone, but we also fail to see that we fall under that abstraction, that death happens to us, too.

Tolstoy also shows us that in the secularized world, people tend to move away from those who are dying. In the novel, Ilych's family actually gets bored and rather annoyed with the inconvenience of his death, while Ilych experiences this unique and incomprehensible tragedy alone.

> **Like Ilych, we are all generally quite happy with an abstract understanding that death happens to everyone, but we also fail to see that we fall under that abstraction, that death happens to us, too.**

At this point in the novel, Tolstoy introduces a new character, a kind, clean peasant boy named Gerasim, who is able to provide some comfort to Ilych. He cares for Ilych in an unpretentious, natural way, not out of some obligation or social pretension. He seems to be honest in a way that others in the book are not and understands the inevitability of death, not just in the abstract but in a concrete sense. Because Gerasim takes his own death seriously, he is able to be honest about death and to engage in meaningful interactions with others. In giving us this cheerful, happy, healthy character, Tolstoy is telling us that the only way we can live a happy, healthy life is if we, too, are honest about death.

As Ilych's health declines, he finds that his accomplishments and possessions, even his family, pale in significance to death. He realizes that he has frittered his life away on the trivial, on the public sphere, instead of confronting the structure of his own existence. He questions whether life is that "senseless and horrible," but of course, that's the point: If we lead a life in which we pay little attention to the concrete reality of our existence and our mortality, a senseless and horrible life is what we're left with.

On the eve of his death, Ilych wonders whether his whole life might have been false; he asks, "But if that is so … and if I am leaving this life with the consciousness that I have lost all that was given to me and it is impossible to rectify it, what then?" Tolstoy's point is that we may all be in exactly that

135

position if we don't move to lead more authentic, meaningful lives now. That terrible possibility with which we are confronted is the consequence of the modern secular life.

At the moment of his death, Ilych has a revelation and finds that he no longer fears death. The message here is that we need to confront the fact that our lives are aimed at death. Not only do we all die, but we're all dying every minute from the moment of birth. That's what structures our lives, and indeed, the most important moment of our lives may be that final one, the one where we need to ask whether it was all worthwhile. ■

Name to Know

Tolstoy, Lev (Leo) (1828–1910): Count Leo Tolstoy was born into one of the most distinguished Russian noble families, but his own youth was undistinguished. He became a great novelist and an important social reformer and political activist.

Important Term

depersonalization: Abstraction from one's own personal interests or place in the world; taking a disinterested view of things.

Suggested Reading

Tolstoy, *The Death of Ivan Ilych*.

Study Questions

1. How does the life of Ivan Ilych as portrayed by Tolstoy compare to the kinds of lives to which most people aspire? Does Tolstoy's indictment of this kind of life seem fair?

2. How does the servant Gerasim contrast with the other characters in Ivan's life? What makes his values different? What kind of life does Tolstoy recommend as meaningful, in contrast to the meaningless lives he portrays in the other characters?

3. In what ways do the values of European modernity contribute to the kind of life that Tolstoy is concerned to criticize?

Tolstoy—Is Everyday Life the Real Thing?
Lecture 27—Transcript

Nice to see you again. Our last few lectures took us to the foundations of European modernity and I'm guessing that was a fairly familiar space. What we're going to do now is to destabilize that space a little bit. We're going to begin to look at critical evaluations of the modernism that most of us take for granted. Today we're going to focus on the critique developed by the great Russian novelist and philosopher, Lev Tolstoy.

Most of us, of course, think of Tolstoy, who was born in 1828, died in 1910, as a great novelist and of course he was a great novelist, he wrote *War and Peace, Anna Karenina,* and so forth. He was also a very important social reformer and political activist in Russia. He was a religious reformer. He was indeed even a supporter of anarchism. A lot of Tolstoy's political and moral thought was in fact influential on the great Indian leader, Mahandas Gandhi whose work we'll address later, and through Gandhi on the great American political leader and philosopher, Martin Luther King. In our own culture we owe a lot of our ideas that are current to Tolstoy.

Tolstoy was radical in that he was one of the first Russian land owners to provide education to his surfs, and near his death moved to liberate them. He tried very hard to make the Christianity of his time less ritualistic and more humanistic. Very late in his life he resolved to become an aesthetic wanderer on the model of the Buddha and left home, but died very shortly afterwards.

Even Tolstoy's novels are intensely philosophical and we will be reading one of his novels, a very short novel, *The Death of Ivan Ilych* which I think is especially philosophical. I also think it's especially beautiful.

Why are we reading a Tolstoy novel now? Well, it's because Tolstoy was above all intensely concerned about the dangers of modernity for human life and spiritual life. In particular, Tolstoy thought that secularization, which as we have seen, is a centerpiece of European modernity and the mass society that results from secularization coupled with capitalism lead to a meaningless life. He thought that they evacuated all sense of value, everything that was worthwhile from life.

In *The Death of Ivan Ilych,* Tolstoy takes as his theme the importance of coming back to what he regards as a pre-modern value, spiritual values including an awareness of death, of value on important, deep human relationships and above all a connection to nature as opposed to a connection to an artificial society.

Tolstoy thought and argues implicitly in *The Death of Ivan Ilych* that a life that's led in a secular world, that's governed entirely by social conventions and laws, like Hume imagined, a life that is governed by our collective social energy, or governed by reason even and public discourse like those imagined by Kant and Mill, he thinks that such a life this kind of secular life with religion pushed off to the side, lives in this public sphere is absolutely hopeless, and that at death it leaves us completely empty and feeling as though we've wasted our lives.

For Tolstoy, Ivan Ilych, who we're going to encounter in the last moments of his life is indeed all of us. Tolstoy wants us to pay attention to Ivan Ilych's life because Tolstoy thinks that that's the life that most of us lead and that his death is the death that we are most in danger of dying. Tolstoy's prose in this novel, as in all of his novels, is absolutely beautiful. So I'm going to do a fair amount of reading the text with you and talking through the philosophical ideas in the text. I'm hoping that after this you'll run out and buy it, because it's a really absolutely lovely little novel.

Let's begin by asking what Ivan Ilych's death meant to those around us, and Tolstoy opens with a lovely scene involving Ivan Ilych's colleagues, people with whom he'd been on very close terms and who had known that he was ill and their conjectures on Ivan Ilych's death. Ivan Ilych, by the way, was a judge at the time of his death, so his colleagues are other colleagues in the law in the judiciary. Tolstoy writes, "

> His post had been kept open for him, but there had been conjectures that in case of his death Alexeyev might receive his appointment, and that either Vinikov or Shtable would succeed Alexeyev. So on receiving the news of Ivan Ilych's death the first thought of each of the gentlemen in that private room was of the

changes and promotions it might occasion among themselves or their acquaintances.

What's going on here? Ivan Ilych has died. What does this death mean to the friends and colleagues that were so close to him? Well we're beginning with his friends. What it means to them of course is there's a vacancy. We've got to start thinking in the shop about who's going to fill that vacancy. But of course it means a bit more than that. Tolstoy writes, "The mere fact of the death of a near acquaintance aroused, as usual, in all who heard of it the complacent feeling that, 'It is he who is dead, not I.' " This is a very important philosophical moment in this text. Which of us, when we've heard that somebody else died thought wow, I dodged a bullet. He's dead, not me. It's sad, I'm worried about it, but I've got to go on living. So we push the thought of our own death away when we encounter the deaths of others. Recall Śāntideva on this. How much of our life is spent pushing the thought of our own death away. Tolstoy continues, "But the more intimate of Ilych's acquaintances, his so-called friends, could not help thinking that they would now have to fulfill the very tiresome demands of propriety by attending the funeral service and paying a visit of condolence to the widow."

We might be embarrassed by this but it's certainly familiar. The idea that we think, damn, I've got other things to do, I've got a life to lead, and now this person has died, it's so inconvenient. I've got to go to a funeral, I've got to make a condolence call. One of the things that death does to us is to force us to think for a moment about our own death and suppress it, and the other to develop this kind of annoyed view that somebody had the temerity to die and screw up our lives right now.

This is what Tolstoy is suggesting that death, often in modern society, means to the friends. How about to Ivan Ilych's wife, who after all is much closer to him? We're now in a conversation between Ivan Ilych's wife and one of these friends and she says, "He suffered terribly in the last few days. He screamed unceasingly, not for minutes but for hours." It wasn't a good death by the way. "For the last three days he screamed unceasingly." Now listen "It was unendurable. I cannot understand how I bore it. You could hear him three rooms off. Oh, what I have suffered." Listen to Ivan Ilych's wife. Ivan Ilych has just died this horrible death and she's told us how painful it was for him and how much he suffered, but it moves immediately to how much I suffered, how much she could not bear.

Tolstoy is emphasizing here the idea that when somebody else dies, we immediately focus not on them but we personalize it. What does it mean to me? How do I feel now? We focus on our own mourning, our own upset. For Tolstoy this is just an indication of the kind of alienation from each other that death brings into focus, an alienation that he thinks is borne of the secular modernity.

Tolstoy now asks, what does his death mean to all of us? Taking it through the silique of one of Ivan Ilych's friends. He writes, "Three days of frightful suffering and death! Why, that might suddenly, at any time, happen to me," he thought, and for a moment felt terrified,

> But—he did not know how—the customary reflection at once occurred to him that this had happened to Ivan Ilych and not to him, and that it should not and could not happen to him, and to think that it could would be yielding to depression, which he ought not to do. … After (this) reflection, Peter Ivanovich felt reassured … death was an accident natural to Ivan Ilych, but certainly not to himself.

Once again, Tolstoy eloquently paints for us what happens when we contemplate the death of another. We immediately realize that it was he who died not me. We immediately decide that thinking about our own death, however natural it might be now, would be depressing, push it aside. Think about other things. Better to lead our lives in ignorance of our own mortality than to focus on that depressing fact.

This all sounds pretty real right? Remember Śāntideva's worry that this is our natural condition. Death appears to be a really big thing to us. To those who remain behind, Ivan Ilych's friends for instance, it's just a reshuffling. One person is gone, other people take the jobs. It's a set of rituals and social obligations. The dead person, Ivan Ilych in this case, slips out of consciousness. Nobody is thinking about him. We think about our own grief and whether or not this death means anything to us. Finally we deny that that death has any relationship to ourselves. Death becomes abstract.

This depersonalization of death, this abstraction of death, is very much how we often deal with our own mortality and with the mortality of others; that's Tolstoy point. The depersonalization and abstraction is an inevitable consequence of a secularism in a modernity.

Who is Ivan Ilych whose death we're talking about? Well Tolstoy points out to us that he's all of us. He writes, "Ivan Ilych's life had been most simple and most ordinary and therefore most terrible." This is an indictment, not a celebration of modernity. This is not Hume or Mill. This is a very different view. Tolstoy tells us that Ivan Ilych had a kind of model career. When he died as a judge at the age of 45 he had done very well for himself. He joined the civil service after graduating from law school. He got a good post as an aide to a governor of a province. Tolstoy explains to us he was a very decent man. He was proper. He was absolutely scrupulous in his duties, nothing corrupt about him. He was honest. He was well-respected. We're told that he was a man of great personal decorum and a man of good cheer. We're also told he had a really nice wife and good children.

Like so many of us, Ivan Ilych, we find out in the novel, had some financial troubles and there's some marital squabbling. But after a while he gets a big promotion to his judgeship and then the financial troubles go away, everybody is happy. He buys a really nice house that Ivan Ilych is really spiffy, but it's a kind of McMansion, it's just like everybody else's house. All the houses that are owned and decorated by the upper middle classes in Russia, Tolstoy tells us, look about the same and Ivan Ilych's is like that, a Russian McMansion.

Nonetheless he has a happy life. We're told he throws good parties, people really enjoy them and look for invitations. He holds bridge nights with his good friends. He enjoys lots of food and drink. He has a very satisfying job as a judge. He does it well. It's not just an imagination, and he enjoys doing it well. He's very well respected socially. He has a lot of material comfort. He is an upper middle class kind of guy. The kids are doing great in school. This is a really good life, this is the modern life. This is the life Tolstoy thinks to which most of us aspire, a really good house, a really good job, a nice wife, good kids who are doing well, a fulfilling job, lots of respect, all that good stuff.

Then Ivan Ilych gets sick, and as soon as he gets sick we start worrying. First, Ivan Ilych is thinking about his own death and realizing that it might be serious and he begins to contemplate what that means. Notice how abstract things get. Ivan Ilych writes, now Ivan Ilych's voice, "When I am not, what will there be? There will be nothing. Then where shall I be when I am not more? Can this be dying? No, I don't want to! It is impossible that all men have been doomed to suffer this awful horror!"

What does this mean? Ivan Ilych is suddenly realizing at this stage of his illness that he might die. The first thing he does is to deny it. He says, it can't be so, death is just too bad. This can't be something that we have been sentenced to. Then he considers this wonderful syllogism, and this is a beautiful exposition by Tolstoy of how we manage to abstract death and depersonalize it. Tolstoy writes,

> The syllogism he had learned [in] logic: Caius is a man, men are mortal, therefore Caius is mortal, had always seemed correct to him as applied to Caius, but certainly not as applied to himself. That Caius—man in the abstract—was mortal, was perfectly correct, but he was not Caius, not an abstract man, but a creature quite, quite separate from all others. He had been little Vanya, with a mama and a papa. ... What did Caius know of the smell of that striped ball Vanya had been so fond of? Had Caius been in love like that? Could Caius preside at a session as he did? Caius really was mortal, and it was right for him to die, but for me, little Vanya, Ivan Ilych, with all my thoughts and emotions, it's altogether a different matter.

Tolstoy points out, we are quite happy understanding that death happens to everybody. We're quite happy with an abstract understanding of immortality. But we always fail to see that we fall under that abstraction, that death happens to us too. It's part of this depersonalization that Tolstoy sees as part of secularization. Unfortunately for Ivan Ilych, his illness is far too concrete. It can't be all made abstract. We learned that he starts having trouble sleeping. The doctors come. He's given opium for the pain and to help him sleep. He's given injections of morphine, but even this doesn't relieve the pain. We're told that he has a special diet prepared for him at doctor's orders, and for a while, that's a little bit better. Eventually the foods become really distasteful and disgusting to him. He loses his appetite and he's going downhill. Tolstoy writes, really emphasizing the concreteness of all of this, "For his excretions also special arrangements had to be made, and this was a torment to him every time—a torment from the uncleanliness, the unseemliness, and the smell, and from knowing that another person had to take part in it."

Let's pause on this for a moment. This I think, even though it seems like a kind of Earthy moment, is for Tolstoy a philosophically very significant moment in the novel. What's upsetting to Ivan Ilych is his embodiment and the fact that he has to be as a physical person who actually excretes smelly stuff involved with another person because somebody has to come and clean him up and take the bedpan out and all of that.

For Ivan Ilych, what happens at this kind of moment having to do with food, with excretion, with physical care, brings the concreteness of his life, brings the concreteness of his illness, brings the concreteness of his death really home to roost and that's why it's so upsetting. It forces him to confront that kind of reality.

Where are we at this point in the text? What we find is that we've got a very nice guy. There's nothing wrong with Ivan Ilych. He's a very good, very ordinary person with a good, ordinary middle class life. He's doing all the right things in life and he's confronting his own mortality in the way that each of us will someday have to confront our own mortality. He tries to do it by abstraction and by denial. Through the syllogism, through thinking that death is a perfectly general thing, denying that it could possibly be true that he's really dying. But life and death, as Tolstoy points out, turn out to be rather concrete. They're realities that we can't abstract away, that we can't depersonalize.

Moreover, Ivan Ilych is turning out to be rather alone in all of this. This is something else that Tolstoy emphasizes about the nature of death. While we might live among colleagues, we might live among family, eventually we die alone. Tolstoy points out that especially in this kind of secularized life, people begin to move away from us if we're dying. They visit less often. They spend less time with us at that time. Ivan Ilych is getting rather lonely. In fact, Tolstoy points out, by this time when we get to this stage of the novel and this stage of the illness, Ivan Ilych's family is actually getting bored. The kids don't like having a dying father around. The wife doesn't like having her social life disrupted. There's a lot of inconvenience. There has to be special physical arrangements made. Rooms have to be readjusted, doctors are going in and out, and—we're in a time before universal healthcare—it's getting expensive, and the wife is worried about the money rolling out to pay for medicines, to pay for doctors and so forth. Everybody in the family is really feeling like this is a grand annoyance.

This is again part of the loneliness of death. For Ivan Ilych what is happening is this unique and incomprehensible tragedy that affects him and him alone. To his family it's just one more annoyance. Can't we get it over with. Can't we just lead normal lives? Again as we read the novel and experience all of this, there's a sense maybe of a kind of compassion or a sense of even contempt for his family and his friends, but there's more of a sense of embarrassment I think. The sense of embarrassment comes from the fact that probably each of us at some point has reacted—even if we didn't like to admit it—to a death or an illness in exactly this way.

At this point Tolstoy introduces a new character into the novel who turns out to be a significant one. I'm going to read with you.

> But just through this most unpleasant matter, [that is the matter of toileting,] Ivan Ilych obtained comfort. Gerasim, the butler's assistant, always came in to carry the things out. Gerasim was a clean, fresh peasant lad … always cheerful and bright. At first the sight of him, in his clean [clothes] engaged on that disgusting task embarrassed Ivan Ilych."

So what happened? We have this kind of sweet, clean, fresh peasant guy coming in and helping Ivan Ilych with his bedpan and cleaning him up and so forth. Ivan Ilych's first reaction to this interaction is serious embarrassment. He doesn't want this boy to see him in this situation and to deal with these functions, and you can understand the embarrassment but things continue. Gerasim turns out to be an uncommonly kind lad. Let's see how Tolstoy puts this. He says,

Gerasim went up to him, grasped his master with his strong arms deftly but gently … lifted him supported him with one, and with the other drew up his trousers. "Thank you. How easily and well you do it all!" [That's the voice of Ivan Ilych, of course.] Gerasim smiled again and turned to leave the room. But Ivan Ilych felt his presence such a comfort that he did not want him to go.

Then Tolstoy describes how he had Gerasim stay and hold his legs up so that he'd feel more comfortable, massage him a little bit, talk to him a little bit, and Gerasim actually provided some concrete, personal, tender human comfort. Gerasim we find out had this wonderful effect on Ivan Ilych. We're told that Gerasim did it all easily, willingly. Tolstoy writes, "Simply and with a good nature that touched Ivan Ilych. Health, strength, and vitality in other people were offensive to him, but Gerasim's strength and vitality did not mortify but soothed him."

There's something about Gerasim that can provide some comfort. What we're seeing, if possible, is Gerasim in a very unpretentious, very natural human way. Not out of obligation, not out of some social convention, but just naturally and spontaneously engages at this personal level with Ivan Ilych. Operating in the private sphere gives a certain kind of comfort. Gerasim is honest in a way that others are not.

Ivan Ilych saw, Tolstoy tells us, that nobody else really felt for him. Nobody else really had serious deep compassion for him in his illness and impending death, for one reason. Nobody even wanted to grasp his position. Nobody really understood what he was going through and that because it was so annoying or so depressing or so terrifying that everybody distanced themselves. It was only Gerasim who recognized and pitied him. Here's how Tolstoy puts it in Gerasim's mouth now. So we hear Gerasim, the butler's boy talking.

> "If you weren't sick it would be another matter, but as it is, why should I grudge a little trouble?" Gerasim alone did not lie, everything showed that he alone understood the facts of the case and did not consider it necessary to disguise them … Once … he even said straight out …

This is an important moment in the novel and an important philosophical moment for Tolstoy. This is the voice of Gerasim the butler's boy:

> "We shall all of us die, so why should I grudge a little trouble?" …
> [H]e did not think his work burdensome because he was doing it for
> a dying man and hoped that someone would do the same for him
> when his time came.

Gerasim is an interesting character in all of this. Gerasim understands the inevitability of death and the meaningfulness of death not just in the abstract but also in this very concrete sense. What does Gerasim represent in this case?

Part of Gerasim's role is to represent the peasant for Tolstoy because Tolstoy, we have to face it, was a kind of peasant romantic. He really thought there was a special, deep kind of wisdom in the Russian peasant through which modern Russians really needed to tap into, this kind of depth and understanding of nature that was absent from the upper classes. There is part of that, but there is a deeper point. Gerasim takes his own death seriously. He says, we, all of us die. He speaks in the first person. When Ivan Ilych thought about death he thought about it in the third person, Caius' mortal. He abstracted it from himself. When his friends thought about death, they thought about it as something that happened to Ivan Ilych but can't possibly happen to them.

Gerasim talks about death in the first person. He's the only person in the novel who's doing that. He says we, all of us, die. Tolstoy's point here is that only somebody who takes their own death seriously can be honest with somebody else about death. If we want to be able to encounter other people in their mortality and to be able to understand the nature of their lives and to engage in meaningful interactions with them, even for their own benefit but for ours as well, taking our own mortality and our own death seriously is an important prerequisite.

The other point here that of course follows from this and is the real punch is that only if you're honest about death can you live a healthy, happy life. That's really central to all of this. Remember all these facts about Gerasim.

He's clean, he's happy, he's healthy, he's cheerful, he's able to be a comfort. That's because of his honesty about his own wife and his own death. This is a theme that we saw developed in Śāntideva. Of course this isn't a modern theme; it's a way pre-modern theme. Śāntideva argued that what makes our lives miserable, what causes us to live in fear, unhappiness and vice is not just a fear of death but pushing death to the periphery of our understanding and of our experience. If we're happy with death and can accept death and our own mortality, the fear disappears.

Now we find ourselves very close to Ivan Ilych's death and we have the question asked, what if his life wasn't the real thing? Tolstoy writes, "All that had seemed joys now melted before his sight and turned into something trivial and often nasty." That is, Ivan Ilych is revealing his life and everything that seemed like it was wonderful, the house, the kids, the wife, the promotion, suddenly seemed really trivial because now he's really confronting his mortality. Death is important, the rest of this stuff pales. What that means is he's finding himself at the end of a life thinking that everything that happened in it was trivial and often nasty. Tolstoy continues,

> And the further he departed from childhood and the nearer he came to the present the more worthless and doubtful were the joys. It is as if I had been going downhill while I imagined I was going up. And that is really what it was. I was going up in public opinion, but to the same extent, life was ebbing away from me. And now it is all done and there is only death.

Ivan Ilych has suddenly recognized that he's frittered his life away on the trivial, on the public's sphere, on a conventional life, an ordinary life, a life that was lived thoughtlessly, a life where he wasn't confronting his own choices and he wasn't confronting the structure of his own existence. "Then what does it mean? Why? It can't be that life is so senseless and horrible." Of course that's the problem. If we lead a life in which we abstract ourselves so much and pay so little attention to the concrete reality of our existence and our own mortality, a senseless and horrible life is what we might be left with.

Might it have all been false? "That night ... the question suddenly occurred to him: 'What if my whole life has been wrong?' " Imagine having to ask yourself that on your death bead. Tolstoy's point is that we may all be in exactly that position if we don't move to lead a more authentic, meaningful life now.

> It occurred to him that what had appeared perfectly impossible before, namely that he had not spent his life as he should have done, might after all be true. ... [H]is professional duties and the whole arrangement of his life and of his family, and all his social and official interests, might all have been false. ... "But if that is so ... and I am leaving this life with the consciousness that I have lost all that was given to me and it is impossible to rectify it—what then?"

That's the terrible possibility with which Tolstoy wants to confront us, the consequence of the modern secular life.

Now at the moment of his death, Ivan Ilych has a revelation.

> At that very moment, Ivan Ilych fell through and caught sight of the light, and it was revealed to him that though his life had not been what it should have been, this could still be rectified. He asked himself, "What is the right thing?"... He was sorry for [his family], he must act so as not to hurt them... He sought his former accustomed fear of death and did not find it. "Where is it? What is death?" There was no fear because there is no death. In place of death there was light.

Tolstoy is telling us here that our lives are indeed aimed at death and that's something that we need to confront. Not only do we all die, but we're all dying every minute from the moment of our birth. That's what structures our lives, and the most important moment of our lives might be that final one, the one where we need to ask whether it was all worthwhile.

Our ordinary conventions, the conventions of modernity Tolstoy thinks, and our ordinary consciousness that pushes death to the side conceals that fact. Tolstoy is challenging us with the idea that that is in fact a dishonest,

149

inauthentic way to live, even if it's the normal way to live. Social propriety, the ordinary conversational customs and our habits and our etiquette conspires in this effort to hide mortality from us. We then find ourselves focusing, as Ivan Ilych says, on the meaningless, on the trivial, on the nasty. We forget that meaning may well emerge at the end and come back to get us.

Tolstoy urges that only a return to the natural and appreciation of our biological nature and our place in the world as concrete individuals can help us. If that happens, he points out, our mortality and the recognition of our own mortality can inspire compassion—as we find in Ivan Ilych at the end—for others and ourselves, that can lead us to an honest life and a meaningful life. In Tolstoy, what we see is a curiously pre-modern response to modernity, a conservative response arguing that all of this modernism and secularism and individualism may not be such a good idea. In our next lecture we'll continue developing the critique of modernity but with a very radical, post-modern critique in the voice of Friedrich Nietzsche. Please stay with me for that.

Nietzsche—*Twilight of the Idols*
Lecture 28

A central theme of Nietzsche's is this idea of creativity and authenticity, that we should lead our lives as works of literature, as great novels in which we are protagonists, novels that we want to leave behind as worth living. Nietzsche challenges us to aestheticize our lives and to lead a life worthy of consideration.

The German philosopher **Friedrich Nietzsche** launched the movement called postmodernism, attacking modernity not from a classical perspective but from a perspective beyond modernity itself. As we have seen, modernism valorized the integrity and transparency of the individual and put forth an image of progress as a constant march forward. **Postmodernity** questions the sovereignty of the individual and rejects the idea that human history is progressive. It questions whether liberal democracy is self-evidently good and whether reason and science are truly foundational. And it criticizes the idea that religion or spirituality is a legitimate option even in private.

Nietzsche's *Twilight of the Idols and the Anti-christ: Or How to Philosophize with a Hammer* is the first clear shot in the battle of postmodernity against modernity. The idols Nietzsche is referring to are the philosophical principles that we tend to take for granted in the history of ideas. Nietzsche uses his hammer to demonstrate the hollowness of many of these ideas, then smashes them. The empty space left behind from previous philosophical activity invites us to novelty, creativity, and authenticity.

Nietzsche opens the section called "Maxims and Arrows" with what he calls questions of conscience, urging us to ask ourselves whether we are leading lives of which we are truly the authors or lives derived from the templates or theories of others. Our lives should arise from a self-creative act, a conscious decision about where we want to be and the enactment of that decision. Nietzsche points out that our ability to take on values from external sources is the greatest danger to authenticity. If we are to live our lives as artists, then we must safeguard our own creativity.

On the theme of knowledge, Nietzsche writes, "Once and for all, there is a great deal I do *not* want to know: Wisdom sets bounds even to knowledge." In modernity, wisdom was a central human value, but Nietzsche asserts that to valorize all knowledge is foolish. On the notion of being natural, he writes, "It is by being natural that one best recovers from one's unnaturalness, from one's spirituality." The spiritual is a kind of decadence that removes us from the natural world into the supernatural. When we move into the realm of religion, we deny our essential naturalness, deprecating the world in which we live. In a deep rejection of religion, Nietzsche asks, "Is man only God's mistake or God only man's mistake?"

> We should, above all, retain responsibility, authenticity, the freedom to act, and an appreciation of diversity and spontaneity; simplifying life is always dangerous.

Nietzsche then tells us, "If we possess our *why* of life, we can put up with any *how*. Man does not strive after happiness … ." There isn't one single, highest good, and the attempt to locate one would have the effect of destroying all creativity. Further, Nietzsche says, "The will to a system is a lack of integrity." In other words, if we establish a system to regulate our lives, we've given responsibility for our lives to that system. We should, above all, retain responsibility, authenticity, the freedom to act, and an appreciation of diversity and spontaneity; simplifying life is always dangerous. In summing up his "Maxims and Arrows," Nietzsche asks whether we are being true to ourselves, reducing ourselves to fulfilling other people's goals, or giving up our responsibilities entirely. Are we serving as representatives for the values of others or are we something represented? Are we spectators in our own lives or truly engaged?

In another section of *Twilight*, Nietzsche takes his hammer to Socrates. The ancient Greek is a touchstone for modernity because his demonstration of the power of reason allowed Hume, Kant, and others to view reason as progressive. But for Nietzsche, the philosophy of the past, from classical Greece to modernity, is a retreat from actually living life—from being creative and engaging with the world—to abstract, airy, meaningless thought. By accepting any one valuation of life—whether it's Aristotle's or Kant's—

we decline the responsibility to evaluate our own lives and live according to our conscience. We must simply accept the fact that we can't know the meaning or value of life; reason won't give us an answer. If our lives are art, then we must put reason aside and live creatively.

According to Nietzsche, the ideas of past philosophers are dead things, "conceptual mummies." The past idolatry of reason leads to a deprecation of the senses and passions, our bodies, and the real world in favor of abstract ideas and principles. The result is an abandonment of authentic values. Nietzsche argues that the desire to find some greater reality outside of the one in which we actually live is simply irrational. To posit the existence of a greater reality is cowardly, life-denying, and inauthentic. Nietzsche challenges us, instead, to create meaning in our own lives and to find significance in the world we actually inhabit. ∎

Name to Know

Nietzsche, Friedrich (1844–1900): Nietzsche grew up in a middle-class Prussian family. He excelled in his studies, particularly in music and literature, and pursued theology and philology at the University of Bonn.

Important Term

postmodernity: An ideological outlook that rejects the fundamental tenets of European modernism—the unity of the subject, the fact that knowledge constitutes a unified system that rests on sure foundations, the conviction that civilization is progressive—in favor of a conviction that subjectivity is variable and often fragmented, a suspicion of unified systems and a conviction that knowledge is socially constructed and fluid, and a suspicion of a single narrative of human progress.

Suggested Reading

Cox, *Nietzsche: Naturalism and Interpretation.*

Nietzsche, *Twilight of the Idols and The Anti-christ: Or, How to Philosophize with a Hammer.*

1. In what ways does Nietzsche build on the insights of Kant and Mill? In what ways and for what reasons does he reject their views?

2. Why would a religious life be inauthentic for Nietzsche? How is Nietzsche's vision of the meaningful life similar to and how is it different from that articulated in Daoism? In Zen?

Nietzsche—*Twilight of the Idols*
Lecture 28—Transcript

Greetings and welcome back. In our last lecture we began to examine critiques of modernity. In Tolstoy as we saw, we had a very conservative critique of modernity, a critique that was based upon ideas that we saw straight out of the classical traditions we examined before. Today things will be very different. We'll be looking at the philosophy of the great German philosopher, Friedrich Nietzsche. We can think about Nietzsche as the person who launched the movement called post-modernism, who really attacks modernity not from a classical perspective, but from a perspective beyond modernity itself.

Nietzsche lived a very short life. He was born in 1844 and died in 1900. In reality his life was shorter than that because he spent the last 12 years in a psychiatric hospital almost completely catatonic after a major catastrophic breakdown. But he was a real prodigy and accomplished an enormous amount before the time of his breakdown. He was appointed to his chair in philology at the university of Basel at the age of 24 which makes him still the youngest person ever appointed to a chair in a European university—just an astonishing achievement.

As I said earlier, Nietzsche was the initiator of this movement we call post-modernity in philosophy. We can think about post-modernity in a very specific sense. Oftentimes that term is bandied about to mean anything very contemporary or very modern or very hip. When we pay attention to what Nietzsche was up to and what his followers took from him, we can really see post-modernity as a very specific kind of response to the themes that we saw articulated in modernism.

Modernism valorizes the integrity and the transparency of the individual. As individuals we are single units. We know ourselves and we're the foundations of society. Post modernity attacks that and questions that. It questions the idea that we really can know who we are and that the individual really is sovereign.

In modernity we valorize the idea of progress that philosophy, science, economics and politics are in a constant progressive march with each generation improving on what the previous generation did. Post-modernity rejects the idea of sustained progress and rejects the idea that human history is progressive. In modernity we valorized liberty and democracy and the equality of human beings. Post-modernity questions whether liberal democracy is a self-evidently good thing and whether we should be thinking of individuals necessarily as equal in relevant senses.

Finally, in modernity we saw a valorization of science and reason as the foundation of human knowledge, of society and of progress, and of religion as something that was an interesting human option. In post-modernity we will be questioning the idea that reason and science really are foundational, that we should take those for granted as the grounds of our human life and of our public life. And we will see Nietzsche also criticizing the idea that religion or spirituality is a legitimate option even in private.

We can really see post-modernity not simply as what comes next, but very much as a critique of the very ideas that are central to European modernism. We'll see that Nietzsche's text poses special challenges to us as readers as well. Throughout this course we have been examining texts that are written in a variety of styles and call upon us to read in a variety of different ways.

Nietzsche gives us yet a new style. Nietzsche wrote in aphorisms, sometimes in poetry, sometimes offering cryptic, sardonic or ironic arguments. Often the arguments are highly implicit, and in the background, Nietzsche challenges the reader not just to understand what he said, but to think about what he's saying and to reconstruct the arguments that lie behind it. When we read Nietzsche, we're going to have to read with a great deal of reflectiveness.

Partly because of that there are many, many interpretations abroad of Nietzsche's thought. I will of course be offering one, it's the one that I like, but you should be aware that I'm reading Nietzsche in a particular way and other scholars might read Nietzsche very differently.

The particular text that we're going to address is called *Twilight of the Idols* and it's the last book that Nietzsche saw into print before his descent into madness. In one sense we can see it as the most mature work that Nietzsche composed. But we can also see it more importantly as what I think of as the first clear cannon shot in the battle of post-modernity against modernity, the first place where a philosopher sets up the idols of modernity, the central thesis of modernity as the targets of philosophical attack.

Once again, while in Tolstoy we saw really a pre-modern response to modernity, in Nietzsche it's going to look very, very different. Nietzsche would have seen Tolstoy as a sloppy sentimental romantic. In Nietzsche, prepare for more bracing, robust stuff. I want to return to the title of the text. The title is *Twilight of the Idols, or How to Philosophize with a Hammer*. That subtitle is really important as well. When Nietzsche talks about the idols in *Twilight of the Idols*, what he means are philosophical ideas or principles that we simply tend to take for granted in the history of philosophy, in the history of ideas.

Once we take them for granted, we think of philosophical reflection as having the task of just explicating and developing these ideas and not of questioning them. We think of philosophy as trying to understand what the individual subject is, trying to understand what moral virtue is, trying to understand the nature of God, or trying to understand how we should articulate personal liberty rather than questioning whether these are the right concepts to operate with in the first place. For Nietzsche, the idols that he really cares about are these assumptions of modernity that we've been examining in the last few lectures.

The hammer metaphor is important as well. He calls this, "how to philosophize with a hammer." When he thinks about philosophizing with a hammer he thinks about the approach to these idols as having two steps. We've got the hammer in our hand, first we tap the idol and discover that it's hollow. We reach back with the hammer and smash it. Nietzsche is arguing that he is demonstrating the hollowness of many of the ideas we take for granted in modernity and then smashing them.

What remains after all this smashing? Hannah Arendt put it beautifully. Hannah Arendt was another post-modernist who was deeply influenced by Nietzsche. She said, "We bestride a landscape littered with the rubble of broken narratives"—littered with the rubble of broken narratives. Nietzsche thinks that when you finish smashing these idols, you end up with an empty space with just the trash left behind from previous philosophical activity. But it's a space in which we're free to create and in which we are invited to novelty, creativity, and authenticity.

A central theme of Nietzsche's is this idea of creativity and authenticity, that we should lead our lives as works of literature, as great novels in which we are protagonists, novels that we want to leave behind as worth living. Nietzsche challenges us to aestheticize our lives and to lead a life worthy of consideration. It's a real challenge to authenticity.

In the present lecture, we're going to be selecting a few particular chapters and a few passages within those chapters for our focus. All of the passages in this lecture are going to be in the "hammer mode." We're going to be tapping and then smashing. The reconstruction, the positive account of what a life ought to look like after the destruction we will address in the next lecture. The sections we'll be focusing on today are those called Maxims and Arrows, the problem of Socrates, reason and philosophy, and how the real world becomes a myth.

We're going to begin with some Maxims and Arrows. Nietzsche opens this section with what he calls questions of conscience. Again, that title is one that bears attention. When Nietzsche approaches us he really asks us to pay attention to our conscience, are we leading our lives in good faith? Are we leading lives that we could endorse, that we could recommend, and that we would regard as lives worth living? He really asks us to interrogate ourselves. He's focusing, that is, on the need for authenticity, that is leading the life of which we really are the authors, not a life that somebody else has prescribed for us, not a life that we've sort of taken up on the template of somebody else's lives, not even a life that we derive from a theory that we like. But a life that arises from a self-creative act where we sit down and say, this is where we want to be, and we enact it. That's a life in which we take responsibility for the decisions that we make, that we don't make decisions and then pawn them off on somebody else.

The same act can be authentic or inauthentic, Nietzsche points out. Self deception is a really easy thing. It's easy to think that we're leading an authentic life when, in fact, the values that we've adopted are values that we took from somebody else or values that we found from an abstract theory. For Nietzsche, this ability that we have to take on the values of others, or the projects of others, or a sense of normalcy in, all things, by the way, that we saw Tolstoy and Mill note are the greatest dangers to authenticity, if we are going to live as artists and that our lives are going to be works of art, then we must safeguard our own creativity and not simply become derivative of those around us.

Let's now enter the text. When Nietzsche writes these Maxims and Arrows, at number 2 he writes, "Even the Bravest of us rarely has the courage for what he really knows... Even the Bravest of us rarely has the courage for what he really knows..." Here we have that real call to authenticity, the idea that we often have knowledge that we can't face, that we know that we are a person of a certain kind and we try to deny that. That we know what the right thing is to do, or the thing that we'd like to do, and it's so scary or so challenging that we tell ourselves that maybe it's rash, maybe we should do something else.

But Nietzsche continues on this theme of knowledge. This is very subtle, he says, "Once and for all, there is a great deal I do *not* want to know: Wisdom sets bounds even to knowledge." This is a real post-modern turn. Notice that in modernity we were really valorizing knowledge as a central human value. That's what Kant thought life was all about. That's what Mill thought life was all about. Nietzsche is arguing, there's a lot I don't want to know. For instance, I really don't want to know what color your underwear are, and you probably don't want to know what color mine are. That's stuff we don't want to know. There's confidential information we don't want to know. There's information that would just clutter up our lives. I don't want to memorize the phonebook for Washington D.C. and neither do you. Nietzsche is arguing that knowledge might be an interesting thing, but to valorize it is always a good thing and is just plain foolish.

Nietzsche continues now on this notion of being natural. He writes, "It is by being natural that one best recovers from one's unnaturalness, from one's spirituality." There is a kind of echo of Daoism here in this emphasis on naturalism. Notice there's a bit of Hume in this too, even though Nietzsche would never acknowledge it. Nietzsche talks here about recovering from one's spirituality. He argues that the spiritual, thinking religiously, is a kind of decadence, that it takes us out of the natural world into the supernatural. Nietzsche thinks of us first and foremost as animals, natural beings in the world who could make something of our lives, and he thinks that when we move into the spiritual realm, into the religious realm, we deny that naturalness. We deprecate the world that we live in, and so we're involved in a kind of self-deprecation not worthy of an artist. You don't start out by saying you're second-rate.

Nietzsche continues this suspicion of God when he asks, "Which is it? Is man only God's mistake or God only man's mistake?" This is only an aphorism but it's a very complete, very deep rejection of religion. Nietzsche sees religion here as a retreat from facing up to reality, something that's unnatural. After all, if there's a god, then theodicy, the problem of evil, is absolutely unavoidable. When he asks, is man only God's mistake, he's pointing out that we are terribly imperfect and we do a whole lot of bad stuff. You would have to blame our creator for that since he, on the grounds of religion, is omnipotent, omniscient, and omni-benevolent.

If there's a god, the god is deeply problematic. But if there isn't one and it's just our mistake to posit a god, then backtrack on the mistake and jettison the god. Either way, Nietzsche thinks, there's no virtue in positing a god.

Nietzsche now turns to thinking more directly about the meaning of life. He asks a question, "If we possess our *why* of life, we can put up with any *how*. Man does not strive after happiness, only the Englishman does that." As I said, Nietzsche is often wry, often humorous, and often sardonic.

What's the point of this? If we really have a sense of what our life is about we can put up with anything. Most importantly is its worry about happiness. When Nietzsche says, man does not strive after happiness, what he means is we don't want to think that there's one single good, one highest good as Aristotle thought, or even a highest good as Mill thought or as Kant thought, to locate one single value is what all life is about, as to flatten life and to make all lives the same and to destroy all creativity. If there's no creativity, no freedom, no ability to create, why bother living? "If we possess our *why* of life, that is something that animates us, we can put up with any*how*." But if there's some single value that we take to animate everything, it makes life look just flat.

Nietzsche continues this theme in the next passage where he says, "I mistrust all systematizers and avoid them. The will to a system is a lack of integrity." The will to a system is a lack of integrity, even if it's a system we construct for ourselves. That is, Nietzsche thinks the real life of integrity, of authenticity, a genuine life, is a life lived creatively. If we establish a system that's going to regulate our lives, we've done just what Kant warned us against when he warned us against having a pastor to form our values for us, having a doctor to formulate our diet for us, and so on, giving our responsibility for our lives over to someone else. Here Nietzsche is pointing out that it's bad enough to give responsibility to your life to someone else; it's even worse to give responsibility for your life to an abstract system, even if it's a system you created. Retain the responsibility. Retain the authenticity. Retain the freedom to act. Retain the appreciation of plurality, diversity, and spontaneity; simplifying life is always dangerous.

Nietzsche sums up these Maxims and Arrows with a wonderful, direct challenge to the reader. He writes, "You run on ahead? Do you do so as a herdsman? Or as an exception? A third possibility would be as a deserter… *First,* question of conscience." So this is a question of conscious. Nietzsche is asking you, when you go on ahead, when you take yourself seriously and leave others behind, are you actually doing it just as a herdsman? Do you want to bring others along with you and so effectively reduce yourself to a servant of others? Or do you treat yourself as an exception, a real individual, somebody who actually has something to say? There is a third possibility, that you've just given up on your responsibilities, that you're a deserter pretending that you're an exception. That's a question of conscience. That forces us to pay attention to our motivations. Are we being true to ourselves? Are we just serving others? Nietzsche sees that as a deprecation. We're just reducing ourselves to other people's goals, or are we shameful deserters?

Then he asks, "Are you genuine? Or only an actor? A representative? Or that itself which is represented?" That is, are you really authentic or are you making believe? Are you acting your life out? Say as we might imagine Ivan Ilych acting somebody's life out. Are you a representative for someone else just taking on their values? Or are you something represented, that is, other people are following you? "Finally you are no more than an imitation of an actor." If you lead your life without taking responsibility for it, you're not even an actor because a real actor is an artist. You're just somebody pretending to be an actor. That's the second question of conscious. These get you deep. Then Nietzsche asks, "Are you one who looks on? Or sets to work? Or who looks away, turns aside? *Third* question of conscience." That is, are you a spectator on your own life? Or are you really engaged in it? Or are you disavowing your life, looking away and effectively leaving yourself abandoned? That's the third question of conscience. Are you really engaged in your own life? It's a hard question to ask but if you're not engaged in your own life, Nietzsche thinks, you've got a meaningless life. You're just a spectator on your own life, forget it. Then Nietzsche asks, "Do you want to accompany? Or go on ahead? Or go off alone? One must know *what* one wants and *that* one wants. *Fourth* question of conscience."

That is, here Nietzsche is asking the question, do you really just want to be along with others, a member of a herd, a member of a group, allowing other people to make the decisions? Or are you willing to go on ahead? Are you willing to be alone? Are you willing to take responsibility for your own desires and your own plans? This is a question of conscience. That's the fourth. For Nietzsche, these four questions of conscience are the questions we have to address in determining whether our lives are genuinely meaningful.

I want to turn to another part of *Twilight*, the problem of Socrates. We should ask ourselves, why does Nietzsche pick on poor old Socrates? Why is he a problem? The answer is simple. Nietzsche thinks that Socrates has become an idol of philosophy, the beginning of the Western philosophical tradition, because we see Socrates as somebody who valorizes reason and who really uses the power of reason to understand reality. For Nietzsche, Socrates represents this triumph of the idea of the supremacy of reason. Socrates in the end becomes a touchstone for modernity because Socrates, in demonstrating this power of reason, allows modern philosophers like Hume and Kant and so forth to see what they're doing as continuous with a classical European tradition, but nonetheless are progressive, because reason is taken to be progressive. All of these are ideas Nietzsche regards as idolatrous—ideas needing the tap and the smash.

Let's look at Nietzsche on Socrates. Nietzsche writes, "The irreverent notion that the great sages are declining types first dawned on me in regard to just the case in which learned and unlearned prejudice is most strongly opposed to it: I recognized"—writes Nietzsche, "the dissolution of Greece ... value judgments concerning life, for or against, can in the last resort never be true: they possess value only as symptoms... One must reach out and try to grasp this astonishing finesse—that the value of life cannot be estimated." I want to repeat that last line. "One must reach out and try to grasp this astonishing finesse—that the value of life cannot be estimated." What's Nietzsche saying here? He's saying first that the philosophy of the past, and he includes everything from classical Greece to modernity as decadent. That it's a retreat from actually living life, from being creative and engaging with the world to abstract airy thought that means absolutely nothing, that just spins out theories, spins out models, and tries to get other people to give up their authenticity by accepting them. He's saying that by accepting any one valuation of life, whether it's Aristotle's or Marcus Aurelius's or Kant's, one is declining ones own responsibility to evaluate one's own life and to lead the life according to one's own conscience.

He's also saying that we have to accept the fact that we can't come to know the meaning or value of life; reason won't get us there. We need to lead our lives. We need to lead them creatively. To think that somehow reason is going to lead us in doing that and that reason is going to ground that leading of a life is the craziest thinking that abstract reason and theory is going to ground and make possible the painting of a beautiful picture, or the creation of a beautiful statue, or the writing of a beautiful novel. If our lives are art, then we have to put reason aside and not rely upon it.

Nietzsche continues on the problem of Socrates. He writes, "

> With Socrates Greek taste undergoes a change in favor of dialectics: what is really happening when that happens? It is above all the

defeat of a *nobler* taste: with dialectics, the rabble gets on top. Before Socrates, the dialectical manner was repudiated in good society: it was considered a form of bad manners... [P]resentation of one's reasons was regarded with mistrust. Honest things, like honest men, do not carry their reasons exposed.

Here we see more modern idols under attack. In the first passage we looked at in this discussion we were attacking the idea of the philosophical tradition as progressive. In this one it's reason an argument being attacked directly as the keys to understanding. Nietzsche is arguing reasoning is just ugly. You reason when you know you're not quite right, you need to persuade somebody. It gives up on the aesthetic approach to life.

There's also something you should note here though that's really cute and that's this: Nietzsche is actually using reason to do his work. He's offering you a rational argument against the use of reason. So there's some real irony at work here. It's also worth taking a moment to think about the resonances that Nietzsche has got to some surprising folks, the book of Job, the *Daodejing*, and Dogen. In each of these cases we saw a deep suspicion of reason as a ground for developing a meaningful life and for understanding our own existence. Now Nietzsche really goes after a reason, and the language becomes a bit stronger. By the way, now we're moving to the section of reason and philosophy. He writes, "All that philosophers have handled for millennia has been conceptual mummies." That is, we're focusing only on dead ideas, things we should have left behind long ago.

Nothing actual has escaped from their hands alive. They kill, they stuff, when they worship, these conceptual idolaters... These senses, which are so immoral as well, it is they which deceive us about the real world. Moral: escape from sense-deception, from becoming, from history... Be a philosopher, be a mummy... And away, above all, with the body... refuted, impossible even, notwithstanding it is impudent enough to behave as if it actually existed!

What's the point of all of this? Nietzsche, in arguing that philosophy creates mummies, that it stuffs reality and leaves it behind is focusing on this idolatry of reason, and the idolatry of reason leads he thinks in philosophy to deprecating our senses, to deprecating our passions, to deprecating our bodies, to deprecating our real world in favor of abstract ideas and thoughts and abstract principles. When we do that, he thinks, we deprecate life itself and life is where we are. So we abandon the authentic values, the authentic life that we actually lead.

Secondly he points out that we involve ourselves in actually denying the importance of our own embodiment, something terribly irrational, because first and foremost we are animals.

This turns up again in Nietzsche's very deep concern with philosophical realism as opposed to philosophical idealism. Nietzsche has got a beautiful diagnosis of the philosophical retreat from reality that he thinks we find ourselves in starting with Greek philosophy and especially ending up with modernity. He takes us through a set of steps for denying the world and for leaving our lives abandoned. Leaving our lives in a way that has to be completely inauthentic. He writes, "*First proposition:* The grounds on which 'this' world has been designated as apparent establish rather its reality—*another* kind of reality is absolutely indemonstrable." That is, he's pointing out as soon as somebody thinks that our senses are deceptive, that we shouldn't pay so much attention to the imminent, the concrete, the temporary, the fleeting, then they want to project themselves into another reality, a permanent reality, a spiritual reality, a reality that's transcendent. He says that is not even demonstrable, that's not a finding of a deeper reality somewhere else. That's an abandonment of ourselves and our own reality. "*Second proposition:* The characteristics, which have been assigned to the 'real being' of things are the characteristics of non-being, of *nothingness.*" That is, when we then go to characterize this transcendent, ultimate reality, talk about it as permanent, talk about it as divine, talk about it as significant or eternal, we find that those characteristics don't characterize anything real at all, and what we've done is to valorize nothingness and to abandon real somethings including ourselves and those around us. "*Third Proposition:* To talk about 'another' world than this is quite pointless, providing that an instinct for slandering, disparaging and accusing life is not within us." That is, Nietzsche thinks that the moment we talk about a transcendent reality that we care about more than this one, all we've done is to disparage the world in which we, in fact, live and to disparage our own lives. That's to be inauthentic. That's to not take responsibility for who we are or for how we're living. "*Fourth Proposition:* To divide the world into a 'real' and an 'apparent' world, whether in the manner of Christianity"—for which Nietzsche of course has complete loathing—"Or of Kant"—who he loathes even more—"Is only a suggestion of *decadence*—a symptom of *declining* life." That is that decadence consists precisely in denying the reality of the world that we live in, of failing to live authentically. What's Nietzsche saying here? He's arguing that the desire to find some greater reality than the one we actually live in, to locate real life, real value, real significance outside of the lives that we inhabit, the lives that we create, and the world in which we have to function is simply irrational. We don't have any reason to go beyond this world, any evidence of the non-existence of this world or any evidence of the existence of a greater reality.

Moreover and more importantly though, for Nietzsche it's cowardly, it's life denying and it's decadent. It's a way of not taking responsibility for who we are or how we live. It's a way of taking the lives that we lead and treating them as second-rate trash in preference to something else.

Finally, in the end it is inauthentic. It is self-repudiating. We leave ourselves in a lurch. In Nietzsche then we see an attack on any account of the meaning of life that's aimed at any transcendent locus. That's many of the accounts we've seen thus far in these lectures, including ancient and modern. Nietzsche challenges us to create our own meaning, to create our own lives, their own significance, and to find that meaning and significance in the world that we, in fact, inhabit. In our next lecture we're going to examine how Nietzsche sees that done, the positive side of *Twilight of the Idols*. I hope you'll join me for that.

Nietzsche—Achieving Authenticity
Lecture 29

Nietzsche is far from a nihilist. Nietzsche urges an important kind of creativity, but Nietzsche actually thinks that modernity is deeply nihilistic; that's the irony. Nietzsche is actually a critic of nihilism, not a nihilist himself.

Nietzsche's oratorical prose and his calls to conscience, his poetry, and his irony can sometimes blind us to the depths of his critiques of philosophy. The idols he smashes are the values of modernity that undergird much of our contemporary intellectual and political culture: progress, reason, systematicity, faith, and the idea of transcendent values.

The section of *Twilight of the Idols* called "How the Real World Became a Myth" is Nietzsche's six-step analysis of how we find ourselves on an inauthentic flight from reality and responsibility for our own lives. We begin with the understanding that wise people or sages dwell directly in reality, understanding its concreteness, impermanence, and beauty. From there, we leap to the mistaken belief that *only* wise people dwell in reality—the unwise dwell in some kind of cosmic illusion—and with that, we disenfranchise ourselves. We believe that knowledge of the real world is practically unobtainable for ordinary people; in fact, we conclude that it is completely unknowable. The next step, of course, is to conceptualize the real world as so remote that it's basically nonexistent. The only rational attitude then is to do away with reality and assert that we live in a world of appearance completely. When we reach this step, we have abandoned any commitment to our own lives as real, let alone meaningful. The alternative to following this path to nihilism is to make beauty and meaning out of the actual lives we live.

Nietzsche offers a completely alternate vision of the ideas of freedom and progress to what we saw in modernism. He rejects the idea of freedom found in liberal democracy because he believes it is shallow; it ends up being the freedom to act like everybody else. Further, liberal democracy ceases to be liberal the moment it is put in place because it establishes an overarching ideology that frames all our thinking.

Nietzsche's conception of freedom is freedom from conformity, freedom to rise above the herd, not to be an equal member of the herd. This is profoundly anti-democratic. Nietzsche sees democracy not as a great achievement but as a disaster for humanity because it treats us all as equal. The person who might move out ahead and create an authentic life is prevented from doing so because of the subtle imposition of a uniform ideology. Further, in Nietzsche's view, truly great art arises from struggle, but liberal democracy makes our lives too easy. A meaningful life is one of striving for self-expression; it's a life of real individuality, not a life of comfort. Nietzsche's conception of freedom is closer to that experienced by Arjuna—the freedom to fight and to realize himself—rather than the kind of abstract, pre-packaged liberty advocated by Mill.

> **Nietzsche's conception of freedom is freedom from conformity, freedom to rise above the herd, not to be an equal member of the herd. This is profoundly anti-democratic.**

Nietzsche tells us that "there exists no more poisonous poison" than the doctrine of equality. He sees most of modern civilization as a degenerate force, a force that levels us and keeps us down instead of lifting us up. This force diverts us from the natural life we would ordinarily lead and directs our thinking to abstract ideas that drain the content from our lives and encourage complacency.

Equality, for Nietzsche, is not justice. When we preach equality of all people, we're saying that everyone is the same and should be treated in exactly the same way, but Nietzsche argues that we're all different from one another. A better sense of justice would be to accord each person the opportunities that he or she is willing and able to take advantage of, rather than giving each person the same opportunities. Nietzsche is an elitist, and he challenges us to strive for elitism, as well.

Nietzsche is distinctively postmodern in a number of ways. He rejects the idea of a sort of preexisting individual in favor of a self-creative individual. He rejects the systematic nature of knowledge in favor of multiple kinds of knowledge, none of them preeminent; as a result, he rejects the sovereignty of reason. The classical idea of progress, too, is reversed: Instead of the steady march of human history from the primitive to the peak of advancement in modernity, Nietzsche sees modernity as the most life-denying, self-alienating approach to life possible. We need to return to our nature and to embrace the possibility of creativity at every moment. Finally, Nietzsche rejects the personal freedom found in liberal democracy in favor of the freedom of individual strength.

For Nietzsche, a meaningful life is one of authenticity, in which we create our own goals and values and live up to them. This life requires intellectual, moral, and aesthetic integrity and demands that we take responsibility for our own deepest values. In this strongly aesthetic conception of meaning, a meaningful life is a work of art on a grand performance scale. ∎

Suggested Reading

Nehamas, *Nietzsche: Life as Literature.*

Nietzsche, *Twilight of the Idols and the Anti-christ: Or, How to Philosophize with a Hammer.*

Study Questions

1. What does Nietzsche mean by freedom? Why is this not the freedom of liberal democratic theory?

2. How is Nietzsche's critique of democracy connected to his critique of modernity in general? Is this critique plausible?

Nietzsche—Achieving Authenticity
Lecture 29—Transcript

In our last lecture we were wielding Nietzsche's hammer. We were tapping and we were smashing and we left a lot of rubble on the ground. Before we go on to replace our hammer with maybe a sculptor's chisel and mallet or a paint brush or even a pen, it's worth examining some of the rubble that we've created. I think that's important because Nietzsche's beautiful, oratorical prose and all of his calls to conscience, his poetry and his irony can sometimes blind us to how deep and disturbing some of the critiques are that we actually developed the last time, and it's worth emphasizing how deep that critique goes.

The idols that we were smashing, or what Nietzsche calls idols, were in fact values that as we emphasized when we were talking about modernity our values that are central to a great deal of our own lives, these are the values of modernity that undergird much of our contemporary intellectual culture but also our political culture.

Nietzsche was concerned to criticize the idea of progress, the idea that each generation we advance over previous generations but philosophical thought, scientific thought, political thought, takes us from more primitive to more progressive states. Nietzsche was concerned to reject the idea that reason is the foundation of our knowledge and that science and rational activity should be at the base of our public discourse. That's another view that we tend to take very seriously in our own culture.

Nietzsche rejected systematisity, the idea that we can have systematic, philosophical frameworks and theories to guide our lives including systematic, political frameworks and theories like those involved in constitutional law, but also including systematic theories of knowledge, systematic theories of morality and so forth. Nietzsche also argued powerfully against faith and the existence of God and against any role for religion. This is really important. We saw in Hume and Kant and Mill a critique of the idea that religion should play some role in public life but very much a commitment to retaining a robust private sphere, we might say the privacy of our own homes or our own churches or synagogues in which our religious faith was a matter of choice and a matter that ought to be protected and indeed respected. Kant talked about circumscribing reason to make room for faith. Hume talked about the reasonableness of faith even if there's no reason. Mill talked about the importance of protecting a plurality of religious views and religious faiths.

Nietzsche will have none of that. Nietzsche argues that even to engage in private in religious faith is an act of bad faith, an act of abandonment of our own authenticity. Finally and maybe most radically the last idol that we saw Nietzsche attacking was the idea that values are transcendent at all. Almost every philosopher whose work we've examined in this course, almost every idea we've taken seriously, has been one in which there's some level of transcendent value to which we ought to orient our lives. Either an entire cosmos that transcends our experience or a divinity or irrationality itself, Nietzsche argues against all of that with these grand, systematizing transcendent values, take us away from the lives that we lead, take us away from the concreteness and in the end are inauthentic and life-denying.

I want to emphasize that because this has been one of the most radical texts that we have read so far. If you understand what Nietzsche is up to, you should be challenged by it but you should also be disturbed by it. Some challenges are disturbing. There's nothing wrong with that, disturbance is often what makes growth possible.

Now it's time to put our hammers down for a while and move towards crafting an account of Nietzsche's positive, post-modern conception of what a meaningful life looks like. I'm going to be focusing on a chapter in *Twilight* that we haven't looked at yet which nature calls *Expeditions of an Untimely Man*. Nietzsche was nothing if not self confident. So he was talking about his own intellectual expeditions and thought of himself as untimely, precisely in the sense of way before his time.

We're going to first pick up where we left up last time with Nietzsche's discussion of what's problematic about the denial of life. I want to emphasize a section that Nietzsche calls how the real world became a myth. This is Nietzsche's final diagnosis of how it is that we find ourselves on an inauthentic flight from reality and an abandonment of responsibility for our own lives.

Nietzsche really thinks that the whole phenomenon of modernity—which he sees as a kind of phenomenon of progressive abandonment of responsibility for individual life and a progressive abandonment of authenticity—requires a diagnosis. How is it that living human organisms develop this life-denying urge to abstraction that he thinks flowers in modernity. He gives a six-step analysis of this process. On this six-step analysis Nietzsche leads us from a position where we start with a basic truth and slowly bend it into dangerous falsehood. Finally he thinks into incoherence and at the end in denialism. I think this is important. Some people interpret Nietzsche as being a nihilist because he attacks so many of the fundamental values that we take seriously. If you think that these values are the obvious values, the ones that we have to take seriously, when Nietzsche abandons those you think nothing is left, just the broken rubble.

Nietzsche is far from a nihilist. Nietzsche urges an important kind of creativity, but Nietzsche actually thinks that modernity is deeply nihilistic, that's the irony. Nietzsche is actually a critic of nihilism, not a nihilist himself. So what are those six steps? Nietzsche begins by saying we first notice, in looking around us, that reality is imminent. That we live in reality, that it's a physical, mental, sensual world that we inhabit. He says we then notice that wise people dwell directly in it. They don't abstract from it. They live in it spontaneously, effortlessly and in this way that we admire. We see some of that, for instance, in Daoism and in Zen. This emphasis on how wise people or sages dwell directly in presence, in reality, understanding its concreteness in permanence and beauty. That's the first step, nothing wrong with that.

The second step is where the twist begins. Nietzsche says, we then say to ourselves, oh, these wise people really dwell in reality. The real world, the way reality is, is known and inhabited only by the wise. That it's only if you're really wise that you really understand reality. The rest of us are somehow misguided and we dwell in an illusion. This is a very subtle twist, right? All it does is go from wise people dwell in reality to only wise people really dwell in reality, and that gives us the idea that unwise people may dwell in some kind of a cosmic illusion.

Once we make that twist though we've disenfranchised ourselves. I've now said my life isn't real and that's only the beginning. But that's the beginning of alienating myself from my own existence, from this kind of inauthenticity or a fulsome conscience. What's the third step? In the third step we say, okay, you've got to be really wise to dwell in the real world. The real world is practically unobtainable. There's no way that somebody like me could ever understand reality. I could at least pause that that is a goal or an ideal and Nietzsche sees that as what animates Christianity. The idea that we're born in sin, we're born in confusion, but there's at least an ideal possibility that we, like Christ, could obtain a certain sense of reality.

Next step, we notice that that goal is so ideal, so distant, that we say in fact the real world is completely unknowable, it's unconceptualizable. It's beyond our understanding. Still, somehow it's an ideal, but you'd have to be really transcendent to get it. Nietzsche thinks that that's what we see in some forms of Buddhism for instance, and he's right. We also see an echo of that in the book of Job, that reality, the universe, God totally unconceptualizable, but still somehow is there in the picture.

Then Nietzsche says, once we've desiccated it so far that it's completely unknowable, we then say to ourselves, there really is no real world. It's so remote that it's basically non-existent. All there is is appearance and the only rational attitude you might say, once we've gone so far as to make reality in principle unknowable is to just do away with it and say we just live in a world of appearance completely. We've seen again a Zen analysis of ordinary experience where we in fact are perceiving but we experience the world through a conception that is a pure haze of illusion is a nice example of how that works.

Finally Nietzsche says, that's the end of the story because if there's no reality only appearance, then even the appearance can't be real, and then we've fallen into total anilism where nothing is real at all. When we do that, we have abandoned any commitment to our own lives as real, let alone meaningful. Here Nietzsche sets out a beautiful garden path to nihilism on how you give up on life. He sets it out because he thinks it's very enticing. Each step leads naturally to the next and you think it's very dangerous.

On this garden path we begin by drawing the contrast between appearance and reality—that's harmless enough it seems—and we valorize reality. By valorizing reality and making it more and more unreachable, we end up deprecating our own existence. What's the alternative for Nietzsche? That's where we're going now. The alternative is to affirm our lives. To make beauty and meaning out of our actual lives, not somewhere else in some idealization according to some artificial framework.

Now let's look at Nietzsche's discussion of his own conception of freedom. We'll see that when Nietzsche talks about freedom and Nietzsche talks about progress he offers a completely alternative vision to that that we saw in modernism. Nietzsche sees modernity as degenerate, as being the end result of this horrible garden path we just sketched. He sees modernism as requiring a total inversion of values, not a rejection of all values but what Nietzsche calls elsewhere a reevaluation of values. Taking what modernity—seen as most important—and seeing it as the mistake and taking what modernity deprecates and seeing that as what's important.

Let's examine Nietzsche's *Conception of Freedom*: "The value of a thing sometimes lies not in what one attains with it, but in what one pays for it. I give an example." And of course this example will not be randomly chosen. Nietzsche is really aiming for the heart here. He says, "Liberal institutions"—and he really means liberal institutions, liberal democracy, the kind of civilization and society that we now inhabit say in the United States, with which he was familiar in Europe, "Liberal institutions immediately cease to be liberal as soon as they are attained, subsequently there is nothing more thoroughly harmful to freedom than liberal institutions." I want to repeat that. This is a deep idea and we're going to explore why Nietzsche believes this in a moment. "There is nothing more thoroughly harmful to freedom than liberal institutions. One knows indeed," he says, "*what* they bring about: they undermine the will to power. They are the leveling of mountain and valley exalted to a moral principle." Notice what he's doing now. He's criticizing the very heart of the values of liberal democracy, the ideas of equality and of liberty for all. "They are the leveling of mountain and valley exalted to a moral principle in plain words"—and here is Nietzsche's deep critique, we're going to explore this in a moment—"reduction to the herd animal." Nietzsche is going to argue that liberal institutions reduce us to the level of, say sheep. He continues, "For what is freedom? That one has the will to self-responsibility."

Let's examine this very challenging passage. Here Nietzsche isn't rejecting the notion of freedom altogether, and some people have suggested that he does that, that's not true. Nietzsche is instead rejecting the very idea of freedom that we find in liberal democracy. The idea of freedom that we saw developed explicitly in Kant and Mill just a few lectures ago. Because those ideas of freedom, Nietzsche thinks, are shallow. They end up being the freedom to act like everybody else, the freedom to be normal, the freedom to lead a life like Ivan Ilych.

What's more, Nietzsche thinks, that kind of freedom isn't just the freedom to lead that life if one chooses. Rather, once we establish liberal democracy, he says it ceases to be liberal the moment it's established. Why is that? It's because it establishes an overarching ideology, a way that we should behave. We should respond to the census. We should vote. We should think about ourselves in terms of democrats and republicans. We should take our institutions seriously. We should pledge allegiance to the flag, we should do all of these things that everybody else does. When we do that, Nietzsche says, that's where we get the leveling of mountain and valley. We get a single, overarching ideology that becomes a dominant ideology that frames all of our thinking and kills creativity. It would be as though we imagined an artistic community that said to itself, now we're going to adopt cubism because cubism liberates us from traditional figurative drawing. Everybody from now on will be cubist. Would that be a creative, progressive, artistic community? It would absolutely not be. It might have been free from something, but it's freed from that into a kind of oppressive uniformity that makes all genuine creativity and authenticity in art impossible. That's what Nietzsche thinks happens in liberal democracy. We replaced one pernicious ideology, the ideology of monarchy or paternalism or the ideology of communitarianism, with a new ideology, the ideology of Kantian or Millian liberal democracy. That just composes a different level of conformity.

For that reason, the freedom to be Ivan Ilych is not just the freedom to be Ivan Ilych, it's a condemnation to the life of Ivan Ilych, and that's what Nietzsche thinks is terrible about democracy. It makes each life most ordinary and therefore, in Tolstoy's words, most terrible.

Nietzsche's conception of freedom is different. It's a freedom from conformity. It's a freedom to create. It's a freedom that's born in strength not in liberty. It's a freedom that is a freedom to rise above the herd, not to be an equal member of the herd. This is profoundly anti-democratic and we have to recognize that. There is no way to be comfortable, harmonizing Nietzsche's own conception of freedom with that say that underlies American liberal democracy. Nietzsche sees democracy not as a great achievement, as say, Kant and Mill did, but as a terrible disaster, a terrible disaster for Humanity because it treats us all as equal. It levels our lives. It makes our lives easy as well. Nietzsche thinks that's a problem. The leveling is a problem because the truly great individual, the individual who has the capacity to create an exciting life and that may well be each of us by the way, they don't have to be exceptional people.

The person who can move out ahead, who can authentically create a life, is prevented from doing so, prevented from doing so because of the subtle imposition of a uniform ideology, a uniformed set of tastes, a uniformed view about what a good life looks like; this kind of hegemony of ideology. Secondly, Nietzsche thinks that truly great art arises from struggle, arises from adversity, arises from having to overcome challenges. A liberal democracy is also welfare democracy. Liberal democracy makes our lives easy for us. By making our lives easy, by allowing us to have malls in which to shop and cinemas in which to go see movies and Netflix and Amazon to order things from and so forth, by making our lives easy it eliminates the conditions that inspire true greatness. Nietzsche values the need to struggle a little bit.

Nietzsche is arguing that a meaningful life is a life of striving and of struggle. It's a life of self-expression. It's a life lived in art where we really set ourselves aside as individuals. It's a life of real individuality, not a life of comfort. It's not that quiet, middleclass life that Ivan Ilych so enjoyed.

If we're thinking about what kind of freedom Nietzsche is advocating, what his conception of freedom is, and why in some sense it's so far from that of our own culture, we can think of this as the freedom of Arjuna, the freedom to fight, the freedom to realize himself, the freedom to be who he is to be, not the freedom of Mill. That is, this kind of abstract liberty that gives us the kind of marketplace of ideas in which we can shop and browse as if we're kind of browsing in a department store with a lot of freedom to choose this, to choose that, to choose this, to choose that, when they're all basically packaged for us in advance. This is the freedom to create art. It's the freedom that we have when we roll up our sleeves and enter the studio, not when we pick up our shopping bags and enter the supermarket.

We should note though there is one really important place in which we can see Nietzsche as sharing a view with Mill and is deriving his own views from Mill, even though I'm sure Nietzsche would never approve of this. Mill really worried in a way that say Kant didn't about the problem of the tyranny of the majority, about the possibility of social expectations and social tastes, exerting as Mill said, a more insidious and powerful tyranny than any tyranny of a single tyrant. Nietzsche shares that, but he thinks Mill has done nothing to eliminate that, only constructed a kind of super majority of an ideology that worries about the tyranny of the majority. So much for freedom, let's worry now about progress.

Once again we saw that while it might appear that Nietzsche is against freedom, he's not. He has a different sense of freedom than that that we see in liberal democracy. Similarly we saw Nietzsche tap the idol of philosophical progress and smash it. You might think that Nietzsche rejects progress in all senses, but he doesn't. He has a sense of progress, and he talks about it in a beautiful passage called *Progress in My Sense*. Here's what Nietzsche says,

> I speak of a return to nature, although it is not really a going back, but a going up, up into a high, free, even frightful nature and naturalness, such as plays with great tasks, and is *permitted* to play with them. ... The doctrine of equality! But there exists no more poisonous poison: for it *seems* to be preached by justice itself, while it is the *end* of justice.

This is a very, very challenging remark. Nietzsche is actually trying to develop an internal critique of this ideal of equality that he thinks animates liberal democracy. Nietzsche sees most of modern civilization and especially liberal democracy as we've seen, as degenerate forces, forces that level us and keep us down instead of forces that liberate us.

What they do that's so terrible is they take people away from nature, from our natural lives, from the lives that we would ordinarily lead, and take us into these abstractions, to these abstract ideas that drain content our of our existence. More importantly, they encourage a kind of complacency in us, a herd mentality. They see each of us as equal to everybody else in all respects. In doing that, Nietzsche thinks, they actually discourage real creativity, real art, and real courage.

Remember when Nietzsche says that equality seems to be justice but it's the reverse. Here's the point. When we preach equality of all people, equal rights, equal justice and so forth, we say everybody is exactly the same and should be treated in exactly the same way in some sense or other. Nietzsche's point though is very different. He says, in fact we are all very different from one another. We have different capacities, different desires, different abilities, and different potentials.

Another sense of justice, a better sense of justice Nietzsche thinks, is to give to each person the opportunities that he or she is willing and able to take advantage of. Justice then involves giving to each what is due to them rather than giving to each exactly the same. Think about it in terms of cutting up a pie. You might say, if you've got six people the appropriate thing to do is to cut the pie into six pieces. That's the liberal, democratic approach Nietzsche would think.

The other one would be to say, ah ha! This person is a very large athlete who needs a lot of nutrition. This is a very small child, he gets a big piece, she gets a very small piece, giving each person that of which she can take advantage. That's what Nietzsche thinks real justice would be, and he thinks that liberal democracy is antithetical to that in its leveling tendency.

Nietzsche looks more like a very militant Laozi then he does like anybody modern, somebody urging this return to this high, wild, dangerous nature. Notice that he does valorize a certain kind of freedom. It's this freedom to create, to make of oneself of what will, and he very much shares Mill's concern that what society ought to be doing is fostering creativity and individuality. That's shared ground. It's just that Nietzsche disagrees dramatically with Mill about what it would take to do that.

Mill thinks, put a lot of stuff on offer and treat everybody equally. Nietzsche says, nn-nn. Don't put stuff on offer. Encourage people to create stuff and make the opportunities for the people who could take advantage of that. Nietzsche is no democrat, he is an elitist, take that seriously. But his elitism is a challenge to each of us. He's challenging us to say, what's wrong with that? Why don't I embrace this? In my own life, don't I at least want to think of myself as elite? Don't I at least want to take myself as seriously as Nietzsche challenges me to take myself? That's a very interesting challenge.

In a number of senses we see that Nietzsche is distinctively post modern. We've seen that he rejects this kind of pre-given unity of the subject that I sort of come out as an individual and encounter the world in favor of a self-creative individual. My task for Nietzsche is not just to lead the life that I'm destined to lead, it's to create my own destiny, to write my own story and then to act it out.

Similarly, Nietzsche rejects the idea of the unity and the systematic nature of knowledge, something that we saw undergirded, Hume's, Kant's, Mill's visions of what reality and knowledge look like, in favor of Nietzsche of a recognition that there are multiple kinds of knowledge and none of them is preeminent, many of them area intuitive, aesthetic and physical.

Because he does that, he rejects the idea of the sovereignty of reason. That's something that we've seen in the Western tradition right since Aristotle. The idea that what makes us distinctively human and what makes our lives meaningful is our ability to reason. We saw that not only in Aristotle, of course we saw that in the Stoics, we see it in Kant. Hume of course distrusted reason in the same sense that Nietzsche did. Nietzsche is reading Hume a little bit. There's a bit of influence there. This vein that runs through the West of the sovereignty of reason, Nietzsche thinks is crazy. In favor he said that we should trust the body, we should trust our senses.

Nietzsche rejects the classical idea of progress. The idea that philosophical thought, political thought and in general, human history is a steady march from the primitive to the better and the better and the better. In fact, he sees us as having been on this terrible decline where we hit the real abyss in modernity where other people see the peak. We hit the abyss because it's the most life-denying, the most leveling, the most self-alienating approach to life that's possible. He sees instead the need to return to our nature and to return to an embrace of nature, and to really embrace many, many approaches to action, the possibility of creativity at every moment.

As part of that move Nietzsche rejects the idea of a systematic unity of knowledge. He thinks that human life and human knowledge is messy. Systematizing is always dangerous, always distorting. Intuitive, spontaneous action is what's required, not careful, deliberate, systematic theory.

Here we see Nietzsche, as I said earlier, more in tune with Daoism. Finally, he rejects the kind of personal freedom and this kind of open, public sphere as a domain of liberty that we see in liberal democracy; rejecting that in favor of thinking about freedom as a very important value, a central human value, but thinking about freedom as individual strength and the possibility of creativity.

So then what does Nietzsche think the meaning of life is? A meaningful life for Nietzsche is a life of integrity, a life of authenticity, a life where we create our own goals, our own values and we live up to them; that we don't abandon our values or abdicate responsibility for our lives to someone else, even to a theory, even to a theory that we endorse. That requires intellectual integrity. That requires moral integrity. That requires aesthetic integrity, and that requires a taking responsibility for our own deepest values. It requires that we pay attention to what's real, to the actual world around us, not some airy set of abstractions to our biological nature, not to some ideal of ourselves as free rational beings. It involves the rejection of everything artificial.

Morally that means we take responsibility for our own actions on autonomy and don't deny them. It means that we need to cultivate our strength, our abilities and our talents, that our task in life is to make ourselves the heroes of really great autobiographies. At the bottom we can see this as a very strongly-aesthetic notion of the meaning of life. A meaningful life for Nietzsche is a successful creative act. It's a work of art. It's art on a grand performance scale from birth to death.

We're now going to turn in our very next lecture to what I think is an even more radical critique of modernity. You might have thought that Nietzsche was as radical as it could get, and he is pretty radical. We're now going to see a critique that integrates both pre-modern and post modern ideas, one that's going to reach back to the Gīta to offer a very stunning critique of modernity, and that one comes in the work of Mohandas Gandhi. Please stay with me for that lecture.

Gandhi—Satyāgraha and Holding Fast to Truth
Lecture 30

> The narrative for Gandhi of Indian spirituality is both philosophical and religious. It's aimed at the future, but it's aimed at grounding the future in an Indian past that reaches back to the Gītā. Gandhi's critique of modernity and of British rule is not just a political critique; it's a very deep cultural critique.

Like Nietzsche, **Mohandas Gandhi** was a critic of modernity, believing that modernity itself makes a meaningful life impossible. During his life, Gandhi lived in India, Britain, and South Africa and, as a philosopher, wove together ideas from many sources into an extraordinarily complex, multicultural vision of what human life is and ought to be.

One idea that animates Gandhi's thought is a deep sense of justice, a sense of the importance of human rights and the obligation of a nation to respect the rights of its citizens. As a young lawyer in South Africa, Gandhi's political sensibility was galvanized by an act of personal injustice he experienced: He was deposited at a remote station in the middle of the night when a white South African demanded his berth on a train. In response, Gandhi mobilized a massive civil disobedience movement to liberalize race laws in South Africa. Later, he was invited to return to India to help lead the fight against colonial rule.

Many of Gandhi's ideas derived from reading the Gītā and from **Jainism**, a religion with a strong emphasis on nonviolence embodied in the principle of *ahimsa*, meaning "non-harming." Jainism also encompasses the idea that no single individual has a complete grasp of the truth; we must always act on our own conception of the truth but hold ourselves open to the fact that others may understand some things better than we do. From Tolstoy, Gandhi inherited an emphasis on personal spiritual development as essential to human life and a powerful critique of industrialism and modernity. He derived a sense of justice from his studies in Britain and an emphasis on civil disobedience from Henry David Thoreau. From the Indian leader Sri Aurobindo, Gandhi developed a sense of the importance of national identity and the need for a revolution in Indian culture, which he thought could be achieved through a union of *svadharma* and *ahimsa*.

Recall that *svadharma* is the idea that we each have a particular duty in society and a meaningful life involves our discharge of that duty. For Gandhi, our *svadharma* derives from our political circumstances, which entail public political duties. Gandhi diagnosed the primary disease of modernity as inconsistency with *ahimsa*; that is, modernity itself is harmful to individuals and causes us to lead our lives in ways that harm others. The only way to confront modernity is to do so publicly and representationally through civil disobedience. Our *svadharma* in the face of an unjust law is to defy it publicly.

> Government could not be an institution that allows some to benefit and others to suffer.

Gandhi endorsed the liberal democratic ideals and fundamental freedoms of Mill, but he believed that they had become the foundation of industrial capitalism, which he saw as intrinsically harmful. The idea of liberal democracy should be reinterpreted to be consistent with *ahimsa*. Government could not be an institution that allows some to benefit and others to suffer.

Another central construct for Gandhi is the idea of **satyāgraha**, meaning a commitment to determining the truth and an insistence that truth prevails. This is a realization of the ideals of the Gītā, specifically, the role of *jñāna* yoga in understanding the nature of reality and *karma* yoga in acting so as to realize that understanding. Gandhi thought that *satyāgraha* must be performed publicly, actively, and nonviolently and should be aimed at enabling others to see and act on the truth. Gandhi follows Thoreau in suggesting that such action always invites resistance and punishment, which one should accept publicly, again, because doing so educates others about injustice.

The second important construct in Gandhi's political thought is **swaraj**, literally meaning "self-rule," a term that can be applied to both politics and the individual. Gandhi believed that political *swaraj* was impossible without personal *swaraj*, self-mastery. For Gandhi, *swaraj* and *satyāgraha* are tightly connected. *Satyāgraha* is the vehicle for obtaining political *swaraj*, but personal *swaraj* is the necessary condition of genuine *satyāgraha*. We can't grasp the truth without first ruling ourselves.

In Gandhi's view, the individualism of Hume, Kant, and Mill was the foundation of capitalism, which inevitably resulted in industrialism and, in turn, the exploitation of workers, concentration of wealth in the hands of a few, and eventually, colonial expropriation of wealth from other countries. Gandhi also thought that secularism—the abandonment of religion in public life—had the effect of eliminating moral critique, which generally arises from religious roots. Gandhi urged a kind of *swaraj* that resisted modern ideas of liberality, individualism, and so on, replacing large-scale government and industry with a commitment to local production. He acknowledged that this commitment would involve the sacrifice of many of the benefits of modernity—technology, medical advances, and so on—but he argued that it's better to do without those benefits than to lose the human soul. ∎

Name to Know

Gandhi, Mohandas K. (1869–1948): Gandhi was born in Porbandar, then a small princely state, in the modern state of Gujarat. His father was *diwan* of that state. Gandhi's parents were both devout Hindus, but much of the surrounding community was Jain; hence, he grew up in a context of great piety and commitment to nonviolence.

Important Terms

ahimsa: Nonviolence, or refraining from harming others.

Jainism: An Indian religion in which nonviolence is the central value.

satyāgraha: A Gandhian term: holding on to, or insisting on, the truth.

swaraj: Self-rule.

Suggested Reading

Gandhi, *Hind Swaraj*.

————, *An Autobiography: The Story of My Experiments with Truth.*

Study Questions

1. What are the roots of Gandhi's account of *satyāgraha* and *swaraj*? Are they consistent with one another?

2. How do the personal and political dimensions of *swaraj* fit together? What aspects of the political program are plausible? Can they be disentangled from the less plausible aspects?

Gandhi—Satyāgraha and Holding Fast to Truth
Lecture 30—Transcript

It is hard to imagine two philosophers more different from one another than Friedrich Nietzsche and Mohandas Gandhi. It's hard to imagine two views of the meaning of life and of the nature of existence more different from one another than those articulated by Nietzsche and Gandhi.

Nonetheless, in the present lecture we move from Nietzsche to Gandhi, and in doing so we're going to discover some surprising commonalities. Nietzsche and Gandhi were both thorough-going critics of modernity. Each of them believe that modernity itself makes a meaningful life impossible in important ways. Each of them believes that a thorough rejection of modernity is necessary if life is going to be truly meaningful.

Gandhi's only critique of modernity is very complex reflecting his own complex life. He was indeed one of the most extraordinary individuals who lived in the 20th century. His life took him from India where he was born, to the United Kingdom where he was educated, to South Africa where he began his career, and back to India. From each of these sources, Gandhi picked up ideas, picked up theories, picked up techniques, and he wove them together in an extraordinarily complex, multicultural and even cosmopolitan vision of what human life is and ought to be.

In India his roots lie both in the Hindu and Jain traditions. He was raised in a devout Hindu family but a family that also boasted Jain relatives and many Jain friends. We haven't talked about Jainism in these lectures, but it was a religion that developed in India at about the same time as Buddhism and had an even stronger emphasis than did Buddhism on non-violence, on non-harming. The Sanskrit term for this is ahimsa, non-harming.

Religious Jains often wear facemasks so as not to accidentally inhale small insects. Jain monks and nuns you will always see walking with a broom to sweep the ground in front of them in order to prevent accidentally treading on a small animal. Jainism has a very, very deep commitment to non-harming of anybody, of any kind of creature.

Gandhi absorbed this idea of ahimsa and Jainism. He also studied the Gītā very carefully, and from the Gītā he developed a deep commitment to the idea of svadharma, of one's own duty and of the importance of leading a life guided by ones svadharma, and of leading that life, guided by the three yogas, the three disciplines that we have studied, namely karma yoga, the yoga of action; jñana yoga, the yoga of knowledge; and bhakti yoga, the yoga of devotion.

But Gandhi also, while in England, encountered the work of the American philosopher, Henry David Thoreau and was taken by his idea of civil disobedience, of the way in which duty could lead one to disobey laws that one regards as immoral and the need to disobey those laws in a public, representational way; in a way in which one's action is not simply a refusal to obey, but a public refusal to obey that symbolizes the immorality of the law one is protesting. Gandhi also corresponded extensively with Tolstoy, and from Tolstoy he developed his deep distrust of modernity as fundamentally soul destroying, as a kind of secularism that took all that was spiritual and worthwhile out of human life.

One of the ideas that animates Gandhi's thought more than any other is a deep sense of justice, a sense of the importance of human rights and of the obligation of a nation to respect the rights of its citizens for a rule to be based upon the consent of the governed. That, he learned in Britain when he studied the law and it's from a British sense of civil justice that Gandhi derives much of his sense of what was wrong with British rule in India. That is what led him to his deep confrontation with colonialism despite the fact he developed these ideas at the center of colonial power.

In Gandhi we see a kind of integration of pre-modern ideas and post-modern critiques. What we're going to be examining in Gandhi will be his challenge, his challenge to modernity, that it makes meaningful life impossible and Gandhi's challenge to each of us that we've got to confront modernity, not to live within it but to roll it back and to develop a very different social order and very different lives in confrontation with that modernity.

Before we can really address Gandhi's thought we need to talk a bit about the historical background of the development of his spot. The British of course ruled India for a very long time and most of us know of Gandhi in the context of his struggle for independence of Great Britain in the mid 20th century. But before 1857, India was not ruled directly by the British crown but bizarrely by the British East India Company. In fact, we can think about the conquest of India over the 18th and early 19th centuries as an unusual example of the conquest of a subcontinent by a private corporation.

The East India Company basically as a private corporation, held a charter to administer India, a charter given to it by the Crown. The East India Company was a fairly rapacious and authoritarian rule for India. It was designed to extract the most possible wealth from India for its stockholders and it worked to do that. It did that by hiring a number of local armies, subverting a number of local Indian kingdoms and republics, and bending them effectively to its will through a combination of corruption and coercion.

In 1857 a rebellion swept Northern India and nearly dislodged company rule. In Britain it's called the Mutiny of 1857, but in India it's generally characterized as the Great Rebellion or the Rebellion of 1857. As I say, it very nearly succeeded and the response in Britain to the near end of British rule in India in 1857 was to remove authority from the East India Company and to impose direct colonial rule by the Crown. True colonialism, that is Crown colonialism, has its origin in the response to the 1857 rebellion.

British legal colonial rule was not a whole lot better than company rule. It became increasingly rapacious, increasingly authoritarian, increasingly racist, and increasingly intent on the maximum extraction of wealth from the Indian subcontinent in order to enrich great Britain. Areas of India that had been previously very wealthy and prosperous like Bengal ended up in terrible famines. Crops that used to be very productive were replaced with crops that were more economically advantageous to British planters and so forth, and India really declined dramatically during this rule.

One of the ways that the British Crown maintained its rule was to construct divisions in India along caste lines and religious lines reinforcing preexisting but rather subtle distinctions and turning them into hard legal distinctions with differences in interest on either side of those distinctions. It was very much a rule of divide and conquer. It distinguished Muslims from Hindus, upper caste Hindus from lower caste Hindus. It distinguished people on linguistic lines and so forth, giving them different degrees of citizenship, different kinds of rights, and different kinds of interests in order to prevent the development of Indian unity.

This reached its apex in the partition of Bengal between predominantly Hindu, West Bengal and predominantly Muslim, East Bengal in 1905 which in turn led to the major agitation in India that eventually resulted in Indian independence. But this British Raj, this British rule, while it deliberately introduced a very complex identity politics to India, really trying to create micro identities, pitting Indians against one another in order to maintain their sovereignty, it had a paradoxical effect. Because Bengal partition so highlighted and so clearly manifested this strategy, the reaction across India was so aggressively hostile that the British had the paradoxical effect of beginning to create for the first time since the fall of Ashoka's great empire in the 1ˢᵗ century CE, a shared Indian sense of national identity across India, and it was that shared sense of Indian national identity that was inevitably going to make independence possible.

One of the manifestations of this sense of identity was a tremendous intellectual and religious renaissance in India. It had its roots in Bengal but it really swept India with other roots in the Punjab as well. The Indian renaissance generated a resurgence of interest in Indian philosophy and religion. There was a recovery of the study of texts that hadn't been studied for a long time, a recovery of religious traditions, and the Gīta was a real beneficiary for this. Because the Gīta had been studied by elites for a long time, it suddenly entered popular culture in a whole new way in the context of the renaissance.

Some of the main figures who were important in this intellectual and religious renaissance and this development of national identity where people like Sri Ramakrishna, who established the Ramakrishna mission in Calcutta, and whose student, Swami Vivekananda, very famously came to the World Parliament of Religions in Chicago and really spread consciousness of Hinduism around the world, but also dramatically reawakened Hindu consciousness in India, and the great first political and then religious leader, Sri Aurobindo, Aurobindo gauche, who like Gandhi was educated in England, returned to India initially as an educator, then as a political revolutionary, and finally lived most of his life as a cultural and religious leader.

The writings of all of these people combine to create a tremendous intellectual ferment. It was this ferment and this revival of interest in Hinduism that made writing and Gandhi's political activity possible.

Who was Gandhi himself? He was born to a merchant caste in Gujarat in 1869. His father was a fairly well-respected merchant in their town. He was a very good student and earned a scholarship to study law in England, and was admitted to the bar in England as a barrister, as a lawyer. His first big job was in South Africa which was then again under British colonial rule as was India.

He traveled to South Africa to begin his practice of law. It was in South Africa that this famous incident occurred that people say galvanized Gandhi's political sensibility and moral sensibility for the first time. Gandhi, as a fairly prosperous lawyer, had a first class ticket in a South African train, and late at night a white South African wanted his berth, wanted his compartment, and ordered that Gandhi be thrown off the train because Gandhi was Indian and did not have the right to a first class ticket. The conductor threw Gandhi and his luggage off the train in a fairly remote station in the middle of the night, and this tremendous act of personal injustice galvanized Gandhi's sense of the injustice of the racial laws in South Africa.

Gandhi mobilized a massive civil disobedience movement modeled on Thoreau's ideas but motivated by British senses of justice and also motivated by Jain senses of ahimsa, of non harmony, and led this huge civil disobedience movement to liberalize race laws in South Africa. He, in fact, achieved a fair amount of success. Some of the race laws were repealed and liberalized, others of course were not. Gandhi, in the course of doing this, gained the attention of Indians in India as a potential leader against the kind of racism that was manifested in colonialism in India.

In 1916 the Indian National Congress invited Gandhi to return to India to help lead the Congress' fight against British colonial rule. Shortly after Gandhi's return to India in the beginning of his activity in the Congress party, one of the most terrible events in the history of British rule occurred in India. This was the massacre of over 1,000 unarmed civilians in Jallianwallah Bagh in Amritsar by Major Reginald Dyer and the British Army who were trying to put down peaceful protest.

This galvanized the quick Indian movement and really mobilized the Congress party from a party that was involved in trying to advance Indian interests to a party that was fully aimed at getting the British out of India, and it committed Gandhi once and for all to achieving not a better life for Indians within a British rule, but rather independence.

Gandhi was shortly after that elected president of the Congress party. He was of course very active in the Indian independence movement, spent a great deal of that time in jail, led many prominent civil disobedience marches, many prominent movements. In the end, Gandhi felt that his efforts were to some extent a failure, because Gandhi, while he succeeded in leading a movement to get Britain out of India, failed to prevent the partition of India into India and Pakistan and the horrible violence that attended that partition.

Shortly after independence in 1948, Gandhi was assassinated by Hindu fundamentalists who regarded him as too conciliatory to Muslims. This is a brief sketch of Gandhi's life. Now let's return to Gandhi's philosophical roots.

He was born into a devout Hindu family and many of his ideas derived from a reading of the Gīta. Many of his ideas also derived from the Jain friends and relatives who impressed him both with the Jain idea of ahimsa and on the Jainian emphasis on perspectivalism, the idea that no single individual has a complete grasp of the truth and so that we must always act on our own conception of the truth but hold ourselves open to the fact that others may understand some things better than we do, and so that we can never act with violence or coercion because we might be trammeling a perspective that actually is more valid than our own.

Tolstoy, from a long correspondence, he inherited an emphasis on personal spiritual development as essential to human life and a powerful critique of industrialism and modernity. From a British sense of justice, from Thoreau the importance of civil disobedience, and from Sri Aurobindo the sense that Indian national identity was important and that a renaissance in India had to be an ideological renaissance and not just a political renaissance, that what was called for in striving for Indian independence wasn't just winning self rule on a political level, but a tremendous revolution in Indian culture, and Gandhi thought that this could be achieved through a union of the idea of svadharma and ahimsa.

Let's recall the idea of svadharma as it's developed in *Bhagavad-Gīta*. It's the idea that in virtue of our particular role in society, we each have a particular duty and that a meaningful life involves our discharge of that particular duty. Gandhi took that up but gave it a real political twist. He twisted it into the idea that our svadharma derives from our political circumstances and that it's our political circumstances that really entail our duties and of those duties are public, political duties.

Ahimsa that he inherits from the Jains is the idea that one should never harm another, that harm is always wrong. In fact, Gandhi diagnoses the primary disease of modernity in terms of ahimsa. He thinks that modernity is inconsistent with it, that modernity is harmful to individuals, and that modernity makes it necessary for individuals in leading their lives to lead those lives in ways that harm others. This idea of modernity as intrinsically harmful owes a great deal to his correspondent of Tolstoy.

Gandhi also argued, following Thoreau, that the only way to confront modernity isn't simply to move away from it, isn't simply to reject it, but to confront it publicly and representationally through civil disobedience. He argued that civil disobedience is always legitimate when we are confronting an unjust law or an unjust order because our svadharma in that circumstance consists of an obligation not to not comply with but to defy and to defy publicly and representationally the unjust social order with which we disagree.

Moreover, that opposition Gandhi thought, had to always be non-violent. From Great Britain, Gandhi of course inherited the Lockean idea that legitimacy of government depends on the consent of the governed, that society is a kind of contract for mutual benefit, and that society is only legitimate insofar as it represents the rule of law.

He also read Mill very carefully and he endorsed Mill's view that speech and thought had to be free. In a lot of ways Gandhi is a beautiful British subject. He endorses the liberal democratic ideals, the rule of law, and the fundamental freedoms that Mill does. But Gandhi thought there were two things wrong with these. First, they're systematically neglected in India, but moreover Gandhi thought that in Britain these things became the foundation of industrial capitalism, and that industrial capitalism was intrinsically harmful to almost everyone who came in contact with it, so that they had to be reinterpreted if they were to be consistent with ahimsa.

Tolstoy and Thoreau were the people who pushed Gandhi in this direction. It was their idea that everyone should benefit from social arrangements, that when we talk about government being legitimized by the consent of the governed and by the benefits that it presents to the governed, that means that it can't be an institution that allows some to benefit and others to suffer. It permits a harm of the many by the few, which is what Gandhi thought that modernity ended up doing through its articulation in capitalism.

Gandhi came back to India in the midst of the Indian renaissance, in the midst of this kind of social ferment and this renaissance of ideas of Indian national identity. Sri Aurobindo was championing this idea that India was a nation and that it was a nation grounded in spiritual values, and this idea of Aurobindos, that Indian nationality was fundamentally spiritual, became the foundation for the anti-British movement, and Gandhi absorbed that immediately.

The narrative for Gandhi of Indian spirituality is both philosophical and religious. It's aimed at the future but it's aimed at grounding the future in an Indian past that reaches back to the Gīta. Gandhi's critique of modernity and of British rule is not just a political critique, it's a very deep cultural critique.

One of the central constructs in Gandhi's sense of what a meaningful life is is the idea of satyagraha. Satyagraha is a Sanskrit compound that can be read in one of two ways. We can see it as a compound of satya and graha which would mean holding onto the truth, seizing the truth, really grasping and understanding it. It can also be a compound of satya and agraha. Agraha means insistence. So then satyagraha means insistence on the truth, and Gandhi read it in both ways, that satyagraha means a commitment to determining what the truth is, and once having determined it, an insistence on making it prevail.

This means that for Gandhi it's extraordinarily important to determine what's right, to get very clear about why it's so, and to insist on making it so. This is a realization of the ideals of the Gīta, of the role of jñana yoga in getting clear about the nature of reality and then karma yoga, acting so as to realize the understanding that we've achieved.

Moreover, Gandhi thought, satyagraha must be performed publicly, actively, and non-violently. Seizing the truth and insisting on it has to be something that educates others and enables them to see the truth, enables them to grasp the truth, enables them to act on the truth. He follows Thoreau in suggesting that this always invites resistance and punishment, and that one should accept the resistance one receives and the punishment one receives and call attention to it, because that courageous calling of attention to the injustice of the oppressor is what educates others to really see the oppression as unjust and to see one's own actions as genuinely representational and genuinely authentic. In fact, sometimes Gandhi satyagraha said, absolutely tragic results is when the great Indian leader, Lajpat Rai was beaten to death by British troops leading a protest against the appointment of the Simon Commission, a commission of British parliamentarians to design Indian rule. Gandhi satyagraha, even though it's sometimes characterized as such, is not passive resistance at all. It's a very active resistance; it's very difficult and it's sometimes very dangerous.

The second important construct in Gandhi's political idea is that of swaraj, literally meaning self-rule. Again this is an ambiguous term. Swaraj can mean something political, that is it can mean Indian political self-rule, and Aurobindo certainly understood it that way. But it could also mean personal swaraj, self-mastery, ruling oneself, something that comes out of the Gīta but also out of Tolstoy.

Gandhi's brilliant insight was that these are mutually entailing, that you can't have political swaraj without personal swaraj. He asked: What use would it be to throw the British out of India if we become British in the process? He argued that one has to achieve personal swaraj, personal self-mastery, before one can engage in political action. So that it's personal swaraj that is the fundamental idea.

Swaraj and satyagraha are very tightly connected. Satyagraha is the vehicle for obtaining political swaraj, but personal swaraj is the necessary condition of genuine satyagraha. You can't grasp the truth without first ruling yourself, that's what yoga is about.

What is Gandhi's critique of modernity? Gandhi sees, along with Hume, Kant, and Mill that modernity is built on the foundation of individualism and that individualism involves an individual right to do whatever he or she might want to do to advance their own good, so long as it doesn't directly harm others. Gandhi saw that this individualism is the foundation in terms of capitalism, the individual right to acquire property, the individual right to invest one's property as one sees fit, the individual right to hire others to work for one, and the individual right to sell one's labor to someone else. Gandhi saw that capitalism inevitably entails industrialism that grows some very large industrial complexes and hence of a laboring class. And that it involves secularism that as we've seen God and religion will eventually be pushed out of the public sphere into the private sphere, and that transcendent values will cease to animate public life.

Gandhi saw that colonialism—the colonialism of his time—and the poverty in India as well as the poverty in England, and the oppression of colonial subjects as well as laborers by industrial groups was a natural outcome of all of this, that it flowed naturally from the kind of industrialism that individualist capitalism gave rise to. He thought that this was true because individualism, Gandhi thought, inevitably leads to greed and greed leads to toadyism, and that leads to complicity in all kinds of authoritarian relationships.

He saw that capitalism is just intrinsically licensed by liberalism, that liberalism encourages this kind of capitalist development. But also that capitalism inevitably leads to the exploitation of workers, to the exploitation of land and resources, and to the concentration of wealth in the hands of the capitalists and eventually in the 19th century to colonial expropriation of wealth from countries such as India and its import to Great Britain. Industrialism we thought was the natural outgrowth, and industrialism inevitably demanded colonialism, the dehumanization of vast parts of the population, and the reduction of people to poverty in order to retain the labor markets that capitalism required.

Finally, he thought, secularism, the abandonment of religion in public life, inevitably has the effect of eliminating moral critique since most moral critique arises from religious roots. This is a very, very broad critique of modern life. Gandhi is urging us to a serious swaraj, a serious kind of self rule that resists all of these modern ideas of liberality, individualism, capitalism and so forth.

For Gandhi this also involved a commitment to swadeshi, or local production, and the use of local products and local government, and a distrust of large-scale government, large-scale industry, and large-scale production. Gandhi thought that these inevitably required large, authoritarian structures that would disregard the benefit of local people and use up much of the world's resources in things like marketing and transportation of goods instead of the production of goods.

Gandhi thinks that a meaningful life has to be a life not only led individually in this sense but led very locally. So this is a critique of large national governments as well. Gandhi acknowledges that if we sacrifice all of this, that is if we sacrifice big industries, a capitalist order, large governments and so forth, we are going to be sacrificing many of the benefits of modernity. Gandhi acknowledges that this kind of critique of modernity involves an implicit rejection of a lot of technology, of a lot of medical development, of a lot of law, all of which emerges from the technical and scientific advances that modernity makes possible. If we say, gee, but you'd be giving up on everything that industry and that an economic order can afford us, wealth, productivity and so forth, Gandhi says absolutely. But Gandhi argued that given the goals of genuine human life, it's better to do without all of those benefits, better to do without those benefits and lead a really human life than to have all of the material benefits and to lose the human soul, to lose what makes our lives worth living in the first place. Gandhi argued, that it's the rejection of modernity that would give us true civilization as opposed to modern civilization which Gandhi thought wasn't civilized at all. It is a rejection of everything that civilization should offer human beings.

Very few of Gandhi's followers in India or anybody else ever followed him that far. That is, very few Gandhians actually suggested we should eliminate national governments and replace them with local governments, that we should eliminate all large-scale industries in production and replace them with small-scale production, that we should eliminate most of liberal democracy and replace it with local village governance.

But most Gandhians, both India and elsewhere, do see this as an ideal and they see this Gandhian ideal of a life that rejects the benefits of modernity in order to avoid the terrible harms that modernity causes, the harms to the working class, the harms to colonial subjects, and Gandhi thinks even the harms to capitalist, the harms that lead capitalists to organize their lives focused on acquisition, focused on greed, focused on acts that are inevitably going to harm and oppress others, and so to deny their own humanity. Many Gandhians see this as a real ideal that if only we could achieve would be a really wonderful thing.

For now, I want you to understand that this critique, A, is very multicultural. We've seen ideas here that have come from Tolstoy, from Thoreau, from the *Bhagavad-Gīta*, from Jainism, stirred together in this kind of creative cosmopolitan synthesis by Gandhi. So it's an unusual critique in that respect.

Secondly I want you to really understand how deep this critique is. I said, at the end of our last lecture on Nietzsche that Nietzsche was radical, but Gandhi is more radical. Gandhi is actually asking us to give up a great number of the material benefits, legal benefits, political, economic benefits that modernity gives us because, he argues, modernity itself is fundamentally evil and that we buy these benefits at the cost of a truly meaningful life. In our next lecture we'll look at the positive end of Gandhi's message: how we can lead a meaningful life in resistance to modernity.

Gandhi—The Call to a Supernormal Life
Lecture 31

Liberalism claims to be the way to make sense of human dignity, the way to encourage freedom, the way to encourage the development of knowledge and progress, but Gandhi argues, in fact, it subverts all of that.

Gandhi insisted that a meaningful life is a supernormal life, and his own was supernormal in a number of respects: his extreme asceticism, his practice of chastity, and his devotion to religion. His concept of *satyāgraha* involved a willingness to sustain injury and deprivation at the hands of his adversaries, and he was imprisoned many times. He was also committed to the idea that every aspect of his life was representational, a potential lesson to others in the possibilities for human life. Of course, his life was also nonviolent in the extreme, and we might say that it was successful in the extreme. This one man mobilized a disunified and largely impoverished subcontinent in rebellion against the most powerful military force in the world.

For Gandhi, a normal, ordinary life involves a rejection of autonomy. He believes that we all too often unreflectively accept social norms, political structures, economic values, and so on. He argues that this abdication of responsibility for our lives is always an acquiescence to and a complicity in violence and oppression, because industrial capitalism and the existence of militaries are themselves inherently violent and oppressive. These entities always involve the concentration of wealth and power in the hands of the few and the impoverishment of many. Because so much of our lives is structured by capitalism and industrialism, we accept these outcomes as legitimate. For this reason, we live lives of bad faith, lives in which we are alienated from our own values and cannot take responsibility for our actions.

One possible justification for living such an inauthentic life might be liberalism of the kind advanced by Mill or Kant, but Gandhi thinks that's insufficient because it ignores the harms of capitalism and industrialism.

According to Gandhi, Mill's harm principle is violated by liberalism itself because liberalism is set up to make harm possible. It argues for freedom, but the freedom it makes possible for the few is bought at the cost of enslavement of the many.

For Gandhi, normality gives others authority over our actions and ideology, allows us to relinquish responsibility for the way we live, and involves a rejection of truth because it requires us to accept ideologies that we know to be false. Further, normality violates the Jain idea of *ahimsa*, because leading a normal life in the context of a system that is built on the legitimation of harm involves leading a life that itself causes harm, even if we don't intend to harm directly. Thus, a normal life is a meaningless one.

Gandhi believes that the principles of liberalism—freedom of speech and of ideas—enable capitalism. People become free to sell their labor, accumulate wealth, and spend their wealth freely. This small-scale capitalism quickly becomes large-scale industrialism; the resulting concentration of wealth and power among the few subverts democracy and encourages consumerism. Further, capitalism and political oppression are built on advertising and propaganda, the purpose of which is to convince us that values we don't actually endorse are

Swaraj, a mastery of ourselves, calls upon us to be deeply self-reflective, to be aware of our motivations and our values.

acceptable. The result is the replacement of knowledge with confusion and a reduction in autonomy. This critique of liberalism is based on the idea of *svadharma* in the Bhagavad-Gītā. Gandhi argued that our membership in society gives us a collective *svadharma* of service, the duty to bring our societies in line with the values we endorse on reflection.

Gandhi's articulation of *satyāgraha*, an insistence on truth, and of *swaraj*, self-mastery, place supernormal demands on us: the duty to engage in constant social and political activity and struggle and the obligation to live a life of relentless nonviolence, consistency of values, and austerity. Such a supernormal life is active in alleviating the suffering of others and in achieving political liberation for the oppressed. Any recognition of harm is an obligation to organize our lives in such a way as to avoid it or eliminate it. Finally, the supernormal life is one of local production and consumption, one in which we attempt to minimize our participation in global economic structures.

For Gandhi, anything less than the supernormal life is utterly meaningless. The kind of self-discipline involved in this life is what gives us freedom from unreflective submission to mass values. Such a life is meaningful because it is the only one that reflects the truth as we know it. Finally, a life led through discipline and service to others connects us to something broader than ourselves: our fellow human beings and genuine sources of values. It's a life that actually serves the values we endorse: genuine freedom, not the artificial freedom of liberalism; genuine equity, not equality of opportunity to suppress others; and complete nonviolence. This is the kind of life that serves the highest good. ■

Suggested Reading

Gandhi, *Hind Swaraj*.

————, *An Autobiography: The Story of My Experiments with Truth*.

Study Questions

1. What aspects of the life Gandhi recommends seem reasonable? Which are unreasonable and why?

2. Do the principles that Gandhi uses to justify the life he recommends in fact entail that life? If so and if that life seems unreasonable, which of these principles might we reject?

Lecture 31: Gandhi—The Call to a Supernormal Life

Gandhi—The Call to a Supernormal Life
Lecture 31—Transcript

One respect in which Gandhi and Nietzsche are fellow travelers, and even fellow travelers with Tolstoy, is their insistence that a meaningful life is a supernormal life, the life of an extraordinary individual and their admonition that we try to be that extraordinary individual.

But there's a difference. Nietzsche after all, despite all of his advocacy of this extraordinary life, lived his life as a university professor, a professor of classical philology. That's actually a pretty conventional life when you come right down to it. I know from experience. Tolstoy, for all of his critique of normality in the death of Ivan Ilych and that wonderful remark that Ilych's life was normal and therefore terrible, led the life of a Russian aristocrat. He was critical of the regime, but he led an aristocratic life right up until the end. Gandhi on the other hand, really did lead a supernormal life and led that life in public as an example to everybody else, as an example of the proposition that a supernormal life is not only desirable, but possible.

Gandhi's life was supernormal in a number of respects. He was ascetic in the extreme. Gandhi deprived himself of all of the kinds of appurtenances that anybody who was politically powerful or potentially wealthy could possibly have. At the time of his death what did he own? He owned a pair of eyeglasses, an extra dhoti—that is the kind of loin cloth that he wore—a shawl, and a fountain pen. That was it. Gandhi through most of his life lived in extreme, self-imposed poverty and also lived a life of sexual chastity, for most of his life.

Gandhi was devotional in the extreme. He was an extraordinarily religious man who devoted an inordinate amount of time to prayer and to reflection and to religious retreat, and urged that his followers did so as well.

Gandhi was courageous in the extreme. As we said, satyagraha was far from passive resistance. Satyagraha involved unarmed resistance committed to doing no harm to one's adversary and a willingness to sustain injury, harm, and deprivation at the hands of one's adversary in public as a representational act.

Many of Gandhi's friends and associates died in the course of the independence movement as a result of satyagraha. Gandhi himself was imprisoned many times and often engaged in very public hunger strikes, sometimes hunger striking so close to death that he was very nearly dead. Gandhi was somebody whose physical courage and personal courage were well beyond the norm. Gandhi was also focused—single-pointedly focused in the extreme. Once he began the quest for British evacuation from India, the quest for Indian independence, that is all that Gandhi did. That's all he devoted his life to, and you can honestly say he devoted every waking moment to that cause.

Gandhi's life was also lived in public in the extreme. Gandhi was committed to the idea that every aspect of his life was representational. Every aspect of his life was a potential lesson to others in the possibility of leading a human life. Gandhi kept nothing private and allowed intrusion into every aspect of his life. Gandhi's life, of course, was also non-violent in the extreme. Gandhi very carefully ensured that even though his actions often posed risks to himself and to those who voluntarily undertook satyagraha, they never imposed risks, harms, or violence on anybody who did not themselves voluntarily undertake those risks. In particular he never permitted violent resistance to violence.

Finally we might say, Gandhi's life was successful in the extreme. Who would have thought that one small lawyer, using completely non-violent means with very limited financial resources could mobilize an extraordinarily diverse, largely impoverished, largely illiterate and extraordinarily disunified subcontinent in rebellion against what was then the most powerful military force in the world and a colonial power that had ruled India for hundreds of years. Gandhi did that. It was an extraordinary success, and Gandhi took it to be the kind of success which demonstrated the value and the meaning of leading a truly super ordinary life.

Gandhi took his own example to be a call to all of us to this kind of super normality. Gandhi concurred, or would have concurred with Nietzsche in calling a normal life, an ordinary life, the life of Ivan Ilych. Or indeed I must say that my life, or most of the lives of people that I know, he would call these the lives of the herd animal, a life that is lived unreflectively, a life that does not involve a truly authentic commitment to the kind of life that we in fact lead. It doesn't involve a harmony of our deepest-held values with the life that we, in fact, conduct.

Normality for Gandhi, this kind of ordinary life, involves an acceptance of heteronomy. That is, a rejection of autonomy. Gandhi thinks that in our ordinary life, we all too often unreflectively accept the social norms into which we socialize, the political structures that we participate in, the economic order in which we buy, sell, work and so forth, and in general an entire set of values that we imbibe from those around us and that we simply accept those and absorb those without thinking about them. It's an absence of responsibility. It's the abdication of the responsibility for authenticity to which Nietzsche called us. It involves exactly the kind of willingness to succumb to the tyranny of the majority that Mill so eloquently criticized, and it's actually from Mill that Gandhi gets many of these ideas.

We see a reflection of this kind of criticism of heteronomy by Kant, Mill, Nietzsche, and Gandhi, but Gandhi goes much deeper. As far as Gandhi is concerned, it's not only that our ordinary life is this kind of inauthentic abdication, but he argues that it is fundamentally and always an acquiescence to and a complicity in violence and oppression. Why is that so? That's so because for Gandhi, industrial capitalism and the existence of militaries are themselves inherently violent and inherently oppressive. They always involve the concentration of wealth in a few hands and the way that that is achieved, he argued, was the impoverishment of many.

They require maintaining labor markets with disproportionately low wages for working people. They involve the concentration of political power in the hands of those who have the money to buy elections, to buy politicians, to advertise their views; and because so much of our lives are structured by capitalism and industrialism, most of our lives involve buying into these as legitimate institutions. Every time we go shopping, every time we buy a brand-named object, every time we take a job selling our labor to a capitalist, or every time we hire somebody else to work for us, Gandhi thought, we are simply accepting as legitimate, accepting as morally okay, accepting as appropriate, a system that is inherently violent.

Gandhi thinks that if we were to reflect on this, if we were to sit and actually ask ourselves the question, do we think that it's morally appropriate for social institutions to be set up like that with enormous disparities of wealth, social systems in which some people are fabulously wealthy and others are homeless, in which some people have access to top quality medical care and others die for the lack of medicine, societies in which some children are able to get educations and others have to work as child laborers. Do we think that's how a society ought to be organized? Gandhi argued, none of us would say that that's morally appropriate. None of us would endorse that.

Nonetheless, in virtue of actively participating in societies just like that, we give aid and comfort to them. We accept them. For that reason, Gandhi thought, we live lives of deeply bad faith, lives in which we are alienated from our own values and cannot take responsibility for our own actions. That's why Gandhi thinks ordinary life is meaningless life. This isn't just Tolstoy, this is Tolstoy ratcheted way up.

Gandhi thinks that the only thing that possibly legitimates this life for us, the only thing to which we can appeal in saying that our lives are okay, is its commonness, the fact that everybody else acts like that. But that's not legitimation, that's just description of a herd, a description of a membership in a society in which everybody is so alienated and so heteronomous.

The other possible justification Gandhi thinks might be a serious defense of liberalism of the kind that say John Stuart Mill would advance or that Kant would advance, Gandhi thinks that's insufficient. It's insufficient because it ignores all the harms. Mill of course is very famous for the Harm Principle. The Harm Principle, Gandhi thinks, is violated by liberalism itself because liberalism is set up to make harm possible. As far as Gandhi is concerned, liberalism is deeply ironic. Liberalism argues for freedom but the freedom that it guarantees and makes possible for a few is bought at the cost of enslavement for many, and that's the only way Gandhi thinks that kind of freedom can be made possible in modernity.

What is wrong then with normality as far as Gandhi is concerned? Several things. The first one of course is heteronomy as opposed to autonomy. Normality gives others authority over our own actions and over our own ideology. We don't act and we don't think in ways that we reflectively endorse, but rather in ways that others describe as acceptable and prescribe to us.

Normality involves an abdication of responsibility. Not only do we act in this way but we are able to convince ourselves that we are not responsible for it, that it's just the only way that we could possibly live. Gandhi emphasizes that we can take responsibility for these actions. We can act in resistance instead of acting in complicity. Normality involves a rejection of truth, a rejection of jñana yoga, of the yoga of knowledge, because it requires us to accept an ideology that we know in our heart of hearts, Gandhi thinks, to be false. It involves a deprecation of our own value and of our own autonomy, and we know that at bottom we are autonomous, that our lives can be valuable, and the only way we can participate in this kind of meaningless normality is to deny that and that is to deny the truth.

Normality, Gandhi argues, is inauthentic. We end up living a lie. We can't possibly endorse the lies we voluntarily lead. Normality is harmful. It violates this Jain idea of ahimsa, of non-harming, because leading a normal life in the context of a political, social, economical and ideological system that is built on the legitimation of harm to some for the benefit of others involves leading a life that itself causes harm, even if we don't intend to do it directly.

Finally, in virtue of all of these features and in virtue of a life that is in the end a life that's just a cog in a vast industrialist machine though life becomes totally meaningless, there's no way, Gandhi thinks, to look at the values we endorse, the lives we lead and to see those lives as those worth living at all.

Gandhi thinks that liberalism is in the end deeply ironic. The liberalism that he has in mind is the liberalism that we examined in our own discussion of modernity. It's the liberalism of Kant and Mill. It's the idea that individuals are free and that individuals are called to gain knowledge, to be autonomous, to think reflectively, to think for themselves, to choose ideas.

This is the fundamental idea of liberal democracy, and we saw that kind of valorization of pluralism, that valorization of free speech, both in Kant and in Mill. Why is it ironic then? It's ironic, Gandhi thinks, because in the end when you start with these principles and you follow them out inevitably, and you look at what people do with them, they end up enabling capitalism. They end up legitimizing capitalism. They end up enabling people to be free, not only to say what they want, but to invest what they want, to sell their labor as they want, to accumulate wealth as they want, to spend their wealth as they want.

This of course moves from small, petty capitalism quickly through efficiency to large-scale industrialism, and large-scale industrialism necessarily concentrates wealth and concentrates power in the hands of a few. That concentration of wealth and power thereby subverts democracy, because these people end up being able to control the very mechanisms of democratic polity such as elections, such as parliaments, and so forth.

Moreover it encourages consumerism. It encourages the idea that we are made happy and that the key to our happiness is the acquisition of goods, goods that are packaged and sold to us through advertising and ideology as the things we need, as the things that will make us happy, whether they're Barbie dolls or new cars or new computers, or new cellular telephones or whatever. None of these are things that we thought we needed before they were manufactured, before they were advertised, and before they were sold to us. But, Gandhi points out, it's the nature of consumer capitalism and the nature of advertising to create these artificial senses of need. When we create these artificial senses of need, we create more demand. We then reinforce industrialism. We reinforce exploitation. We reinforce the division of classes and the concentration of wealth, and we cause more and more harm all the time. Even a purchase in a shop becomes an instance of a causing of harm and a reduction, not a creation of freedom.

The central idea here is that what looks like the freedom to choose among many different products, the freedom to lead our lives as consumers in liberty, becomes a freedom bought at the expense of the reduction of freedom in many others. All of these facts end up reducing the net amount of freedom. They end up reducing our knowledge as well though. They reduce our knowledge because Gandhi argued that capitalism and political oppression are built on advertising and propaganda. Advertising and propaganda are there to convince us that values that we don't actually endorse are actually okay. The products we don't actually need are, in fact, necessary and so forth. What they do is to gradually replace what could be knowledge with confusion, with ignorance, and they decrease our autonomy in the end because we end up being driven by these messages that come to us from outside, rather than from our own moral compass.

This is why Gandhi thinks that liberalism is, in fact, ironic. It's, in fact, a disguised attack on freedom, a disguised attack on liberty, a disguised attack on knowledge, a disguised attack on human dignity, and that's what it claims to value. Liberalism claims to be the way to make sense of human dignity, the way to encourage freedom, the way to encourage the development of knowledge and progress, but Gandhi argues in fact it subverts all of that.

The critique that Gandhi has advanced is based entirely in the *Bhagavad-Gīta*. Remember the Gīta saw the idea of svadharma as one's own duty, as tied to caste, or as we put it to one's social role. That makes a certain kind of sense. It generates an individual duty and the Gīta argued that it's recognition of that kind of duty and leading life in harmony with that kind of duty that gives meaning to our lives. Then we saw the superstructure of the yogas that makes that possible.

Gandhi takes up that idea of svadharma, but he socializes it. It's not our particular social role, not my role as a teacher or your role as a doctor or a lawyer or a carpenter or a dentist, that determines our svadharma. But rather, Gandhi argued, that our very membership in society gives us svadharma, the same svadharma, a collective svadharma, a svadharma of service. That is the duty to bring our societies in line with the values that we endorse on reflection. That's really important. Gandhi argues that if you reflect carefully and to think about what you really regard as most important, it will be that people are generally happy, that there is less oppression, that there's a reasonably equitable distribution of the world's goods, that knowledge flourishes, and so forth. Gandhi thinks that our contemporary societies are organized in ways empithetical to all of that.

What that does is it gives you a duty, a svadharma, an individual obligation as a member of the collective to bring your society in line with those values even though it's difficult, even though it's challenging.

Social goals, collective goals, hence for Gandhi, in gender, individual goals and individual duties—it's really interesting, by the way, to reflect on how Martin Luther King, who was so deeply influenced by Mohandas Gandhi takes all of this up in arguing that every individual in a nation has a personal obligation, a personal duty, to devote his or her life to the alleviation of repression, the alleviation of oppression, and the achievement of equality and dignity for all human beings. This isn't an idea that flourished only in India; it's an idea that came from India to the United States as well in Martin Luther King's work.

This kind of articulation of satyagraha, of grasping an insistence on the truth, and of svaraj, gaining control of oneself and achieving genuine independence in a political and social sense truly are supernormal demands on us. Why is that? In a practical sense they each impose on each of us, that is the demand of satyagraha and the demand on svaraj, to engage in constant social and political activity and struggle; they each impose this universal responsibility on us because we constantly find ourselves living in social orders and living in circumstances in which we know that things are happening that are wrong that we don't endorse and in which our collective social order does not match our deepest values.

We take Gandhi seriously. That recognition imposes a demand to struggle to alleviate that situation. That means they impose a universal responsibility on each of us to lead a public life committed to these goals; that's the practical demand. There's also a kind of ethical, spiritual demand that takes us well beyond the normal. They impose an obligation on us to achieve this deep kind of self mastery. Svaraj, a mastery of ourselves and that mastery for Gandhi is very much the mastery of the *Bhagavad-Gīta*. It's the mastery of the yoga of action, the yoga of knowledge, and the yoga of devotion.

We are called upon to be deeply self reflective, to be aware of our motivations, to be aware of our values, to be aware of what they call upon us to do, and we are called upon to a life of relentless non-violence, a life in which whenever we see an action that could be harmful to others, to refrain from doing it and to actively engage to minimize harm. We are also called upon to a life of enormous value consistency, to refining our values so that they form a system, and to living our lives in harmony with them.

The life of the satyagrahi, of somebody who embraces satyagraha in Gandhi's sense, is a hard life. It's a life that rejects material acquisition. Gandhi was fond of saying that the world has enough for everyone's need, but it doesn't contain enough for anyone's greed. The idea that he had there was very simple. That most of us have a lot more stuff than we need, and having more than you need is made optional by liberalism. As far as Gandhi is concerned, it's morally impermissible, and if we reflect deeply we'll see that it is morally impermissible and undermines the meaning of our lives.

Why is that? It's because if we think reflectively, we see that our material acquisition is always at the expense of the possession of even enough to get by for some very poor people. I have to look at the fact that my assets, if divided among the world's hungry, could do a lot of good. By not dividing them I'm actually accomplishing harm. Gandhi calls me to relinquish possessions in order to do less harm.

The satyagrahi is called upon to devote his or her life not only to this kind of austerity but also to the active alleviation and suffering of those who are suffering, and to the active achievement of political liberation for those who aren't liberated. Because if we recognize harm and we recognize that it's wrong, that imposes a constant obligation, not an obligation to write a check to our favorite political party once a year, or even a lot of checks to our favorite charities, but an obligation to organize our lives in a way that achieves those goals.

The satyagrahi leads a collective life because it's a life that doesn't conduce to individual privacy. Individual privacy and individuality require this kind of acquisition and fencing off that makes that life impossible. It's a sober life. You don't have time to party if you actually recognize that there's a lot of suffering in the world and it is your constant duty to alleviate it. It's a very sober life. You might even say an almost monastic life. Gandhi led most of his life in exactly that way. While we might say, this is an impossible demand, Gandhi's life always stands there as the demonstration that hard, yes, impossible no.

Finally, the satyagraha's life is a life of local production and of local consumption, a life in which we really attempt to minimize our participation in and reliance on global economic structures that we recognize to be necessarily harm-producing. It's a challenging life indeed. Here's the thing, this is what makes Gandhi so radical. Remember I said he was even more radical than Nietzsche. The thing is that for Gandhi, this is the only kind of meaningful life possible. Anything less is utterly meaningless. For one thing, the kind of self discipline that is involved in this life, the kind of yoga if we're to use the terminology of the *Bhagavad-Gīta* is what gives us freedom from our unreflective submission to mass values. Remember the Gīta. The idea that yoga or discipline isn't somehow antithetical to freedom, but it's through discipline that we attain freedom.

Gandhi sees our actual loss of freedom in contemporary society as our factual submission and slavery to mass values. That's our current source of un-freedom that is pervasive. The only way he sees that we can become free from that is through this kind of discipline, through this kind of yoga, of svaraj and satyagraha.

For another thing, this kind of life is meaningful and only this kind of life is meaningful because only this kind of life really reflects truth as we know it. That is, Gandhi thinks, if you reflect, you will see that the world is as he describes it. That kind of truth entails this kind of obligation. This is the only kind of life, Gandhi thinks, that you can reflectively endorse, that you can live authentically.

Remember what Nietzsche says in terms of a call of conscience. Are you working in your life, or are you turning away, or are you just a spectator? Gandhi is arguing that if you don't dedicate yourself in this deep and profound way to social action, to satyagraha, to ahimsa, then you are at best turning away or living as a spectator to your own life and not showing up for work.

Moreover, this is a life, Gandhi argues, that through service, through service to others, through discipline and yoga, connects us to something broader than ourselves. It connects us to our fellow human beings. It connects us to our social orders. It connects us to our only genuine sources of values. It's a life that actually serves the values that we all endorse. Genuine freedom, and not the artificial freedom of liberalism. Genuine equity, and not the equality of opportunity to strive to oppress others, but genuine equity in social relations and real non-violence. This was the kind of life that Gandhi argues, that serves the highest good.

If we lead this kind of life, Gandhi argues, we can generate a civilization that we can all legitimately endorse, the kind of civilization of which we would actually choose to be a part. Remember how thinkers of disparate as Aristotle, Confucius, and Nietzsche all argued that what we really want to do is to live in a society whose values we endorse, the kind of society we would want to achieve.

This might sound crazy. It might sound highly demanding. But it's not as crazy as it seems, because it seems to emerge organically out of values that we all endorse; and as I said, Gandhi's life demonstrates that it's in fact possible.

While Gandhi's life sounds inspiring but unrealistic, Gandhi argued that it's, in fact, very realistic and lived a life dedicated to demonstrating that fact. If you think it's unrealistic you have to ask yourself why, because the life that we've been looking at, this view of what a meaningful life is, draws very heavily on many of the ideas that we have actually been exploring in this course. Ideas ancient and ideas modern, and many of the ones that are most compelling, ideas of community, ideas of the value of freedom, of individual obligation, of the relationship between discipline and meaningfulness, and of the connection of our own lives to lives of others and to something transcendent in order to give them meaning.

Gandhi really does challenge us to rethink many of our deepest values and commitments. He forces us to really rethink the value of modernity and the plausibility of the promise of liberal democracy. He forces us to think about a very profound question, can we, without this kind of commitment to moral seriousness, without this kind of seriousness of purpose, without this kind of dedication, can our lives have any value at all? Gandhi argues that without this level of commitment, there's no point at all. It's hard to argue with that. It's a very challenging call to conscience.

This might be the most challenging text to our ordinary lives that we've encountered, at least the most challenging since Job. Take it seriously, think about it, and in our next lecture we're going to move from India, move from Europe, to a very different tradition, that of Native American reflection on the value of life. I look forward to seeing you in that lecture.

Lame Deer—Life Enfolded in Symbols
Lecture 32

Modernity doesn't only construct a prison for us, but it's a prison without any windows. It's a prison that we can't even see out of and imagine alternatives to.

In some respects, **John Lame Deer**, a medicine man of the Lakota Sioux, shares insights with some of the other critics of modernity whose work we've examined. Along with Nietzsche, he is a critic of "mass-produced people." With Tolstoy, he shares the belief that society's focus on consumerism and normalcy alienates us from interpersonal relations. Lame Deer also agrees with Gandhi that modernity forces us to lead lives in which we're complicit in harmful social structures. He connects modernity and mass culture to alienation from ourselves and the world of nature that we inhabit. He also points out that the values of modern life tend to assume a kind of universality that makes it impossible for us to see alternatives. We adopt a regime of ideology and morality that takes over our way of seeing the world; as a consequence, we lead lives that are unreflective, self-alienated, and meaningless.

The context in which the Lakota seek the meaning of life encompasses both the social and the natural world. It embodies a sense that, first and foremost, human beings are animals living in a natural ecosystem. We should treat other animals as our peers, members of our culture who have obligations to us and to whom we have obligations, and should care for the environment. This natural context also means that we must internalize a sense of temporality, because the natural world itself is marked by temporal cycles.

An important issue for the Lakota is the nature of symbols and the pervasiveness of the symbolic. The world is defined by its symbolic character, and that symbolism is central to the meaning of life. To the Lakota, life as a whole is permeated with symbols, things that mean something in a linguistic sense. Part of the meaning of life is the meaning of those symbols, and part of what makes our lives meaningful is that our lives themselves can be seen as symbolic.

Lame Deer offers an eloquent example of the meaning found in nature in his description of a cooking pot. He writes, "The bubbling water [in the pot] comes from the sky: it represents the rain cloud." The water itself is symbolic of the cloud; it's not just caused by the cloud, but it represents the cloud. Lame Deer continues, "The fire comes from the sun which warms us all—men, animals, trees. The meat stands for the four-legged creatures, our animal brothers, who gave of themselves that we might live. ... These things are sacred." Each of these commonplace things is a symbol that calls to mind something sacred, something greater than us. For the Native American speaker, simply looking at the pot is to look at a host of symbols that remind us we live in a vast, sacred order. The symbols around us are actually language, the language of the universe teaching the meaning of life.

The symbols around us are actually language, the language of the universe teaching the meaning of life.

Understanding the world in this symbolic dimension effects a transfiguration of the commonplace into the sacred. Opening our eyes and seeing these symbols enables a much deeper connection to a sacred natural world that gives our lives meaning. Lame Deer points out that the human world of symbols—names and rituals, for example—is part of the natural world. Human language is just one instance among thousands of the symbolic; the symbolic is a much grander affair than something that we instantiate.

Lame Deer describes the Native American sun dance as a ritual that served as a symbolic sacrifice of the dancer's body, sensations, and endurance. These are the only things humans have to sacrifice; everything else already belongs to the universe. The ritual of the sun dance reinforces a vision of unity of the universe through devotion, as well as the symbolism of the dancer himself. The dancer becomes a symbol of his own devotion.

The symbol of the Native American is the circle, which not only resembles and describes the character of nature but is also a representational symbol. In the repetition of circles in the universe—the planets, the stars, the rainbow— Lame Deer sees "symbols and reality at the same time, expressing the harmony of life and nature." Symbols and reality don't stand apart from each other; the universe is already saturated with the symbolic, and the symbolic is natural to the universe, not imposed by our conceptual activity. In contrast, the symbol of non-Native Americans is the square, seen in houses, office buildings, and walls. Our world, too, is full of symbols, but they are the wrong symbols—symbols of separation. The truly meaningful life is the organic life, the life that is in unity with nature and represented by the circle. What's wrong with modernity is not that it fails to be meaningful but that it means the wrong things. ■

Name to Know

Lame Deer, John (1900–1976): John Lame Deer was a Lakota Sioux medicine man born on the Rosebud Reservation and educated in Bureau of Indian Affairs schools.

Suggested Reading

Black Elk and Lyon, *Black Elk: The Sacred Ways of a Lakota.*

Lame Deer and Erdoes, *Lame Deer, Seeker of Visions.*

Study Questions

1. How does the notion of meaning found in Lame Deer's writing—symbolic meaning—differ from the understanding of "meaning" that we've explored to this point in the course?

2. In what ways is Lame Deer's critique of modernity familiar to us from other thinkers and in what ways is it different?

Lame Deer—Life Enfolded in Symbols
Lecture 32—Transcript

Welcome back. In these next two lectures we're going to be turning to a very different intellectual, philosophical tradition, and a very different account of the meaning of life. It will be addressing Native American traditions.

When we address Native American culture and Native American traditions, particularly in the contemporary, social, cultural, and political landscape, in the wake of tremendous genocide against Native American people, we have to tread very, very lightly. For one thing, we have to be careful not to treat all Native American cultures as though they are the same. North America contained hundreds of Native American cultures before the coming of Europeans, and still contains and is home to hundreds of Native American traditions, and we can't pretend to be representing all of them.

The particular text that we'll be looking at is a very particular tradition, namely that of the Lakota Sioux. These traditions included many different languages, many different kinds of beliefs, many philosophical perspectives. Until very recently, all of these traditions were oral, they did not include written texts, and not all of the Native American traditions are even available to people outside of the tribal cultures.

This of course is because some of these spiritual traditions, some of these philosophical traditions, are regarded as private, are regarded as available to inside people, but not made public.

Even those of us who are privileged to be able to read in English published work from particular cultures in which people have chosen to make the philosophical beliefs and arguments available, we don't have the oral tradition that underlies these; and given that so many of these texts arise from oral traditions and are addressed primarily to people who are steeped in those cultures and oral traditions, we have to be aware of the fact that in our reading and our interpretation, we may unconsciously be distorting those traditions.

I think we need to read with a great deal of delicacy and a great deal of respect, and a great deal of care. The two principal texts that we have available to us as readers of the English that represent Native American philosophical views are both those of Lakota Sioux. One is the great text by Black Elk, called *Black Elk Speaks*. The second, the one that we'll be discussing today, is by John Fire Lame Deer and it is called *Lame Deer, Seeker of Visions*.

I'm really quite taken by Lame Deer's work. It's very philosophically systematic in a way that Black Elk is focused more on ritual, more on religious practice, and remarkably eloquent. I hope you're going to enjoy working through parts of that text with me, and I hope especially that you will enjoy some of Lame Deer's beautiful prose.

In some respects we're going to see that Lame Deer shares insights with some of the other critics of modernity whose work we've examined. In particular, along with Nietzsche, we're going to see that he's a real critic of mass-produced people, as Nietzsche referred to them as herd animals. Lame Deer will sometimes use fairly similar metaphors actually. He's really worried about the ability of modern culture to dumb down, to homogenize, and to alienate people from their own, real existence.

Lame Deer also shares part of Tolstoy's critique. We saw that Tolstoy had this deep insight that modern mass culture is connected in very deep ways to a valorization of consumption and a particular kind of lifestyle taken as normative, a middle class lifestyle. Tolstoy saw that this kind of consumerism and this kind of focus on normalcy, on living as people ought to live, is ruinous to our spiritual lives and in a deep way, alienates us from interpersonal relations and alienates us therefore from what makes life worth living. Lame Deer will share that insight as well.

Gandhi argued that modern life alienates us further from our moral values. That modernity forces us to lead lives in which we're complicit in harms and social structures that we can't possibly endorse, and that it's necessary if we're going to save ourselves from this kind of alienation to rebel against modernity and to construct an alternative. We'll see that Lame Deer agrees with that as well.

Lame Deer goes a bit deeper. Lame Deer connects modernity and the mass culture that it generates to an alienation not just from other people, not just from moral values, but from ourselves, from our own nature and from the world of nature that we inhabit. Lame Deer's critique goes very deeply. He argues that modernity is poisonous not just because it alienates us from other people and from the lives we want to lead, but because it makes us strangers to ourselves.

Lame Deer adds one further insight to this critique. That is, Lame Deer focuses on an aspect of modernity that might have escaped some of these others, that was one that Mill was hinting at and that is the totalizing character of modernity. Lame Deer points out that when we accept the values of contemporary modern life they assume a kind of universality that makes it impossible for us to even see alternatives. We end up adopting a regime of ideology, of morality, of taking up with lives, and a conception of normalcy that takes over our way of seeing the world. As a consequence we end up not only leading a life that's unreflective, self-alienated, and eventually empty and meaningless. That's not all, more deeply, not only do we lead such a life but within that life we don't even see that there are alternatives. We don't even take seriously the possibility that there are alternative values that might give us or others meaningful lives to lead.

As a consequence, Lame Deer thinks, modernity doesn't only construct a prison for us, but it's a prison without any windows. It's a prison that we can't even see out of and imagine alternatives to. It generates in us a very deep amnesia about freedom. That deep amnesia that forgetting what it is to be free, forgetting what it is to lead a meaningful life ends up making us accept our imprisonment and adopt it willingly to construct our own prisons and to be complicit in our own confinement.

As I said, we're going to be working through Lame Deer's text and I'm going to do as much as possible of this through Lame Deer's own words.

Lame Deer lived from about 1903—we're not sure of his exact birth date— to about 1976. He was a really interesting person. He grew up on a Lakota Sioux reservation—on the Rosebud Reservation—and his early life was quite wild. He rode in the rodeo, he was apparently somewhat fond of drink and womanizing and was often on the wrong side of the law, and led a fairly rowdy youth.

At some point, as he recalls it, after a fair amount of wildness, he accidentally stumbled into the home of another Lakota Sioux, an elderly woman who was keeper of the Lakota Peace Pipe, the pipe that was, according to legend—according to tradition—handed down from the very beginning of the Lakota nation. She told him, I've been waiting for you and thus began his apprenticeship and his subsequent career as a very eminent Sioux medicine man and speaker for Native American people. As I said, his book which was published in 1972, *Lame Deer, Seeker of Visions,* is I believe the most eloquent statement of Native American philosophy available in English.

The context in which the Lakota seek the meaning of life is a very large context. It's not only the social world, as we might have seen for Aristotle or Confucius. It's this large context of the natural world. All of the texts we've been reading so far have been emphasizing that in order to lead a meaningful life we need somehow to connect our small, finite lives to a much larger context, almost always though either a universal context, as we've seen in the Gīta or the book of Job or for the stoics, or a social context as we've seen for Aristotle, for Gandhi, for the Confucians.

The Lakota emphasized something kind of in between. That is the context of nature and that context embodies a sense—again shared with Nietzsche—that first and foremost, human beings are animals, living among animals in a natural ecosystem including animals and plants, and that our community thus transcends the human community in very fundamental and very important ways.

Taking this seriously entails developing a kind of reverence for other animals, not just as beautiful, not just as elegant, not just as cute, but in some sense as our peers, as members of our culture who have obligations to us, and to whom we have obligations, with whom we are in social relations. It also entails developing a respect and a care for the environment that sustains not only us but the other animals and plants who are members of our relevant, moral community.

It also, of course, entails developing a very deep, internalized sense of temporality of time. That's because the natural world is marked by so many temporal cycles, cycles of day and night, cycles of the months of the moon, annual cycles, cycles of seasons, reproductive cycles, and so forth. We'll see that in the Lakota tradition this awareness of temporality and of connectedness to the natural world plays a very, very important role.

Another issue that we'll see is very important for the Lakota is the nature of symbols and the pervasiveness of the symbolic. Lame Deer sees the world as defined by its symbolic character and sees that symbolism as absolutely central to the meaning of life. We're going to begin by talking about the nature of those symbols and the nature of interpretation of those symbols. Moving from there we'll talk about the ubiquity of those symbols. We'll talk a little bit about names as symbols and finally the role of symbols in ritual.

Let's begin by talking about the nature of symbols themselves and their connection to meaning. Way back at the very beginning of this course in the first lecture, we talked about the many meanings of the word "meaning" and we noted that one of them is the one that we've been focusing on that is significance in this greater sense. A second one was the notion of the symbolic, where a word means something, the word "bachelor" means unmarried man. The word "Jay" means me. The word "sun" refers to that thing in the sky. So far, that notion of meaning, the symbolic, has not figured at all in our discussions. But that notion of meaning is the one that is central, as we will see, to Lakota thinking. To the Lakota, as Lame Deer will emphasize, life as a whole, our entire lives, are permeated with symbols, things that actually mean something in this linguistic sense. Part of the meaning of life is the meaning of those symbols, and part of what makes our lives meaningful is that our lives themselves can be seen as symbols, as symbolic.

For that reason, our life in nature is meaningful because the nature of which we are a part is meaningful. Notice, just saying that we need to live our lives naturally means nothing if nature itself isn't meaningful. The meaningfulness of nature, Lame Deer will emphasize, consists in its symbolic character.

Lame Deer himself puts the point so eloquently like this. He says, from birth to death we Indians are enfolded in symbols as in a blanket. Let's turn to one of his favorite examples. Lame Deer, making this wonderful description of an ordinary object says, "It doesn't seem to have a message, that old pot."—he's pointing to a cooking pot now—"And I guess you don't give it a thought, except the soup smells good and reminds you that you are hungry… But I'm an Indian. I think about ordinary common things like this pot. The bubbling water comes from the sky: it represents the rain cloud." Pause on that for a moment. It represents the rain cloud. The water itself is symbolic of the cloud, not just caused by it, but it represents it. When I see the water, the clouds come to mind. Just as when I say the word "cloud," the clouds come to mind. "The fire comes from the sun which warms us all—men, animals, trees. The meat stands for the four-legged creatures, our animal brothers, who gave of themselves that we might live." Once again it's representational not just causal. "The steam is living breath. It was water, now it goes up to the sky, becomes a cloud again. These things are sacred."

That's a really important point. Each of these commonplace things, the water in the pot, the steam, the heat, is a symbol that calls to our mind something sacred, something greater to us. For the Native American speaker, simply looking at the pot is to look at a host of symbols that remind us that we live in this vast, sacred order.

Lame Deer continues,

> Looking at this pot full of good soup, I am thinking how, in this simple manner, Wakan Tanka (the Great Spirit) takes care of me. We Sioux spend a lot of time thinking about everyday things, which in our minds are mixed up with the spiritual. We see in the world around us many symbols that teach us the meaning of life.

That's it. These symbols around us are actually language, the language of the universe teaching the meaning of life.

> You [now he's talking to non-Native Americans] see a lot that you no longer notice. You could notice it if you wanted to, but you are usually too busy. We Indians live in a world of symbols and images

where the spiritual and commonplace are one. What to you seems commonplace to us appears wondrous through symbolism.

Notice that by understanding and living in the world as a world full of symbols, the world becomes wondrous because the world itself becomes saturated with representation of the sacred. Every possible thing, even an old cooking pot, becomes something potentially sacred. Lame Deer continues, "This is funny, because we don't even have a word for 'symbolism,' yet we are all wrapped up in it. You have the word, but that is all."

There's a lot here. There's a stinging indictment of the modern way of seeing the world. Lame Deer is pointing out that if we simply understand the world in this symbolic dimension, this affects a kind of transfiguration of the commonplace, the ordinary, the everyday, the trivial into a sacred world through the symbolic activity. He's also pointing out to us the absolute ubiquity of symbolization, that it's every place and that it's totally natural. We don't have to make it up. All we have to do is open our eyes and observe. By observing these symbols and taking them seriously, we develop a much deeper connection to the natural world. That connection is a connection to a sacred, natural world that is eminent in which we dwell and that gives our lives meaning.

He's also emphasizing the importance of developing the skill of noticing and also attend to how spontaneously he sees the world that way. He sees the world that way. That wasn't a studied, careful reflection about a pot. That was a spontaneous articulation of how the world appears when it's seen this way. Lame Deer points out that there's also a human world of symbols, and as natural animals, that's part of the natural world too. He points to names and to rituals that when we name ourselves or name our children we're establishing symbols. He's pointing out that this isn't the model for symbols, it's not as though we begin with names and begin with linguistic words and then we extrapolate from that to find things like cooking pots or steam to be symbolic. Instead, human names, human language, is just one instance among thousands of the symbolic, that the symbolic is a much grander affair, a much more natural affair than just something that we instantiate.

Lame Deer says, "Words, too, are symbols, and convey great powers, especially names. ... We receive great gifts from the source of a name; it links us to nature, to the animal nations it gives power." In discussing names, Lame deer contrasts the names that Native American people use in which the significance of the name is very clear, very public, and well known to everybody.

He contrasts these with the names that non-native people use, names like Jay or Bob or Sam, which even though they in fact do have meanings and have lexical roots in Greek or Hebrew that have got meanings, most of us don't even know the meanings of our own names, and so the names themselves, even though they are potentially symbolic and potentially link ourselves to something greater, are eviscerated of all of their significance.

A beautiful discussion that Lame Deer enters with regard again to symbolism and a link to the sacred is this discussion of the Native American sun dance. The sun dance is an extraordinary ritual. It involves a day-long dance in hot sun in which the dancers have leather thongs literally sewn through their chests so that they're bound by their skin and attached to a pole. They dance around and around this pole for hours with a bone whistle between their teeth whistling. They are allowed no food, no drink, no rest, their chests are bleeding. It's extraordinarily exhausting, extraordinarily painful, and by the end of the dance the leather thongs pull free and blood rushes down their chests and there are these big wounds, it's a very painful ritual. Many people have looked at this and seen it as horrible, as barbaric, as masochistic, as a crazy ritual.

Lame Deer emphasizes that this ritual was in fact a deep symbolic sacrifice. It's a sacrifice of oneself, a sacrifice of one's body, of one's sensations, of one's endurance. That's important he argues, because we are the only things that we in fact have to sacrifice. Everything else already belongs to the rest of the universe. Sacrificing possessions is to sacrifice something that comes and goes. To sacrifice ourselves though is serious. Connect this if you will to the insight in the *Bhagavad-Gīta*. The insight of Bhakti yoga, the yoga of devotion is necessary in order for our lives to really be lived in a meaningful unity with the universe.

Here what we see is this ritual not only as reinforcing a vision of unity of the universe through devotion but also establishing myself—not myself—but the self of the person in this ritual as a symbol him or herself. The dancer himself becomes a symbol of his own devotion and it's the symbol with which others interact. It makes our own lives representational. That is, it makes our lives meaningful.

Lame Deer continues this with a wonderful contrast of Native American symbols with what he sees as the symbol of modernity. This will get to a very deep issue about the structure of Lame Deer's critique of modernity. Let's follow his thinking. Lame Deer says, "To our way of thinking"—that is the Native American way—"The Indian's symbol is the circle, the hoop. Nature wants things to be round. The bodies of human beings and animals have no corners. With us the circle stands for the togetherness of people who sit with one another around the campfire."

So again, we're thinking about the circle not only as resembling and describing the character of nature, the being without corners, but it also stands for or represents the idea that people sit in a circle around a campfire. It's a representational symbol. He continues, "The nation was in itself only part of the universe, itself circular" again, when we look at the universe in the skies we see this kind of celestial spheres as the Greeks would have put it. The sky looks like a great circle above us, the planets and the stars move in circular motion. "And made of the earth, which is round"—again circles—"Of the sun, which is round, of the stars, which are round. The moon, the horizon, and the rainbow—circles within circles within circles, with no beginning and no end. To us," this is Lame Deer, "this is beautiful and fitting, symbol and reality at the same time, expressing the harmony of life and nature." Again, notice that, symbol and reality at the same time is very important for this conception of meaningfulness in symbols. Symbols in reality don't stand apart from one another. Often when we think about symbols we think immediately of the distinction between the symbol and that to which it refers. The name Jay is different from the person Jay. The word sun doesn't give you sunburn like the real sun does. We really focus on the distinction between symbol and reality.

If on the other hand, we see with Lame Deer the idea that the universe itself is already saturated with the symbolic and that that symbolic is natural to it, not imposed from outside by our conceptual activity, but part of nature, then we see that there's no distance between symbol and reality. Each reality is a symbol. Each symbol is perfectly real, and sometimes things are even self-symbolic like the circle which symbolizes itself as well as other things. Lame Deer continues, "Our circle is timeless, flowing, it is new life emerging from death—life winning out over death." Now he draws the contrast.

> The white man's symbol is the square. Square is his house, his office buildings, with square walls that separate people from one another. These all have corners and sharp edges—points in time, white man's time, with appointments, time clocks and rush hours— that's what the corners mean to me.

Let's focus on that for a minute. You might think that what Lame Deer was about to say is that while the Native Americans have a world rich with symbols, non-native people, European people, live in a world that's devoid of the symbolic. That would be interesting. He's gone one step deeper though. What Lame Deer is really suggesting here is not that our world is devoid of the symbolic but that it's full of symbols. They're just the wrong symbols. They're symbols of really unfortunate things. Squares for him are symbols of separation. They are symbols of sharp edges. They're symbols of seeing the world as pontic points in time with appointments, time clocks, rush hours, instead of continuous and flowing as he suggested the circle is.

This is deep because what it means is not that we simply fail to live in a symbolic order but that we live in a symbolic order that, A, we don't recognize to be symbolic and so it gets to work on us subconsciously without conscious interpretation, and B, it's symbolic of exactly what deprives ourselves of our humanity, of our connection to nature, and eventually even of our connection to each other, to the things that we value.

As he concludes, "You become prisoners inside those boxes"—that is those office buildings and those houses. Lame Deer is emphasizing the pervasiveness of symbol even in the lives that we lead, even if we don't notice them. He's also emphasizing the view that a really meaningful life is the organic life, the life that's in unity with nature, the life that's represented by the circle as opposed to the artificial square life. This gives the depth, the deep part, of Lame Deer's critique of European modernity. It should feel somewhat familiar; a critique in terms of alienation, a critique in terms of the power of modernity to alienate us from what we actually value most even reflectively. But it's also somewhat new because of this symbolic nature, this emphasis on representation, and this emphasis on nature itself as being the object from which we are alienated.

The idea is, we're surrounded simply by the wrong symbols. Even though we don't notice them, we end up responding to these symbols, that's central. The central point to take away from Lame Deer's understanding of what the universe is like and of what is wrong with modernity. What's wrong with modernity is not that it fails to be meaningful, not at all. It is meaningful. It is symbolic. It is representation. What's wrong with modernity, as far as Lame Deer is concerned, is that it means the wrong things. When we pay attention to what, in fact, gives our lives meaning as we live them, they're not the values that we would reflectively endorse. They're not the values that we would hope to endorse. They're rather these values that keep us prisoners, that keep us square.

In our next lecture, what we're going to do is to examine how Lame Deer suggests we respond to this critique. What Lame Deer thinks that a meaningful life looks like and how we can lead a life that's enfolded in more positive symbols. That's going to require first a deeper understanding of the nature of the alienation, and that's where we're going to begin.

Lame Deer—Our Place in a Symbolic World
Lecture 33

We end up living in a world that's square, not a world that's circular; a world that's a prison, not a world that's organic. That's not a world that any of us would choose to live in, despite the fact that every day, in every action, we make choices that entail the necessity of just such a world.

"My grandparents grew up in an Indian world without money," writes Lame Deer. Most of us take for granted that money must play a role in the world, but for this philosopher, that's part of the totalizing character of modernity: We can't even envision a world that different from ours. Most of us also spend a great deal of time thinking about money, possessions, and so on. Those things become the objects around which we organize our lives. But we would never reflectively endorse the idea that the focus of our lives should be money. Lame Deer tells us that after the Battle of the Little Bighorn, the victorious Native Americans gave the soldiers' money to their children to play with. Thus, the money became useful in precisely the way it should be useful— not as the central organizing principle of our lives but as something that has a useful subsidiary role.

The Battle of the Little Bighorn was over gold in the Black Hills, and Lame Deer points to another "battle" based on money: the poisoning of prairie dogs to preserve grass for cows. According to Lame Deer, the rancher "looks at a prairie dog [and] sees only a green frog-skin [a dollar] getting away from him." But when a Native American looks at a prairie dog, he sees another member of the community to which we all belong. The prairie dog, if it's symbolic of anything, is symbolic of the natural order that enfolds us. The Native American sees the dollar as a symbol of what it can do. The rancher, in a deep reversal of priority, sees the natural world as symbolic of the artificial symbol. In the European view, everything— grass, prairie dogs, Black Hills—comes to be seen in monetary terms. That view imposes a new symbolic order on our world, one in which everything stands for money.

Lame Deer points out that the bald eagle appears on our money as a national symbol, but our money is killing the eagle, and the destruction of this symbol means that we've lost the ability to connect with symbols as symbols. If we lose the ability to appreciate the symbolic character of the eagle, then we'll be happy to simply let it become endangered and disappear. The disappearance is bad enough, but the alienation from the natural order we inhabit is the disease of which that's a symptom.

> **The end of this path of rejecting the symbolic and the natural, of fetishizing commodities, and of denying that we are biological animals is a completely ersatz life, a life that's a stand-in for a real life.**

For Lame Deer, the symbolic and natural orders go hand-in-hand. Symbols are part of reality; reality is completely symbolic. Commodity fetishism and the systematic disregard of symbols also go hand-in-hand. When we see things only in terms of their economic value and we see the economic value as all that matters, we abstract ourselves from the natural world, precisely because we abstract ourselves from its symbolic character. In doing so, we commodify the world and, in the end, we commodify ourselves.

Modern European culture draws a clear line between the biological world of plants and animals and the nonbiological world of minerals. But for Lame Deer, this line is dangerous because the biological world depends on the nonbiological one. To call rocks and minerals "dead" gives a kind of implicit permission to commodify that world and despoil it. Further, domestication has changed animals from creatures with beauty and integrity to artificial things that can live only on feed lots or in cages—things that are symbolic of exactly what might be uncomfortable for us. Ultimately, we no longer even think of ourselves as biological animals who live in an ecosystem but in terms of our functions in an economic order. We thus imprison ourselves and are complicit in our own imprisonment.

The end of this path of rejecting the symbolic and the natural, of fetishizing commodities, and of denying that we are biological animals is a completely ersatz life, a life that's a stand-in for a real life. For Lame Deer, the nature of modernity is to turn us into spectators, not even of our own lives but of other people's lives. We become prisoners looking at televisions that give us views into other people's cells.

Finally, Lame Deer argues that modernity alienates us from death. As we've seen in so many other views we've examined, confronting the reality of death and coming to terms with it is essential to leading a meaningful life. But Lame Deer argues that modernity sweeps that under the rug. We live in a culture of violence, war, and pollution, but we sanitize it away through television and other means. To come to terms with death, we must think about it, plan it, and accept it. That leads to an authentic life, a life that understands us as natural objects that are indeed mortal. ∎

Suggested Reading

Black Elk and Lyon, *Black Elk: The Sacred Ways of a Lakota.*

Lame Deer and Erdoes, *Lame Deer, Seeker of Visions.*

Study Questions

1. Why does modernity, in Lame Deer's view, necessarily alienate people from the natural world and its symbolic order? How does commodity fetishism lead to the destruction of nature and of meaning?

2. What is added to our understanding of the meaning of life through Lame Deer's emphasis on the natural world as the ground of meaning?

Lame Deer—Our Place in a Symbolic World
Lecture 33—Transcript

It's lovely to be back with you. In our last lecture we were addressing the Lakota vision of the nature of reality and of how reality is saturated with meaning in virtue of its symbolic character. We saw Lame Deer saying Native Americans see themselves as enfolded from birth by symbols, surrounded by things that aren't merely natural objects and are not artificially symbolic but are naturally symbolic, naturally representational.

This took us back to thinking about meaning in a different sense from that that we've been thinking about for the remainder of these lectures. That is to go back to the idea that meaning doesn't only mean broader significance, but also means symbolic reference. For the Sioux, the pot for instance was pregnant with meaning. It entailed symbols that meant the sky, symbols that meant the animals, symbols that linked us in our interaction with that pot to an entire sacred order of reality.

We also saw that it's not enough to recognize that the world is pregnant with symbolism in this sense, but that it's deeply important that we learn to notice these symbols if we are to lead our lives meaningfully. That is to lead our lives in recognition of the meaning that surrounds us, and in recognition of the symbolic character of our own behavior, of our own lives, of our own comportment.

The point here, and we concluded last time with this point but I want to recall it, is that the critique of modernity implicit in this Lakota Sioux vision is not that the Native American world is a world rich with symbols and that the European or non-native world is devoid of symbols. Rather, as we saw in that wonderful contrast of circles versus squares, of the circular symbols so central to a Native American vision and the square symbols that Lame Deer saw permeating a European tradition. The important thing is that Native Americans recognize the value of the symbols, recognize the meanings of these symbols and live in constant awareness of that symbolic character, and so can respond to it.

Lame Deer's deep critique of modernity is that modern Europeans, although we live in a world full of symbols, many of them symbols of our own contrivance, we don't notice their symbolic character. Because we don't notice their symbolic character, they work on us subconsciously. Because they work on us subconsciously, we don't even see them as symbolic. We just take them as natural, as ordinary, as the only way the world can be. We don't allow ourselves even a vision beyond them that allows us to see that there's an alternative. Instead we lead a life constrained by them, complicit in that constraint without even an awareness that we are constraining ourselves or that that constraint is an option as opposed to the only way to live.

Today we're going to begin to examine the role of money in all of this and the role of the economy in all of this. We're going to see here a lot of echo of Gandhi's critique of modernity in Lame Deer. That is we saw that Gandhi thought that money, the modern economy and liberal capitalism articulated through industrialism, turns most human beings into working machines instead of actual persons.

For Gandhi though, remember what a meaningful life turned out to be is a life of constant service, a life of constant work, a life of constant engagement. Gandhi was focusing, for his account, of a meaningful life really on the Gītā, the idea of karma yoga, a yoga of action, a yoga of devotion.

Lame Deer is not going to follow him there. For Lame Deer the meaningful life is going to be a life of calm reflection, a life in which we really come to appreciate and to live in harmony with the symbolic order that surrounds us. Let's begin.

Lame Deer, writing about his own youth here and his own perspective on reality even before he embarked upon his career as a medicine man, just the way that he was brought up as a Native American. Let's hear what he says. He says, "I was like many other fullbloods. I didn't want a steady job in an office or factory. I thought myself too good for that, not because I was stuck up but simply because any human being is too good for that no-life." "That no-life," he says.

This is very cool. Look what Lame Deer is saying. He's saying, I didn't want a real job. I didn't want a job in an office. I didn't want a job in a factory. I didn't want a job working for somebody else because I'm too good for that. One way that we might hear that I'm too good for that is a bit of personal arrogance. Other people can do that job, other people can work like that but not me, I'm too good for that. That's not what Lame Deer is saying. Lame Deer is saying I recognize myself—that is Lame Deer—to be a human being and no human being deserves a life like that. As he puts it, any human being is too good for that no life because as far as Lame Deer is concerned, that's not a way of life, that is working a constant job, governed by a time clock and so forth. It's not a way of life, it's an abandonment of life.

This leads directly to one of Lame Deer's most poignant critiques of modernity, his critique of the emphasis on money and commodity fetishism. I'm going to read to you one of my favorite passages from Lame Deer's discussion. It's one that focuses on the battle at the Big Horn in which General Custer's army was eliminated by Sitting Bull. It's going to focus on Lame Deer's sardonic look at money. "The green frog skin—that's what I call a dollar bill." This is not meant to be, by the way, a positive evaluation of a dollar bill. "In our attitude towards it lies the biggest difference between Indians and whites. My grandparents grew up in an Indian world without money." Notice that we take for granted that a world has to be a world in which money figures. That's part of the totalizing character of modernity that Lame Deer worries about, that we don't even have a vision of a world that different from ours. But Lame Deer is emphasizing, there's an alternative. My grandparents grew up in an Indian world without money.

> Just before the Custer battle, the white soldiers had received their pay. Their pockets were full of green paper and they had no place to spend it. What were their last thoughts as an Indian bullet or arrow hit them? I guess they were thinking of all that money going to waste. That must have hurt them more than the arrow between their ribs.

Here Lame Deer is focusing on what we notice, what we think about, what's salient in our lives. Even if this remark about Custer's soldiers isn't literally true, what he's pointing out is the fact that for most of us we are very often thinking about money, thinking about possessions, thinking about our debts, thinking about our salary and so forth. That becomes salient in our life. That moves to center stage. That becomes the object around which we organize our lives.

Ask yourself, as Nietzsche would have asked you, as Gandhi would have asked you and as Lame Deer is asking. If I really reflect and I really ask myself the question: Is that how I think a life ought to be organized, is that the way I want to lead my life, do I, on my deathbed want to say, I thought all the time about money and that's a really good way to have spent my life? Lame Deer is suggesting that that's not something that even we Europeans would reflectively endorse. That's a problem because that means that modernity has alienated us from who we are.

He continues,

> The close hand-to-hand fighting… had covered the battlefield with an enormous cloud of dust, and in it the green frog-skins of the soldiers were whirling around like snowflakes in a blizzard. Now what did the Indians do with all that money? They gave it to their children to play with, to fold those strange bits of colored paper into… toy buffalo and horses. Somebody was enjoying that money after all.

The point here is a very straightforward one of course. He's focusing on a metaphor. The money was enjoyed after all. It was useful. It was useful in precisely the way that money can be useful. It was useful instrumentally. It was useful as a way of creating nice toys for children. Lame Deer is pointing out that if we think about money clearly we can think about it the way that these Native American children thought about it, something useful, not something that deserves to be the focus of our lives, but something that can play a subsidiary role, something that can symbolize something that can be used for something but not the central organizing principle.

Lame Deer continues, "The green frog-skin—that was what the fight was all about."—notice how he brings the symbol, the metaphor back down to reality. The green frog-skin a moment ago was just this symbol of the way we organize our lives. Now he's pointing out that that symbol was in fact the reality here. "The gold in the black hills. ... The prairie dogs are poisoned because they eat grass." I want you to notice this, he has moved from the gold in the Black Hills, talking about what Custer was fighting for to the contemporary moment, to the present day. He doesn't see a difference there and that's important too.

> The prairie dogs are poisoned because they eat grass. A thousand of them eat as much grass in a year as a cow. So if the rancher can kill that many prairie dogs he can run one more head of cattle, make a little more money. When he [that is the rancher] looks at a prairie dog he sees only a green frog-skin getting away from him.

That's a very, very profound remark. Lame Deer is pointing out that when a Native American looks at a prairie dog he sees an animal. He sees another member of our civilization, another member of the community of which we belong.

The prairie dog, if it's symbolic of anything, it's symbolic of a natural order that enfolds us. When the rancher looks at the prairie dog, he sees a symbol as well. But Lame Deer points out that what he sees a symbol of is a dollar bill flying away. He sees a symbol of a symbol, a symbol that has come to be the principle around which he organizes his life. It's a reversal of what's important. The Native American, he suggests, sees at best the green frog skin—the dollar bill—as a symbol of what it can do. The rancher sees the natural world as symbolic of this artificial symbol, and that's a very deep kind of reversal of priority and a very deep kind of alienation. This is what we might call the fetishism of money, treating money not as an instrumental good, but as something sacred in its own right, something that acquires a value well beyond what its actual value is.

We also see here this emphasis on totalization, the idea that everything, grass, prairie dogs, the Black Hills comes to be seen only in monetary terms. That everything becomes seen in terms of its instrumental value, and its instrumental value in terms of its economic use value. When we do this, Lame Deer is pointing out, we're not fleeing from a world of symbols. We're not fleeing from a world that's pregnant with meaning. We're moving from one kind of symbolic world to another. We are imposing a new symbolic order on our world, a symbolic order in which everything stands for money. That's not a productive symbolic order, that's a destructive one. It's a destructive one because it takes us away from our own being, from our own nature, from our own context into a completely artificial context that transforms us from what we would like to be to something that we would never want ourselves to become but which we, nonetheless construct a modernity that ensures that we will become like that.

Referring to our own symbols Lame Deer says, "The bald eagle is your symbol." Now referring to our national symbol of course. "You see him on your money, but your money is killing him. When a people start killing off their own symbols they are in a bad way." That's a very nice insight. We might put the bald eagle up there on the money, put the bald eagle on the great seal, and see the eagle as a symbol but our own way of life, by destroying habitat, by destroying fisheries, manages to turn the bald eagle into an endangered species.

As he says, when people start killing off their symbols they're in a bad way. Not just because there's a deep irony there, not just because it shows that they don't care, but that it shows that they've lost the ability to connect with symbols as symbols. If we lose the ability to really appreciate the symbolic character of the eagle, then we are quite happy to simply let it become endangered and let it disappear. The disappearance is bad enough but the alienation from the natural order we inhabit is the disease of which that's a symptom.

For Lame Deer symbolic and the natural orders go hand-in-hand. Symbols are part of reality, reality is completely symbolic. Commodity fetishism and this systematic ignoring of symbols, this systematic living in a world in which we are ignorant of the significance of what goes on around us also go hand-in-hand. When we can modify things, when we see them only in terms of their economic value, and then when we see the economic value as all that matters we abstract ourselves from the natural world, precisely because we abstract ourselves from its symbolic character. When we do that, we commodify. We commodify the world, we commodify the prairie dog, we commodify the grass, we commodify the mountains, we commodify the water. In the end we commodify ourselves. We see other individuals in terms of what they can do for us, how much money can I make them bare labor? Or how much salary would he or she pay me? Or how much would it cost to hire him to do this? We end up commodifying each other. When we manage to commodify everything, we end up literally killing the world. We kill the world because a world that we would care to live in would be a world that would be meaningful, a world that would be rich with symbolism and not this kind of dead commodification.

We end up living in a world that's square not a world that's circular. A world that's a prison, not a world that's organic. That's not a world that any of us would choose to live in despite the fact that every day in every action we make choices that entail the necessity of just such a world. In that kind of world there's no possibility for real life. All we get is what Lame Deer called the no life that everybody is too good to live.

This critique of alienation continues for Lame Deer because he argues that we alienate ourselves deeply from nature, including not only the natural world but our own nature. This is a beautiful line. Lame Deer writes, "You have not only despoiled the earth, the rocks, the minerals, all of which you call 'dead,' but which are very much alive." Notice that that's a very nice point. Lame Deer is emphasizing that while we draw a very clear line, that is modern European culture, between the biological world, the biotic world of plants and animals and the non-biological world of minerals, that line is a very dangerous one to draw precisely because the biological world depends for its integrity, depends for its life on that non-biological world. To call these things dead is to artificially carve them off from the biosphere. In doing that it gives us a kind of implicit permission, a permission that we take advantage of all too often to despoil this stuff, to commodify it, forgetting the dramatic impact that it has on everything else around us. But he continues, "You have even changed the animals, which are part of us, of the Great Spirit, changed them in a horrible way, so no one can recognize them." Here he's talking about the phenomenon of domestication, a very serious phenomenon for Lame Deer. He says, "There is power in a buffalo—spiritual, magic power—but there is no power in an Angus, A Hereford."

He's saying, look what we end up doing through the kind of domestication and selective breeding of animals is to get rid of the natural animals that have got a kind of beauty and of integrity and a place in an ecosystem and to create these strange, artificial animals which can only live on feed lots or which can only live in cages, which can only live in domestication, the kinds of things which are symbolic of exactly what might be uncomfortable for us, instead of symbolic of what could be beautiful for us.

When you think about a wolf, when you think about an eagle, when you think about a buffalo, you think about things like freedom, power, ecological interdependence and so forth. When you think about an angus or when you think about one of those hens bred for batteries, you think about a very uncomfortable, tragic, no-life of domestication.

Lame Deer is calling upon us again, this kind of call of conscience as Nietzsche would have put it to ask, can we endorse the world that we've created? Is this the world that we would have said to ourselves at the beginning we want to create? Is this the kind of life we would have said to ourselves, we want to live? His conviction is that when we ask ourselves those questions directly in a way that hits our conscience, the answer has to be no. If that's so, his critique is very much like Gandhi's, telling us we've managed to create a life that none of us could endorse. The only reasonable option is to step out of it to see that there are alternatives and to embrace them.

He continues on this theme. He says, "You have not only altered, declawed and malformed your winged and four-legged cousins, you have done it to yourselves." Now the critique really comes home because now Lame Deer is going to be arguing that we've managed to destroy our own humanity. "You have changed men into chairmen of boards, into office workers, into time-clock punchers." What does this mean? It doesn't just mean that we've given people jobs and made them work hard, made them put on suits and ties or whatever. What it means is that we've changed what we think it is to be human into something else. Imagine this for instance. I think this is the kind of phenomenon that Lame Deer might have very much in mind. When you meet somebody, suppose you're sitting on an airplane or you're waiting for a bus or you're just having a conversation in a checkout line or something like that and you introduce yourself, hi my name is so-and-so, my name's so-and-so. Pretty soon you ask something like, what do you do? What do you do? And then we answer, I'm a dentist, or I'm a teacher, or I'm a lawyer, or I'm a carpenter or I'm a bricklayer, whatever, I'm retired. We answered the question who we are in terms of our occupation, an terms of a place that we play in cogs in a larger machine in square cubicles, in square buildings. That's what Lame Deer means. We don't think of ourselves as human beings anymore, as biological animals who live in an ecosystem with other biological animals who can see, feel, taste, who live in time, who are going to die, who have children and so forth. We think of ourselves in terms of our functions in an economic order, and not otherwise. That is, the symbols in which we understand ourselves are now these artificial economic symbols, not the symbols of a larger, natural life. "You have changed women into housewives, truly fearful creatures." Now of course there's a lot of humor there. But part of what's fearful isn't just this kind of caricature that Lame Deer is worrying about, but the idea that somebody could identify themselves as a being whose purpose and whose nature is to live inside and to manage a confined house in a bunch of square walls.

That is a kind of voluntary prisoner whose job is to maintain her prison. That's what Lame Deer finds so devastating. This is not the kind of life that one would say, this is not what human beings evolved for, to live indoors and to confine themselves and to maintain them. He emphasizes that in this wonderful statement. "You live in prisons which you have built for yourselves, calling them 'homes,' offices, factories."

This idea is one of being complicit in our own imprisonment, complicit in our own oppression and complicit in it in a completely unreflective way that makes it impossible for us to even imagine a life of freedom outside of the walls that we've so carefully constructed. This idea leads to Lame Deer's final kind of analysis of alienation and to an ersatz life, into what he thinks of as spiritual suicide. He talks in a wonderfully contemptuous way about the use of deodorants and perfumes. He points out that human beings in modernity, as European modernists, are even disgusted by the natural odors of a healthy human body, by the odors that come from under our armpits, from off of our skin and so forth, and so we scrub ourselves with deodorant soaps to make the natural odors go away. We put on underarm deodorants. We put on artificial perfumes to make us smell like something else.

He points out that that's a really life-denying, self-abnegating act to perform. What it does, here you can see again Lame Deer following Nietzsche—what it does is it represents the fact that we try as hard as we can to deny the fact that we're biological animals, that we actually lead lives. Denying that is denying who we are. It's a profound self-alienation, a deprecation of our own fundamental nature. The most terrible thing you could do to yourself. To say, I'm the kind of being that I just don't even want people to know that I am, that is alive, biological, with an odor.

He writes,

> I think white people are so afraid of the world they created that they don't want to see, feel, smell or hear it. ... Living in boxes that shut out the heat of the summer and the chill of winter, living inside a body that no longer as a scent, hearing the noise from the hi-fi instead of listening to the sounds of nature, watching some actor on TV having a make-believe experience when you no longer experience anything for yourself.

This is a powerful and profound indictment. You can imagine Tolstoy nodding at this one. You can imagine Nietzsche nodding at this one. But you can imagine them nodding saying, this has just gone a step further.

What Lame Deer is pointing out is, that the end of this path of rejecting the symbolic, of rejecting the natural, of fetishizing commodities, of denying that we, ourselves are biological is to lead a completely ersatz life, a life that's a stand-in for a real life, a no-life that forces us to become spectators to other people's lives. Remember Nietzsche's wonderful question of conscience? Are you an actor or are you a spectator? Lame Deer is pointing out that the nature of modernity is to turn us into spectators, not even of our own lives, spectators of other people's lives, because we've already deprecated our own as not even worth living. We're just prisoners looking at televisions that give us views into other people's cells. That's a fierce indictment of modernity.

Lame Deer's analysis begins with an analysis of our alienation from nature and our alienation from the symbolic. It carries us through to alienation from ourselves as natural objects. If we can't appreciate our own natural character, Lame Deer urges, then we can't appreciate our place in nature. If we can't appreciate our place in nature, we can't appreciate the symbolic blanket that enfolds us. If we can't appreciate that, we can't apprehend meaning. If we can't apprehend meaning, there is no meaning in our lives. The totalization that modernity implies, the fact that it sets itself up as the only option, that fetishism becomes natural, precludes our ability to see anything else. Lame deer is banging on our prison doors pointing out that they're locked from the inside, asking us to open them, to come out, to consider another way to live, to consider a way to live that is far more meaningful, far more genuine.

Lame Deer points out that many anthropologists and many educators think of Indian values, Native American values, the values of community, the values that reject money, that valorize nature, that would allow the sun dance, as outdated, as primitive, as tribal, even as pathological as leading to laziness and a lack of progress.

Lame Deer argues that that's wrong, that the pathology is in modernity and the pathology arises precisely from these very pillars of modernity that we explored when we looked at Hume, Mill, and Kant, its commitment to progress where progress is seen as material progress, economic progress, progress away from nature, and its emphasis on reason as opposed to an emphasis on perception and symbolic appreciation. These are built into modernity, and for that reason, Lame Deer thinks, a certain kind of intolerance is built into modernity, an intolerance of the Native American view for instance. That intolerance, in fact, prevents us from learning from others, even in learning from Lame Deer. So we get a kind of internal critique. Modernity is built on this idea of reason and progress but its very nature makes it impossible for it to learn, for it to progress in important ways.

Finally, Lame Deer argues, modernity also alienates us from death. As we've seen so many of the views about the meaning of life that we've examined, those of Daoism, of stoicism, of Śāntideva, of Tolstoy, of Nietzsche, remind us that facing death, confronting the reality of death and coming to terms with it, is essential to leading a meaningful life.

Lame Deer argues that modernity sweeps stuff under the rug even though it markets it in another guise. Remember again Śāntideva who argues that our suffering is caused by a pervasive awareness of death coupled with a denial of it. Lame Deer argues that we cannot possibly live authentically if we don't take our own mortality seriously. What we end up doing is causing death to others needlessly precisely because we think of it as trivial. We end up getting violence and inauthenticity as mutually reinforcing pathologies of modernity.

Lame Deer says, "You are spreading death, buying and selling death. With all your deodorants you smell of it, but you are afraid of its reality, you don't want to face up to it. You have sanitized death, put it under the rug, robbed it of its honor. But we Indians think a lot about death." Notice what he's talking about. He's talking about a culture of violence, a culture of commodification, a culture of war, a culture of pollution, a culture of dessicration of the natural order, all done in this kind of sanitized way through video games or by watching wars on television and so forth, or by using undertakers to put the bodies away.

> But we Indians think a lot about death, I do. Today would be a perfect day to die—not too hot, not too cool. A day to leave something of yourself behind, to let it linger. ... Other days are not so good. They are for selfish, lonesome men, having a hard time leaving this earth. But for whites, every day would be considered a bad one, I guess.

That is, if we're going to understand our lives we have to come to terms with our death. To come to terms with our death we've got to actually think about it. Plan it. Accept it. Lame Deer is pointing out that a really authentic life, a life that understands us as natural objects, understands that we are indeed mortal.

Some of what Lame Deer has been saying we've seen before, but the meaning of life derives from connection to something greater. That it requires facing our own human nature and that it requires facing death. A meaningful life is a life lived in social harmony with others, it's a happy life. Like other critics of modernity we've examined, Lame Deer thinks that modernity is really dangerous to a meaningful life in virtue of its consumerism and mass culture. But some of what Lame Deer does is distinctive. His emphasis on the natural context, of the fact of our alienation from nature in modernity, and the ensuing self-alienation is a new insight, and his emphasis on the symbolic and sacred order of reality is a really special feature of the Lakota position.

In our next lecture we're going to turn to a figure who really tries to synthesize the pre-modern and the post-modern with a modern view, the present Dali Lama. Please join me for that talk.

HH Dalai Lama XIV—A Modern Buddhist View
Lecture 34

> [The Dalai Lama] has argued repeatedly that as far as he is concerned, it's the deliverances of science that tell us about the fundamental nature of reality, not classical religious scriptures, and he has repeatedly said that where Buddhism or when any religion conflicts with science, we should go with science, not with the deliverances of religion.

The **Dalai Lama**'s view of the meaning of life is, of course, deeply inflected and motivated by Buddhism, but he articulates it primarily as a modern secular vision, a vision with roots in ideas of individual liberty, freedom of speech and religion, democratic theory, and the importance of science. He follows Aristotle in seeing the universal goal of human life to be happiness, but that happiness can only be attained in the context of social interdependence. Like any Buddhist, the Dalai Lama sees the problem of life as constituted by suffering, whose modern sources he finds in consumer capitalism and industrialism. He sees the sources of happiness in purposive action in a human context.

The Dalai Lama agrees with Aristotle that happiness, flourishing, meets the criteria for the highest good in life: finality and self-sufficiency. The components of happiness in a modern life include food, shelter, physical security, peace, education, access to health care, the opportunity for free expression of ideas, a certain amount of leisure, and possibility for personal development. The fact that people around the world are willing to fight to achieve these goals must mean that they are universal.

Because the Dalai Lama's is a Buddhist account of the nature of reality, it is rooted in the doctrine of dependent origination, in which all things are interdependent in three senses. The first is causal dependence; everything occurs as a consequence of innumerable causes and conditions, and every event produces innumerable effects. The second form of interdependence is part-whole dependence; parts depend upon the whole for their nature and functioning, and wholes depend upon parts in order to exist. The third form of interdependence is dependence on conceptual imputation, that is, dependence of things for their identity and function on the way in which we think about them.

The Dalai Lama argues that interdependence provides us with the deepest analysis of the fundamental nature of reality. Everything around us, in particular, our own lives and the lives of the communities in which we participate, is characterized by this threefold interdependence. Moreover, the Dalai Lama emphasizes that this is completely consistent with the deliverance of modern science. Physics, for example, demonstrates that everything is part of a uniform, causal whole and interdependent in all these ways. He argues that if our lives are to be meaningful, they must be grounded in reality, and given that interdependence is the fundamental nature of reality, a meaningful life is one that responds to and reflects an appreciation of interdependence.

For the Dalai Lama, human interdependence deserves special emphasis. Social reality develops for us distinctive kinds of part-whole interdependence because so much of our lives and our identities are determined by the wholes of which we're parts. Conceptual imputation in the construction of identity and roles is also salient in human affairs in ways that it's not in physical affairs. Our decisions that a particular person is a

© iStockphoto/Thinkstock.

Interconnection also constitutes our happiness because so much of our happiness is social. We become happy when our actions actually match the goals and values we endorse. That's often only possible socially because so many of our goals and so many of our values are collective social values.

criminal versus an upright citizen, a colleague versus a competitor, and so on determine the nature of our relations, the nature of our lives, and the nature of our happiness.

Each of the dimensions of interdependence is implicated in the arising of suffering and the production of happiness. All these forms of interdependence give us the possibility of having complex effects in our actions. Everything we do ripples through societies instantly and in countless ways and in ways that we can't always control but that demand our reflection. And because our actions have so many effects, we have obligations to make sure that those effects are beneficial, and we have responsibilities to those who can be affected by our actions.

> **Everything we do ripples through societies instantly and in countless ways and in ways that we can't always control but that demand our reflection.**

According to the Dalai Lama, modern capitalism has brought the original source of suffering—primal confusion that results in attraction and aversion—to new heights. Advertising, for example, creates both need and fear, attraction and aversion, and it isolates us in a marketplace with a given commodity, forcing a decision on whether or not we need something. The Dalai Lama thinks that commodification has also infected politics because it creates politicians and ideas as commodities, then generates attraction or aversion. The mass media and mass culture are, thus, sources of confusion and suffering.

Oddly, the sources of happiness in the modern world are similar to the sources of unhappiness. One such source is our interconnection with others, which enables us to produce both the material and the collective social goods we want and allows us to discover truth in learning from one another. This interconnection also brings us happiness in the form of social interactions and activities with friends and families. It offers us the opportunity to work out the kinds of social values and ideals we endorse and lead a life of integrity and authenticity. ∎

His Holiness the Dalai Lama XIV, Tenzin Gyatso (b. 1935): The Dalai Lama lineage in Tibet is regarded by Tibetans as a reincarnate lineage: Each successive Dalai Lama is recognized as a rebirth of his predecessor, and all are regarded by Tibetans as emanations of Avalalokiteśvara, the Buddhist celestial bodhisattva of compassion.

Suggested Reading

Dalai Lama XIV, *Ethics for a New Millennium.*

———, *The Universe in a Single Atom: The Convergence of Science and Spirituality.*

Prebish and Baumann, eds., *Westward Dharma.*

Study Questions

1. In what sense is the Dalai Lama's diagnosis of modern life Buddhist? In what sense is it modern?

2. What is the difference between the analysis of modernity presented by Gandhi and that presented by the Dalai Lama?

HH Dalai Lama XIV—A Modern Buddhist View
Lecture 34—Transcript

Welcome back. We're now going to spend two lectures examining the extraordinary view of the meaning of life that's articulated by a great contemporary leader both in spiritual, political, philosophical affairs, the XIV Dalai Lama of Tibet, Tenzin Gyatso.

Let me begin by talking a little bit about who the Dalai Lama is so that we can contextualize some of the views that we're going to be considering. The present Dalai Lama—and by the way, the term Dalai Lama isn't a name of course, it's a title. It's a title that was conferred by Mongol rulers of Tibet in the 15th century, and the present Dalai Lama is the XIV in that lineage.

It's a reincarnate lineage which is something that Western people sometimes find a little bit surprising, so that the XIV Dalai Lama is regarded as the rebirth of the XIII Dalai Lama who in turn is the rebirth of the XII Dalai Lama and so on and so forth. When a Dalai Lama dies, after a few years a search party is sent out to try to find the rebirth of the next Dalai Lama.

In the case of the present Dalai Lama, that search party found him in a very tiny village called Taktser in far northeastern Tibet in the region known as Amdo along the Chinese border. When he was discovered, at age four, he and his family were brought to Lhasa, to the capital of Tibet where he received a traditional Tibetan monastic education that culminates in the Tibetan philosophical Ph.D. or geshe degree. So he wasn't raised by his family but rather was raised as a monk in a monastery from the age of four.

This Dalai Lama lived in times that were very challenging, very difficult, and have been very difficult for Tibet. After the victory by the People's Liberation Army in China, and the establishment of Communist rule in China, the Chinese government set its sights upon the conquest of Tibet with the view that Tibet had traditionally been part of China from a Chinese perspective, even though from a Tibetan perspective Tibet was an independent country. Shortly after the success of the communist revolution, Mao's troops moved on Tibet and very quickly, in 1949, overran a good deal of Tibet.

At age 14, the Dalai Lama, still being educated, still being groomed for leadership was forced to confront the invasion of Tibet, a very sparsely populated and poor and unarmed country by a very large, well-equipped and experienced army. The Tibetan people insisted that he assume leadership at that point. So at the age of 14 he became Head of State and Head of Government of a country at war. That's a significant challenge in life. He led Tibet for about 10 years under Chinese occupation trying to negotiate an accommodation in which Tibet would retain its cultural autonomy, its traditional cultural practices and its religious practices under this new Chinese sovereignty. But Chinese rule tightened and became more and more oppressive, more and more difficult for Tibetans, and finally in March of 1959 there was a large, spontaneous uprising of Tibetans against Chinese rule. It was hopeless because the Tibetans were certainly outgunned and outnumbered at that point by armed Chinese. But the suppression of the uprising was aggressive, quick, and brutal, and in fact also included an artillery attack on the residence of the Dalai Lama.

The Dalai Lama, realizing that his own life was in danger as part of the consequences of this uprising, fled Tibet in disguise and went into exile in India. Many of his followers in Tibet—hundreds of thousands—followed him into exile in India and have continued to escape from occupied Tibet right up to the present day.

Right now there's a large Tibetan exile community of a few hundred thousand, primarily in India but also centered in Himalayan countries like Nepal and Bhutan, but now also abroad, Tibetan exile in the West including a substantial Tibetan community in the United States and in Europe.

The Dalai Lama, after arriving in India, very quickly moved to establish a Tibetan exile leadership structure. So a government in exile was established, headquartered right now in a tiny Himalayan town of Dharamsala north of Delhi. The Tibetan government established schools very quickly, and some of the best schools in India in fact, also monastic institutions, monastic universities, some quasi secular universities, a Tibetan medical care system, and all of the appurtenances of a government in exile.

The Dalai Lama leads this government in exile as Head of State but it's important to note that he is not now Head of Government of the Tibetan government in exile because a few years ago the Dalai Lama insisted that Tibetans, if they were going to live in a modern world, needed a democratic government, and so led a commission that drafted a Tibetan constitution which paradoxically, against the will of most Tibetans, imposed democracy on them. So the Tibetan government now, under the Head of State leadership of the Dalai Lama has a parliamentary form of government with an independent head of government.

Nonetheless, for Tibetans all around the world and indeed for Buddhists all around the world, the Dalai Lama is recognized as an important spiritual leader, somebody to whom people turn for advice, for comment, and for leadership. The present Dalai Lama is not only informed by Buddhism. He's somebody who has always been a champion of a Gandhi an account of non-violence. He was very enamored by the work of Mohandas Gandhi, the work that we'd examined, the idea of satyagraha, the insistence upon the truth, and of a refusal of violence.

Partly in recognition of his emphasis on democracy and his emphasis on spreading democracy through the world, and on his Gandhian non-violence he was awarded the Nobel Peace Prize to recognize this tremendous contribution to non-violent struggle, not only for Tibetan independence, but his advocacy of non-violent struggle worldwide, and his advocacy of the spread of democracy and fundamental human rights.

The Dalai Lama isn't only a Buddhist and isn't only a Gandhian. These of course are both as we've seen, kind of anti-modern tendencies. He's also a passionate modernist, and herein lies some of the complexity and the tension in the views that we're going to be examining in this lecture and the next. The Dalai Lama has been deeply engaged with science, primarily physics, but also cognitive science, psychology, linguistics, computer science, and neuroscience—sciences that he finds extraordinarily important. He has argued repeatedly that as far as he is concerned, it's the deliverances of science that tell us about the fundamental nature of reality, not classical religious scriptures and he has repeatedly said that where Buddhism or when any religion conflicts with science, we should go with science, not with the deliverances of religion.

He has also, by the way, been committed to the view that the fundamental tenets, or not all tenants of Buddhism, are absolutely consistent with modern science and can be enriched and informed by science, and that science can, in turn, be enriched and informed by Buddhism.

The Dalai Lama is also a superb scholar, a superb scholar of classical Buddhism with a very eloquent PhD, but also somebody who has studied Western philosophy very seriously and understands Western philosophy, Western religion very seriously including Christianity, who has written commentaries on Christian scriptures, and somebody who is also a real scholar, as I've pointed out, of science.

He is the author of over 50 books, some of these are popular books on Buddhism. Some are deeply scholarly analyses of classical Buddhist texts, and some are important philosophical texts articulating his own modernist synthesis of Buddhism, democratic theory, and science. The text that I'm going to be primarily relying on in my presentation of the Dalai Lama's views is his book called *Ethics for a New Millennium* published in the year 2000.

Let's begin with a broad outline of the Dalai Lama's view of the meaning of life. The first thing to say is that while it is deeply inflected by Buddhism and motivated by Buddhist ideas and incorporates Buddhist ideas, he intends it and articulates it primarily as a modern secular vision, a vision that's going to have its roots in ideas of individual liberty, in freedom of speech, and freedom of religion, and in democratic theory, and in the importance of science as a source of knowledge.

He's going to follow Aristotle in important ways in seeing the highest good, and the universal goal of human life to be happiness, and to be even understanding happiness as a broad kind of human flourishing. We're going to see an Aristotelian emphasis in the Dalai Lama. But the Buddhist underpinnings are going to guarantee that this happiness must and can only be attained in the context of a Thoreau gully interdependence, of a recognition of the fact that all human beings and all phenomenon are interdependent in all of the ways that Buddhism respects. For the Dalai Lama that is predominantly and preeminently going to include social interdependence.

Like any Buddhist he's going to see the problem of life as constituted by suffering and the task of a meaningful life as a solution of the problem of suffering. The Dalai Lama is going to follow Gandhi, and we might also say Lame Deer—though he's never read Lame Deer—in seeing the main sources of modern suffering in consumer capitalism and industrialism. He's going to see the sources of happiness as lying very much in purposive action in a human context, in acting in ways that we can reflectively endorse. He'll argue that acting in that way requires the cultivation of a deep sense of compassion, very much in the sense articulated by Śāntideva

We'll be talking about most of the positive end of this in our next lecture. But in the present lecture we're going to really talk about the analysis of the nature of reality that underlies the Dalai Lama's characterization of the meaningful life.

We're going to begin by talking about his view about the goal of human life and as we're going to see, that's going to be happiness, and his argument for that will remind us a great deal of Aristotle's function argument, and we'll also see that he's got a very Aristotelian view of happiness spelled out as a very broad sense of human flourishing.

For the Dalai Lama, the account of happiness is not going to be one set out in terms of virtue, but rather in terms of satisfaction, in terms of lack of conflict, in terms of material goods. It's going to be a much more modern, much more familiar sense of happiness.

We'll then be talking about the components of happiness in a modern life. Let's talk a bit about happiness right now. When the Dalai Lama argues that happiness is the highest good and the goal of human life, his argument, very much as I suggested, follows Aristotle. He doesn't follow Aristotle in talking about the function of a human being, but remember these two fundamental criteria Aristotle establishes for something being the highest good or the goal of life, one is finality and the other is self sufficiency.

That the goal of human life, the highest good, should be something for which other things are done, but it's something which is never done for the sake of other things. That's the sense of finality. It's the thing we seek for its own sake, not for the sake of others.

Moreover, it should be self sufficient. We should be able to say, if we ask is a life good? We should be able to say, it's got that quality, and not then ask what else it has. It should, of itself make a life worth living. The Dalai Lama argues that it's happiness that does that. All of us seek happiness. We don't seek happiness in order to become wealthy. We don't seek happiness in order to become powerful. We don't seek happiness in order to get anything else. Rather, we seek other things for happiness. Moreover, if I ask whether somebody led a good life and I say, she was happy, that's enough. I don't then ask, but was she also rich? Was she also powerful? But if I say, she was rich, we might ask, yes but was she happy? She was powerful. Yes, but was she happy?

For that reason the Dalai Lama argues with Aristotle, happiness is really what we seek. Happiness must be understood as happiness in a complete life. What are the components of happiness in a modern life? Well there are things that we all want the Dalai Lama thinks. The Dalai Lama thinks we all want food—adequate food—adequate shelter, personal physical security, peace and education which makes everything else possible, access to healthcare, the opportunity for free expression of ideas—political ideas, religious ideas, artistic ideas.

We want to live in a democratic order. We would like to have freedom of religion. We would like to have a certain amount of leisure and not be working all of our days. We would like to have possibilities for the kind of personal development that we find important. Why does the Dalai Lama think that these are the central components for happiness? The reason is simple and it also follows a kind of Aristotelian framework.

He argues that in fact we see that these are universal goals. People all over the world are willing to fight and strive for democracy, not to fight in order to become oppressed. People are willing to fight and strive to attain freedom of religion. They don't fight and strive to have their freedom restricted. They might fight and strive to restrict other people's freedom, but nobody asks that their own freedom be restricted. It's something that shows that we each really value freedom, at least in our own case.

People will strive for leisure. They don't strive to lead lives of unending toil and so forth. It's the universality of these goals, the fact that everybody sees these as components of happiness that the Dalai Lama shows us that these really are the components of human happiness and that this universality demonstrates the importance of these goals in our human life.

Now of course this is a Buddhist account of the nature of reality and so it's going to be rooted in the fundamental Buddhist doctrine of dependent origination. This is an idea that we reviewed a number of lectures ago in our lecture on the ideas of the Buddha, but it's worth reviewing them right now. When we say that things are dependently originated or that things are all interdependent we mean that in three very important senses, and the Dalai Lama emphasizes each of these in his analysis of the nature of human life. The first of those is causal dependence. Everything occurs as a consequence of enumerable causes and conditions and every event produces enumerable effects. Things don't just happen, things aren't isolated.

That means that our own actions, our own states of minds, our own emotional states, and our own values also arise dependent on enumerable causes and conditions, and everything that we do has enumerable effects. That gives us both reason to examine the world around us and to care about changing it, to care about making it the kind of world that will give rise to the kinds of lives we want. But it also forces us to attend to the actions we perform because they are going to have ripples of effects beyond the possibility of our imagination. That's the first dimension of interdependence.

The second dimension of interdependence is part whole interdependence. Parts depend upon the wholes of which they are parts for their nature and for their functioning. Wholes, in turn, depend upon their parts in order to exist. The example that we used a while ago was the example of an automobile. We only have a fully-functioning automobile in dependence upon all of its parts—its brakes, its steering wheel, its engine, its exhaust system, and so forth. But to be an exhaust system, to be a steering wheel, to be an engine, to be a brake, is to play a particular role in the whole, not simply to be shaped in a certain way, to be made out of a certain material, or to have a certain label.

In human affairs, of course this is extraordinarily important. Human institutions, universities, hospitals, communities, armies, corporations, social clubs, depend upon their parts, depend upon their members for their functioning. But in order to be a member of a chess club, in order to be secretary of a Town meeting, in order to be a chief of medicine at a particular hospital, in order to be professor at a university, those parts depend for their identity and for their functioning on the wholes. We can no more reduce complex human affairs to their parts than we can reduce parts to the wholes. There's a mutual interdependence here.

Finally the third form of interdependence is dependence on conceptual imputation. That is, dependence of things for their identity, for their function on the way in which we think about them, the way in which we name them, the way in which we reason about them. This is extraordinarily important in human affairs.

For instance, if I imagine one of those green frog-skins that Lame Deer talked about, a dollar bill—and I ask, what is it that makes that dollar bill worth one dollar? It's not something in the value of the paper. I could analyze the paper as long as I wanted to try to figure out whether it was worth a dollar. Instead, what makes it a dollar bill is the place it plays in an entire complex banking system. It's a partness in that whole that's important. But more than that it's the fact that we all agree to treat that dollar bill as having the value of one dollar, that we're willing to give four quarters and change for it. That we're willing to sell something whose price is one dollar for it and so forth, that's conceptual imputation.

If we decided that these green frog-skins were no longer going to be recognized, suppose we decided to go to dollar coins and we're only going to recognize dollar coins, not dollar bills. No matter what part that dollar used to play, no matter how much that paper is worth, it's now worthless because we no longer impute the value of one dollar to it. Interdependence has all of these three dimensions: causal, part whole, and imputational.

The Dalai Lama argues that interdependence, in this sense, provides us with the deepest analysis of the fundamental nature of reality. Everything around us and in particular our own lives and the lives of the communities in which we participate is characterized by this three-fold interdependence. Moreover, he emphasizes, this is completely consistent with the deliverance of modern science. That physics demonstrates that everything is part of a uniform, causal whole, and interdependent in all of these ways. If you're worried about imputation, think about quantum mechanics and the role of observation in giving identity and reality to quantum phenomenon. Social science and psychology also reveal that our cognitive lives, our emotional lives, and our social lives are interdependent in all three of these ways.

The Dalai Lama argues that if our actions and our lives are to be meaningful at all, they've got to be grounded in truth, they've got to be grounded in reality. Lives that are grounded in a false vision of things are just a mistake. If it's interdependence that gives us the fundamental nature of reality, that means that a meaningful life has to be a life that responds to, is grounded in and reflects an appreciation of interdependence. The Dalai Lama is not alone in this kind of insight that meaningful lives are lives grounded in appreciation of reality. We've seen Gandhi's idea that the meaningful life is constituted by satyagraha, grasping and insisting on truth. We've seen this idea from the Buddha, which is where the Dalai Lama gets it most forcefully that the Four Noble Truths or the four truths for one who would be noble are the foundation of a meaningful life. We've also seen this idea worked out in a very different way by the Stoics, who argue that since the universe is fundamentally rational, then a recognition of that rationality is what grounds our lives as rational, and hence as meaningful.

Human interdependence, the Dalai Lama argues, is only a special case of this broader truth. But it's a very important special case and it's a special case that deserves special emphasis because of the fact that what we're asking about is what is it to lead a distinctively human life, a meaningful human life?

Social reality develops for us special kinds of part whole interdependence. We're not just cars. So much of our lives are lived as members of families, employees of institutions, citizens of cities, states, nations, members of clubs, social organizations, political parties, and so much of our identity is determined by wholes of which we're a part. So much of our responsibility to each other is helping in our participation to determine the characters of those wholes. Part whole independence plays a very deep role in trying to understand exactly who we are and what we are. Ignore that and you can't understand your own identity even at the beginning.

Conceptual imputation, the construction of identity and roles of imputation is also quite salient in human affairs in ways that it's not in physical affairs. When we say of somebody that they're a leader, it's because we impute to them leadership qualities. We are willing to follow them. When we say of somebody that she's a criminal, it's because we've decided that what she does is something that we don't like and that it is our conceptuality, our assessment, that gives her that role. When we decide of somebody that they are a Nobel Prize winner it is because somebody has conferred that prize on them. This kind of conceptual imputation, this making decisions about identity, deciding that somebody is one of us or one of them, which is often very important, is absolutely startling. Deciding that somebody is a criminal versus an adversarian war, deciding that somebody is a colleague versus a competitor, all of these things determine the nature of our relations, the nature of our lives, the nature of our happiness, and they all depend upon this kind of social construction.

Given that our suffering and our happiness arise out of this matrix of interdependence, each of these dimensions, causal interdependence, part/ whole interdependence, the interdependence in terms of conceptual imputation, is implicated in the arising of suffering and in the production of happiness. It's my actions that can cause pleasure for others. It's my actions that can cause pain for others.

It's my participation in a beneficial organization that can cause happiness for me and others, my participation in a criminal organization that can cause unhappiness for myself or for others and so forth. All of these forms of interdependence give us the possibility of having very complex effects in our actions. Everything we do ripples through societies instantly and in countless ways and in ways that we can't always control, but demand our reflection. What this also generates is a set of complex obligations and responsibilities.

Because our actions have so many effects, we have obligations to make sure that those effects are beneficial, and we have responsibilities to those who can be affected by our actions.

So what are the sources of modern suffering, specifically the suffering that characterizes modernity and the lives that we lead? Recall the trio of sources of suffering that we examined in that First and Second Noble Truth when we talked about the view of the Buddha. We said that suffering is rooted in confusion or ignorance about the fundamental nature of reality that gives rise to attraction to things that we want but can't have and aversion to things that are present with us that we don't want. It's attraction and aversion that immediately cause suffering, but that are rooted in confusion.

Modern capitalism, the Dalai Lama notes, following Gandhi very straightforwardly here, developed these three sources of suffering to new heights. Commodity fetishism again—just as Lame Deer would have agreed—add to this, advertising and the fetishism of objects as the sources of happiness give us this artificial creation of need. Advertising artificially creates fear, creates fear of not having the best new car, creates fear of having last year's model, creates fear of being seen as wearing last year's clothes and being seen as some kind of a dork right? Advertising creates both need and fear, attraction and aversion, and it isolates us in a marketplace where there's me and the commodity, and I've got to make a decision, do I need it? And the answer is always, yes.

It's this kind of engine of capitalism to create confusion and then to create attraction and aversion that the Dalai Lama thinks creates much of our modern suffering. He also thinks that this commodification infects politics as well because it creates politicians as commodities, creates ideas as commodities, and creates confusion that then generates attraction to ideas or politicians to whom we should not be attracted, aversions sometimes from those we should. For this reason, the attraction and aversion that permeate our modern lives begin in confusion, and the Dalai Lama pinpoints the mass media and mass culture as sources of this kind of confusion as well as, of course, potential sources of its opposite, that is of knowledge, but at this point confusion and so is sources of suffering.

He has a wonderful metaphor when he says that what we do in advertising, by getting people to really want commodities, to want the newest thing is we first create thirst and then we offer the thirsty man a glass of salt water.

So much for the sources of unhappiness in the modern world, what could the sources of happiness be? Well they're in a funny way the same things, the Dalai Lama points out. They are the interconnection with other people. This can facilitate our happiness and can constitute our happiness because it's our interconnection that enables us to work together. It enables us to produce the goods that we want. the material goods, the spiritual goods, the collective social goods. So much of that requires collective action, not something we can do individually. It's our interdependence that allows us to produce the goods that are constitutive of happiness. It's also our interconnectedness that allows us to discover the truth because we can learn from each other, learn from other perspectives, integrate other ideas.

Interconnection also constitutes our happiness because so much of our happiness is social. We're often happiest when we're with friends, when we're with families, when we're engaged in social activity. We become happy when our actions actually match the goals and values we endorse, when we're living authentically in a way that Nietzsche recommended, in a way that Gandhi recommended, in a way that Lame Deer recommended. That's often only possible socially because so many of our goals and so many of our values are collective social values.

Interconnection makes happiness possible materially because a lot of the material goods we want can't be produced by us alone, Hume pointed that out of course. Interdependence facilitates happiness in a deep, constituative way because, the Dalai Lama argues again following Gandhi, integrity, authenticity, leading the kind of life we could endorse, is important in its own right. If we don't lead that kind of life, we are always feeling uncomfortable and self-alienated. It's only the interdependence and the ability to interact with others that allows us to work out the kinds of social values and social ideals that we would endorse.

This kind of propulsive action, the Dalai Lama argues, requires genuine compassion, karuna, and as we said when we talked about Śāntideva, karuna is not an emotion, not a feeling. It's a commitment to act. The root of the word karuna is kr meaning action and that means that happiness in this sense, a meaningful life in this sense, according to the Dalai Lama, requires not just caring about others but being committed in our action. This kind of commitment to action, this kind of compassion, even though it had affected dimensions arises as a commitment to act through the recognition and through the understanding of interdependence, and through the understanding that only an interdependence and only in compassionate action can we generate collective happiness. For that reason, the Dalai Lama thinks compassion is an absolutely essential ingredient both of happiness for others and of happiness for ourselves. For that reason, as we're going to see in our next lecture, karuna, compassion, the altruistic commitment to act for the welfare of other sentient beings is going to be the foundation of a meaningful life.

HH Dalai Lama XIV—Discernment and Happiness
Lecture 35

> The union of compassion and discernment is a union of moral perceptual skills—where, when we see a situation, we see the sources of suffering, we see the possibilities for happiness—and the interpersonal skills that allow us to see what kinds of interventions will be most useful and commit us to those kinds of interventions.

As we saw in the last lecture, dependent origination grounds the possibility of both suffering and happiness. For the Dalai Lama, the source of suffering in the modern world is the ideology of commodity fetishism, and the only solution to suffering is to develop a deep kind of compassion, an attitude that respects interdependence and commits us to the creation of happiness.

The Dalai Lama notes that unhappiness doesn't derive directly from external circumstances but from our emotional reactions to adversity. Such emotional reactions arise from both attachment and aversion and can be either individual or collective. The Dalai Lama thinks of emotions that cause suffering as pathologies; examples include greed, lust, hate, and so on. In some cases, such as when we speak of righteous anger, we mistake pathology for virtue, but as we've seen, anger never results in positive outcomes. If we're going to understand the nature of suffering and happiness, we must be able to distinguish between beneficial and pathological emotions.

According to the Dalai Lama, pathological emotions are grounded in confusion, a misperception of reality. We see something else as the source of our unhappiness instead of ourselves; we see some object as necessary instead of simply an option. To cultivate positive emotions, we need a clear, accurate understanding of reality and not just on a theoretical or abstract level. We must seek instinctive, spontaneous responses to the world as causally dependent, part-whole dependent, and dependent on imputation. This instinctive cognitive habit is difficult to accomplish, and that's why the notion of *karunā*—compassion—is so important. *Karunā* gives us commitment, that altruistic aspiration to act, impelling us to develop spontaneous ways of interacting with the world in place of our ordinary approaches. The use of moral imagination is important here because we need to be able to understand that the interests of others are, in a deep sense, just like our interests and that their pain is just like our pain.

The Dalai Lama argues that the cultivation of compassion comes in two parts: the cultivation of restraint and the cultivation of virtue. By restraint, he means the holding back of instinctive negative reactions, actions of anger, greed, carelessness, and so forth. By virtue, he means developing a positive commitment to benefit others. Restraint cuts off the roots of suffering by prompting us to reflect on the causes of pathological emotions, thus subverting primal confusion and ignorance. Reflection also highlights the impermanence of the world, including the impermanence of the things that cause us to experience suffering and our own emotional reactions. Through reflecting on selflessness, we're able to suspend the ordinary cognitive habit of thinking of ourselves as subjects and everything else in the world as objects. That way of thinking reflects the nature of reality as determined by a polar coordinate system with oneself at the center and everything else arrayed in terms of its relationship to the center. This conception gives rise to conflict, but by reflecting on selflessness, we come to take our own importance less seriously.

To cultivate positive emotions, we need a clear, accurate understanding of reality and not just on a theoretical or abstract level.

Restraint keeps us from doing bad things, but it doesn't by itself motivate us to do the things that are necessary for own happiness or the happiness of others. To do that, we need to cultivate generosity, the willingness to detach ourselves from our possessions. As Śāntideva reminded us, virtue also requires patience, not only with others but with ourselves. The moral development that we come to demand of ourselves when we adopt this understanding of the nature of our lives isn't acquired in a moment.

The concept of virtue that the Dalai Lama emphasizes requires attentive concern, mindfulness, discernment, and compassion. The dimension of attentiveness commits us to truly understanding the nature of the problem and the solutions that would rectify it. The dimension of concern is a commitment to take action. Mindfulness of our own emotional states enables us to focus on virtuous rather than nonvirtuous emotions. Discernment is necessary to allow us to understand the details of any particular situation: What are the causes, conditions, and effects? Finally, we need compassion in the sense of *karunā*, an altruistic commitment to act. For compassion to be genuine and efficacious, it must rest on discernment, a deep analytical understanding of suffering.

The Dalai Lama emphasizes that this kind of compassion entails a Gandhian universal responsibility, a responsibility for the welfare of all, because there are no limitations on compassion. Any limitations could originate only in pathological distinctions between ourselves and others. Compassion must be rooted in the de-centering of the individual, which will make such distinctions impossible. What we're seeing here is a modern version of the bodhisattva path: the altruistic resolution to act for the benefit of all sentient beings. ∎

Suggested Reading

Dalai Lama XIV, *Ethics for a New Millennium*.

Queen, *Engaged Buddhism in the West*.

Study Questions

1. In what sense is the Dalai Lama's recommendation for a meaningful life different from those of Gandhi and Lame Deer? In what respects is it similar?

2. Why is compassion, as opposed to a sense of duty, the foundation for a meaningful life in the modern world, according to the Dalai Lama?

HH Dalai Lama XIV—Discernment and Happiness
Lecture 35—Transcript

Greetings. In our last lecture we were reviewing the Dalai Lama's conception of the fundamental nature of reality and of human happiness. But of course as Aristotle even said, to say that happiness is the highest good is a bit trite and one needs details. We spent a fair amount of time in our last lecture filling out the details of the Dalai Lama's view of what human happiness is.

We saw that the Dalai Lama concurs with the general Aristotelian idea that happiness isn't a kind of fleeting emotion but is the goal of human life, the highest good, and constitutes a global state of flourishing, of living well. We saw that the Dalai Lama differs from Aristotle, doesn't see happiness necessarily as analytically connected to virtues. Rather, for the Dalai Lama happiness is comprised as a broad set of goods, social, material, would involve certain kinds of liberty, certain kinds of freedom, certain kinds of social interactions and so forth.

Nonetheless for the Dalai Lama we are very much aimed at happiness. That is the goal of life, and for very much the reasons that Aristotle thought that happiness is something we choose always for its own sake, never for the sake of something else. That we choose other things in order to be happy and that if you're happy that's enough, it's self sufficient. We also saw that the Dalai Lama as a Buddhist really emphasizes the idea the fundamental nature of reality is given by dependent origination in its three forms: causal dependent origination, part whole dependency, and conceptual imputation. We saw that that's especially true when we think about social reality, the reality that we preeminently inhabit.

The fundamental truth about the reality in which we live, our social reality, is this complex network of dependent origination. Dependent origination, we saw, grounds both the possibility of suffering and the possibility of happiness. When we think about dependent origination in its aspect as the root of suffering, the Dalai Lama takes us back to the Four Noble Truths or the four truths for one who would be noble. What we find is a social structure, an economic structure that through the ideology of commodity fetishism, through the activity of relentless advertising and consumerism, systematically paints a distorting view for us of what we actually need and of what we should actually fear, of what candidates are actually desirable and which ones are scary, of things without which we cannot possibly live, or things that we must not do. This fundamental confusion is what conditions most of our current desires, and felt needs, and most of our fears, most of our aversions.

This source of suffering, this fundamental confusion generating attraction and ignorance generates a kind of cycle, and it's the cycle that we metaphorically described as offering salt water to a thirsty man. We buy yet another object and that other object just leads us to desire one more. We saw that the Dalai Lama is drawing inspiration not only from Buddhism but also from critics of modernity like Gandhi. We concluded by reminding ourselves that for the Dalai Lama the only possible solution to this is the development of a very deep kind of compassion, because our interdependence is in virtue of being the nature of reality not only the source of actual suffering, but also the source of potential happiness. If suffering is grounded in reality, happiness must be grounded in reality too. The development of an attitude that respects this kind of interdependence and commits us to the creation of happiness, that's what we mean by compassion is necessary in order to make life meaningful. Today that goal is to find out how that can be achieved.

The Dalai Lama begins his analysis through an analysis of our emotions. By the way, this is also a respect in which it makes sense to say of the Dalai Lama that even though he's a great Buddhist leader steeped in the Buddhist tradition, he's also very much a modernist because the whole category of emotions—things that just come out of us, right? Emote—just move out of us, is very much a Western psychological notion, and there's no neat translation of the term "emotion" into any Buddhist language. The Dalai Lama in adopting this framework is very much adopting a Western, secular model of psychological life in order to understand both unhappiness and happiness. It's very much informed by his study of Western cognitive science.

The Dalai Lama notes that our unhappiness—the suffering that we actually experience—doesn't derive directly from external circumstances. Things may go wrong. We may even be in pain. We may lose things. We may not get what we want, but that by itself is not suffering. That's just adversity. Suffering arises from our emotional reactions to those adversities or to our emotional reactions to not having what we want. Not having a Mercedes Benz is not itself a source of suffering. But feeling bereft of something that I need, feeling a deep hollow in my soul because I don't have a Mercedes Benz, that's suffering, but that comes from the pathological emotion, not from the fact that I've got a Toyota not a Mercedes Benz.

The Dalai Lama points out that these emotional reactions and these attachments come not only from attachment but also from aversion. That is, my adoration of somebody could become a source of suffering if that person does not particularly want to be adored by me. Positive emotions can also constitute attachments and become pathological. Here we should be noting very deep resonances not only to Śāntideva, who the Dalai Lama reads very closely and whose text he teaches very frequently, the text that really animates most of his moral thinking, but also the Stoics. Remember that metaphor of the arrow. We can control the shooting of the arrow but not what happens outside.

We can control what belongs to us, not what's outside. For the Dalai Lama the important point is that suffering has its sources internally not externally. These pathological emotions, the emotions that cause our suffering, the Dalai Lama thinks of as pathologies of attachment and pathologies of repulsion, and there are a lot of them. Pathologies of attachment are things like greed, lust, this feeling of terrible neediness, the needing of approval, pathologies of aversion, hatred, racism, distaste for things, and so forth.

The Dalai Lama's view is that these have individual as well as social dimensions. That's really important, that we are social beings. So many of the pathologies—these kind of pathologies—might just be individual psychological states. I really want that kind of car, or I really don't like that person. There's also social dimensions. We don't like them, or as a country we need this kind of military security. There are collective attractions, collective repulsions as well as individual attractions and individual repulsions. No matter what, the Dalai Lama urges that these set up a kind of self perpetuating cycle of emotional pathology. It goes like this, I decide that I don't like what you've said to me and so I become angry.

Notice, what you said to me isn't a harm, it's just something you said, but I become angry. Now all of a sudden I experience harm, and what do I do? I project you as the cause of the harm rather than my own anger.

So I say something nasty back to you and the same thing happens. You become annoyed and you throw a rock at me. Now I've got some blood coming down my forehead and now I'm really mad so I pick up a stick and the escalation goes. The injury generates anger that generates more injury and we get this self-perpetuating cycle.

In the case of attraction we get the self perpetuating cycle of need that we have that advertising generates. In interpersonal relations we are certainly familiar with self- perpetuating cycles both of positive and negative emotions, positive and negative emotions that undermine genuine relationships. It's important to note that we very often, in thinking about the emotions, mistake pathology for virtue. I think this is a deep part of our modern predicament, and it's one that the Dalai Lama really emphasizes. Sometimes people will talk about justified anger or righteous anger and think of that as a virtue. Ask yourself when is the last time that anger did anything positive for you or for anybody else that you know.

Go back to Seneca who talks about the horrors or anger and who thinks that if what you want to do is to motivate punishment, think calmly, think calculatedly, think carefully. Anger only blunts your faculties. It makes you behave irrationally, it distorts things. Even love can often be thought of as a virtue when in fact it's pathological, when it becomes obsession, when it becomes a fascination that gets in the way of seeing another person clearly.

Patriotism and honor sometimes sit that way too. We think of somebody as deeply patriotic when in fact they may have simply have fetishized a particular policy or a particular country. It's very important if we're going to understand the nature of suffering but also if we're going to understand the nature of happiness to be able to distinguish emotions that are indeed beneficial from emotions that are pathological, and very often they are so close to each other that it's very hard to tell unless we actually engage honestly, reflectively, and deeply with our own inner life.

The Dalai Lama argues that given that so much of our emotional life is pathological, even if we don't experience it that way, what we need is an antidote are positive, non-pathological emotions. Pathological emotions, he argues, are grounded in confusion. Attraction and aversion are grounded in misperceiving reality, seeing something else as the source of our unhappiness, rather than ourselves, seeing something else as necessary instead of simply an option.

Here we're really reflecting ideas that we saw in Śāntideva, the idea that we really have an erroneous perception, a misperception of reality that has to be the foundation of this kind of pathology. If we're going to cultivate positive emotions, this means that we need to cultivate not an erroneous understanding of reality, not a distorted understanding of reality, but a clear, accurate understanding of reality. This clear, accurate understanding can't just be a kind of theoretical thing. This is kind of important. It's easy having maybe read a book or listened to a lecture or two about Buddhist philosophy or about physics or about calculative science to convince ourselves that it really is true that we live in a world that is completely interdependent, in which everything is causally conditioned, and in which everything produces innumerable effects, where parts are dependent on their wholes, wholes dependent on their parts, where things depend for their identity on conceptual imputation and the green grass grows all around all around. We're able to mouth these words, we're able to say them. We're able to engage theoretically and analytically with reality that way.

Maybe we are even able reflectively to say, damn, when I was angry yesterday that's because I didn't make sense of this. I didn't understand this kind of interdependence and I projected a kind of special importance to something that I shouldn't have done. Or to say, I really don't need that. I'm really reifying it in a way that it's not necessary.

That kind of theoretical engagement—that kind of abstract engagement—is not enough to constitute an antidote to real emotional pathology. It's really just an addition of insight to injury. If we're going to cultivate an antidote to these habits, what we need to do is to cultivate clear, cognitive habits, that is instinctive, spontaneous responses to things as interdependent, as causally dependent, as part whole dependent, as dependent upon imputation. It's that instinctive, innate, spontaneous cognitive habit that can be so difficult to accomplish, so difficult to cultivate, and that's why it requires work. That's why the notion of karuna, of compassion, is so important. What karuna does is give us that commitment, that altruistic aspiration to act, and an important part of the action is an action of deep self-cultivation and the development of different spontaneous ways of taking up with the world than those that animate most of our ordinary ways of taking up with the world.

The use of moral imagination is important because we need to be able, for instance, when responding to another, to understand that their interests are, in a deep sense, just like our interests. That their pain is in a deep sense just like our pain, and to take their pain as a motivation to act for alleviation, just as we take our own pain as a motivation to act for alleviation, to take another person's need as a motivation to act to alleviate it, just as we take our need as a motivation. That requires the kind of moral imagination that projects us into that person's perspective.

It requires habituation, it requires practice, it requires doing this again and again. Note the echoes of David Hume here. The idea that it's our imagination and convention and habits, childhood upbringing and re-imagining that enable us to extend the narrow emotions, the emotions that obey that inverse square law into real emotions like compassion and real emotions like justice. It's no accident that the Dalai Lama has studied Hume as well as Śāntideva.

The Dalai Lama argues that this kind of cultivation of compassion comes in two pieces. The first part he calls the cultivation of restraint, and the second he calls the cultivation of virtue, these are his terms. By "restraint" he means the holding back of instinctive negative reactions, actions of anger, actions of greed, actions motivated by carelessness, and so forth. By "virtue," he means a development of the positive commitment to do benefit, and he sees these as related to one another, the first as the prerequisite for the second. Why is restraint so important and how should we cultivate it?

The Dalai Lama argues that restraint is actually what cuts off the roots of suffering because remember, from a Buddhist perspective we think of suffering very much as a positive phenomenon. It's attraction and aversion conditioned by ignorance, and ignorance itself is a positive thing, not the absence of knowledge, but the superimposition of a mistaken understanding on reality.

What restraint does is to cut off those roots. Restraint, this ability to stop the anger, to stop the greed before it really moves into prominence in our cognitive lives, has to be cultivated, not just by telling myself I'm not going to get angry, I'm not going to get angry, I'm not going to get angry. Or I'm not going to act on greed. I'm not going to act on greed. I'm not going to act on greed, but by the reflection on causes, and of course remember, we saw this same kind of reflection recommended to us by Marcus Aurelius and by Seneca. Think about what gave rise to the other person's actions. Think about that and you will no longer be angry. People aren't responsible for their own stupidity. People aren't always even responsible for their own greed or their own thoughtlessness.

Those emotions, those tendencies were built into them through causes and conditions as well. As Śāntideva says, I don't get angry at a stick when it beats me, so why should I get angry at the intention that motivates the stick that itself is generated by antecedent causes and conditions?

If we reflect on causes, if we reflect on what actually gives rise to our suffering, then it goes down a little bit. Secondly the Dalai Lama urges, we need to reflect on impermanence. We need to reflect on the fact that these things that we want so badly are going to disappear and dissolve at some point, they're not all that permanent, they're not that important. These things that are causing us the experience of suffering right now, themselves are impermanent as well, and that our own emotions, our own mental states, those are impermanent too. We don't need to care about them so much. We can let them go. We can watch them proceed one after the other just like everything in the universe proceeds, one after the other, rising, enduring for a moment and passing away.

Finally, by reflection on selflessness, by reflecting on the fact that we ourselves are not substantial entities that are disconnected from and distinct from everything else in the world, that might seem like an obvious point but it's not an obvious point. It's not an obvious point for the following reason: Our ordinary cognitive habit, our ordinary way of taking up with the world is to think of ourselves as subjects, everything else is object. The first person pronoun encodes that. There's I and everything else. When we do that we think of everything else in relation to ourselves. There's me and my friends and my enemies. There's me and my car and the cars that aren't mine. There's me and the stuff that I care about and the stuff that I don't care about. Everything in the world becomes experienced instinctively, not reflectively instinctively in terms of its relation to me, the subject. But what's wrong with that? What's wrong with that you might ask? After all I am the person experiencing all of that. There is of course something deeply wrong with that because that way of taking up with the world, however natural it is, reflects the nature of reality as determined by a bizarre, polar coordinate system with me at the center and everything else arrayed in terms of its relationships to me.

To think that reality is really like that, I have to really think that I am pretty damn special. The problem of course is that everybody thinks that way, and there's where conflict comes from. If we're each the center of the universe and the center of the universe can only be in one place, conflict naturally arises. By reflecting on selflessness, by reflecting on the fact that the universe does not revolve around us as we saw in the book of Job, we are able to take our own importance less seriously. I'm not right here and everything else there. From another standpoint I'm over there and I'm just one passing phenomenon among many passing phenomena.

We see in this kind of method for cultivating this strength, this method for undermining the afflictive or the pathological emotions, the Dalai Lama is offering kinds of remedies, recommendations that have these Buddhist roots because they've got these roots in the understanding of selflessness, impermanence, and causal interdependence. But they also have very much Stoic roots. Roots that in the understanding that what we can control is what's inside us, our emotional reactions. Also the Stoic idea that really is understanding reality rationally that enables us to bring our emotions under control, an idea that we saw developed not only in stoicism but also in Buddhist moral theory in the hands of Śāntideva in *How to Lead an Awakened Life*; so much for restraint.

Why isn't restraint enough? Why do we need to move beyond it to positive virtue? The Dalai Lama argues that we need to move beyond it to positive virtue because while restraint keeps us from doing bad things, it doesn't by itself motivate us to do the things that are necessary for our own happiness or for the happiness of others. To do that, we need to cultivate generosity, the willingness to detach ourselves from our possessions and to give, because others need things from us. Generosity comprises not only material generosity, giving of physical gifts, but the giving of our time, the giving of our attention, the giving of our concern, the giving of our knowledge, the willingness to be beneficial, and this is so important because we live together and we benefit together and if others don't benefit from us, we don't benefit from those interactions.

Virtue requires patience, and as we saw in our discussion of Śāntideva's *Bodhicāryāvatāra* that comprises not only patience with others—which actually isn't that difficult to cultivate once you practice—but patience with oneself, noticing that the moral perfection that we come to demand of ourselves when we adopt this understanding of the nature of our lives isn't acquired in a moment. That kind of moral development requires time, it requires work, it requires meditative practice, it requires accustoming ourselves to certain ways of thinking, and that means that we need to be patient with ourselves as well as patient with others.

The virtue the Dalai Lama emphasizes requires attentive concern. Not just ideally thinking, yeah it's really important to me that other people be happy. Not just thinking, yes I want to make sure that my kids go to good schools and that other people's kids go to good schools too. Not just concern that it's a bad thing that people are suffering in that place, whether it's Darfur or Chad or Haiti or wherever, but actually attentive concern. And attentive concern involves two different dimensions. One is the dimension of attentiveness and the other is the dimension of concern. The dimension of attentiveness commits ourselves to really understanding the nature of the problem, to thinking about it, to thinking about what's going wrong and what would be necessary to rectify it. Concern means actually being committed to do it. Not just saying, oh it's so sad that those children are suffering, please turn off the TV, I can't take anymore. But rather, an actual commitment to do something, that's part of the root of virtue in this sense.

Mindfulness: Mindfulness in the sense that we need to be able to pay attention to our own emotional states, to our own reactions, to our own motivations, moment-to-moment in order to cultivate the virtuous ones instead of the non virtuous ones.

Finally we come to discernment and compassion. I treat these two together as does the Dalai Lama. Discernment is necessary because we need to really understand in any particular situation what the details are in order to act. What are the causes, what are the conditions, what are the affects, what kinds of mental habits are imputing the kinds of characteristics that are causing difficulties here?

What are the whole networks and what are their parts that are important? Finally compassion: What is compassion? Compassion here, as I keep emphasizing, is not an emotion. It's not a feeling of caring about others. Compassion in the sense of *karunā* is an altruistic commitment to act, an emotion that just says I feel so awful I wish somebody would do something is not compassion. It's what the Dalai Lama likes to call sloppy sympathy. That doesn't get us anywhere. All it does is compound somebody else's suffering with your own, better not to even notice.

Compassion is this commitment to actually doing something. For the compassion to be genuine, for the compassion to be efficacious, the compassion has to rest on discernment because to be committed to doing something, and for that something to make a difference, you'd better be committed to doing the right thing. That's why compassion isn't just "I've got to do something," but compassion rests in a commitment to develop a deep, analytical understanding of suffering in order to alleviate it. That means in each situation a deep, analytical understanding of the nature of suffering in that situation in order to alleviate it.

Compassion in this sense is not just abstract understanding, and not just abstract desire. The union of compassion and discernment is a union of moral perceptual skills where when we see a situation we see the sources of suffering, we see the possibilities for happiness, and the interpersonal skills that allow us to see what kinds of interventions will be most useful and commit us to those kinds of interventions.

The Dalai Lama emphasizes that this kind of compassion, if we really cultivate this altruistic attitude, entails a kind of Gandhian universal responsibility, a responsibility for the welfare of all. Why is that? What could a limitation on compassion be? What could it be for me to be compassionate for these people but not for those? That could only originate in a pathological distinction between say my friends and my enemies, back to that polar coordinate system. That's then not genuine compassion. Whatever I feel for these people becomes then a kind of pathological attraction or a pathological attachment. What I feel towards these people is a pathological anger or detachment.

Compassion has to be rooted in the de-centering of the individual. For that reason, distinctions between individuals become impossible as objects of compassion. This is what generates universal responsibility and an unlimited scope of compassion. That's an idea that we saw in Śāntideva. But *karuṇā*, compassion, requires the resolution that I be the source of benefit for all sentient beings. That's what universal responsibility is. That's why what we're seeing here is a modern version of the bodhisattva path.

While the Dalai Lama might be a modernist in many ways, and we've seen all of those ways, the reliance on science, the reliance on a very modern conception of the nature of happiness, and a modern understanding of the nature of suffering, it all comes back to the bodhisattva path. It's the altruistic resolution to act in every way that I can for the benefit of all sentient beings as the only kind of state that could possibly make my life worthwhile. And that's not just an affective state, not just an emotional state, and it's not even just conative state, not just a state of desire but it's an affective state, a conative state, and a rational understanding of circumstances coupled with a resolution to be a source of happiness and not a source of suffering. It's a superlative moral standard. A moral standard that's as superlative as that of Gandhi's, even if it's a little bit more modernist in its field.

But there is a moral standard that connects us as moral agents to a universal community, and in this way it harmonizes so beautifully with so many of the positions we've seen. It has the same kind of universality of commitment that we saw in the Gītā, the same kind of universal context that we saw valorized by the Stoics. While we're seeing an enormous modernism in the content, the specific content of the recommendation of the Dalai Lama for a meaningful life, this recommendation for a meaningful life based on compassion is also deeply traditional and are rooted in very ancient traditions but animate his way of thinking and show us how the traditional can enter modernity.

What is a modern Buddhist view of the meaning of life? A meaningful life is a life that is lived in recognition of truth, of the fundamental nature of reality. This echoes ideas we've seen from as far back as the *Bhagavad-Gīta*, but also in post modernists like Nietzsche who urges us to focus on the truth and live in the way that has fidelity to it.

It's a life that involves a realization that we are fundamentally members of vast universal social totalities. That way again we remember the Gīta, but we also remember Marcus Aurelius who asks us, what are you? You're a family member, you're a citizen, you're somebody who's a member of a large universe, and of course Gandhi.

This is a view of a meaningful life that demands of us, if we're going to live meaningfully, very deep cognitive, very deep emotional transformation. This does not allow us to remain content with our ordinary, everyday instinctive consciousness but calls upon us to deep personal transformation. It forces us to attend to the mundane circumstances around us in order to be effective just as Mill or Hume or Aristotle would recommend.

But also to rise above attachment to the mundane as Tolstoy would ask us to do or Gandhi. This is what makes it modern and traditional. It also reminds us that a meaningful life is, in the end, a life that's genuinely happy. It's a life that's led in the context of a genuinely happy community. Here we find our echoes of Aristotle and Hume but reflected through this Buddhist context.

So in the Dalai Lama we have this remarkably cosmopolitan synthesis of so many of the ideas that we've been examining throughout this course. Next time we'll try to do some serious summing up.

So, What Is the Meaning of Life?
Lecture 36

Often, one is led to find superficial similarities and to overemphasize those and, therefore, to lose a lot of the texture and detail that's bequeathed to us by the textual traditions that we've been examining.

We've encountered a great deal of diversity in this course, but we can still point to certain recurrent themes. For example, almost every position we've considered has emphasized the importance of a connection between our own lives and some larger context, of temporality, of some ideal of human perfection, and of spontaneity. In conjunction with spontaneity, we've seen an emphasis on freedom. We've also seen the need to understand the nature of the world we live in and the nature of our own lives in order to live an authentic life. In this lecture, we examine each of these themes to see what general conclusions we might draw.

The larger context required for a meaningful life has sometimes been conceived as a universal, divine, or cosmic context, as in the Bhagavad-Gītā, the book of Job, and the Stoics. For the Daoists, this larger context is similar but more impersonal; it's the context of the *dao*, the way of things. Sometimes, this context is a bit more narrow—a global context or a natural one. Lame Deer, for instance, emphasized that the context of our lives that matters most is that of nature, and the Dalai Lama, along with Aristotle, Confucius, and others, emphasizes a social context. In each case, the key to finding meaning in our lives is to first identify the larger context in which our small lives make sense, then to understand how we can make our lives meaningful by connecting them to that context.

With regard to temporality, the Stoics emphasized the eternality of the universe and the fact that the period of our existence is brief and bounded by infinite gulfs of our absence. Buddhism also emphasizes a constant awareness of impermanence, the beauty of impermanence, and the urgency that impermanence gives to our lives. Tolstoy, Lame Deer, and Nietzsche pick up on the theme of mindfulness of death: At each moment in our lives, we need to be aware of our own mortality and finitude.

In the texts we've examined, we've often seen the question of the meaning of life addressed in terms of an account of human perfection. Aristotle offered us an ideal of the perfect human life in the concept of *eudaimonea*, flourishing, and tells us that this ideal can be achieved through a life of activity in accordance with virtue, through moral strength and practical wisdom, and through friendship. The Daoists and Zen Buddhists give us the sage as the ideal of perfection, one who pays attention to the empty spaces and who lives spontaneously, effortlessly. Śāntideva and the

This spontaneity is motivated by the idea that our actions and values don't need to be brought together artificially.

Dalai Lama extend this account of perfection to encompass the cultivation of a certain kind of compassion, a commitment to altruistic action on behalf of others. For Kant and Mill, human life is focused on reason, discourse, and participation in liberal democratic societies. That ideal was challenged by Nietzsche, who emphasized that what makes our lives beautiful is our artistry and spontaneity, our ability to re-evaluate the values we're taught and lead our lives in harmony with values we ourselves create.

Many of the philosophers and theologians we've examined have urged us to cultivate spontaneity in our lives. This spontaneity is motivated by the idea that our actions and values don't need to be brought together artificially. For Aristotle and Confucius, the model here is that of the artist, one who practices endlessly to achieve a second nature. For Daoism and Zen, the emphasis is on the need to pare away the artificial second nature and return to naturalness. Ultimately, Lame Deer tells us that we need to understand that we are fundamentally part of the biological world, a world of circles rather than squares.

For the thinkers we've explored, a meaningful life necessarily entails freedom. The Gītā emphasized the fact that freedom emerges from discipline, while the Daoists urged us to free ourselves from social standards. Hume and Kant emphasized the need to attain freedom from authority, an idea that Mill extended to an insistence on absolute freedom of thought. Nietzsche was concerned with freedom from philosophical ideas and from an intellectual tradition that makes creativity impossible. Gandhi emphasized self-mastery similar to that in the Gītā, the kind of discipline that frees us from consumerism and other external constraints.

The answer to our original question is deeply complex and conflicted; it requires us to cultivate an awareness of reality in all its complexity and adversity, to understand that our lives are finite, and to develop a commitment to achieving individual excellence and to creating meaning in the lives of others. Perhaps the first step in finding meaning is to ask the question, then to engage, as we have done in this course, with the wide diversity of answers that have been given throughout history and around the world. ∎

Study Questions

1. What are the major dimensions along which accounts of the meaning of life differ from one another? How would one go about choosing one approach over another?

2. What common insights survive these differences? Why do these ideas transcend the different approaches? Are they consistent with one another?

So, What Is the Meaning of Life?
Lecture 36—Transcript

Well here we are together for the last time in this series of lectures. This is the lecture in which we would hope to be able to tie up all the loose ends, draw everything together and come to a wonderful, grand conclusion regarding the nature of the meaning of life.

That might be a bit much to hope for though. While it's tempting to try to draw everything that we've said together over this course into one, big, happy unified picture, showing how everybody somehow agrees and each theory is somehow like the others, that might be a nice dream but it would really be fallacious.

That is because perhaps more than anything else we've encountered a great deal of diversity. True, there are analogies but we must pay attention to the diversity. Often one is led to find superficial similarities and to over emphasize those and therefore to lose a lot of the texture and detail that's bequeathed to us by the textual traditions that we've been examining.

For instance, we might be tempted to say, ah, the Gīta, Buddhism, they both come out of India and they both arise in India at roughly the same kind of era. So they must somehow agree. There must be some common Indian identity. That would be wrong. Even though they're both concerned in some sense with release, or with salvation, or with finding a meaning of life, they're both concerned with big questions, in the context of the Gīta we're talking about a union with a transcendent, deified reality. That's what we're talking about, and we're talking about cultivating a particular kind of discipline conditioned by devotion.

With Buddhism that's not what we're doing. With Buddhism we're talking about interdependence, we're talking about selflessness. The Gīta emphasizes the importance of the self, the reality of the self, the permanence of the self, the union of the self that the God had.

Buddhism emphasizes that the self is a losery and that interdependence is all that we find. We can't run these things together no matter how much we might be tempted to do. We might be tempted to do that same thing with the book of Job, with the Stoics, and with the *Bodhicāryāvatāra* of Śāntideva. After all, all of them emphasize patience. All of them emphasize the pervasiveness of suffering in the world and the need for us, to in some sense, insulate ourselves from that suffering and find meaning of life in that context.

But they're not doing the same thing. The book of Job, after all is theistic. The Stoics are theistic too but the god of Job and the rational god Zeus are as different as night and day. The *Bodhicāryāvatāra* comes out of the Buddhist tradition, which is resolutely atheistic. Some of these, like the book of Job and the Stoics are asking us to find meaning in something totally transcendent. Where the *Bodhicāryāvatāra* is really counseling us to focus on what's eminent.

Similarly we might be tempted to say, ahh, Aristotle, Confucius, The Laozi, all of them are emphasizing the importance of effortlessness, of virtuosity in our lives and the importance of cultivating this effortless glide through life. They're not doing the same thing either. Aristotle and Confucius are really emphasizing the importance of social cultivation, of our social roles and role of society in finishing us.

Whereas the Laozi emphasize the idea that society in fact ruins us and that we need to get out of that kind of social construction in order to find the meaning of our lives. Moreover, we've been looking at classical traditions, modern traditions, and post-modern traditions and these offer very different perspectives. The classical traditions emphasize the collective. They emphasized the importance of particular textual traditions and views. They emphasize transcendence.

The modern tradition emphasized the sovereignty of the individual, the importance of science, the foundational role of the individual in the political, the epistemic and the social realms.

When we returned to post-modernism we again saw that rejected, but not with a re-embrace of the classical but with the rejection of systematisity itself, with the rejection of the importance of the individual, with the rejection of the idea that knowledge is foundational. We've seen all of these different views; what are we going to do with them at this point in order to help us answer the question that motivated this entire course: What is the meaning of life?

First let's note that despite all of this diversity there are certain important recurrent themes and appreciating those themes can be extraordinarily helpful. Almost every text has been examined, almost every position we've considered has emphasized the importance of a connection between our own lives and some larger context. That's not surprising since as we saw in our very first lecture the very idea of meaning carries with it the relationship of something small, finite, and determinate, something outside of itself.

Almost every position that we've examined has emphasized the importance of temporality, of focusing on time, on impermanence and on what's permanent. That's not surprising then either considering what raises the question in the first place. How is it that something that comes up and is cut down so quickly, as we say in the book of Job, has any meaning at all?

Each of these positions that we've examined involves consideration of some ideal of human perfection. That's something we might not have expected, because we might have thought that it's our own imperfection that poses the problem. One of the things that we've seen over these lectures is that if we can imagine what a perfect life would be, we can begin to imagine what the trajectory of our lives might be towards that goal.

Finally, we've noticed that almost every text we've examined, almost every position we've considered, has emphasized the importance of some kind of spontaneity, an effortlessness, as I put it repeatedly, a virtuosity in our lives, some way of getting our actions to conform naturally to our values without calculation. That may have been one of the surprises in this course.

In conjunction with spontaneity we've seen an emphasis on a certain kind of freedom even though that freedom had been differently conceived at different points in this course, freedom from external constraint versus political freedom for instance. Freedom has still played an important role in thinking about the meaning of life in almost every tradition we've examined.

We've emphasized the need in leading a meaningful life to face up to reality, to really understand the nature of the world that we live in, and the nature of our own lives and the need to do that in order to live an authentic life, a life of which we are the authors and a life that we can reflectively endorse.

Let's try to examine each of these themes in a little more detail to see what kind of general conclusions we might draw despite the diversity. First, we talked about the need to live in a larger context, and that's something we can certainly take away. Sometimes that context is conceived as universal, divine, or cosmic. We've seen that view articulated in the *Bhagavad-Gīta* where the context is the context of the entire universe.

Also in the book of Job where the context is also in a certain sense, universal, where that universality is conditioned by the creation of a particular divinity. The Stoics also emphasized a very universal context, a context again conditioned by a divinity. Curiously the Daoists also give us this very large context, but it's a much more impersonal context. For the Daoist, remember the context is the great Dao, the way of things, the nature of things, and that our lives have to be lived in that context, and so the Dao of our own lives needs to be brought into harmony with the great Dao, the way that the universe works.

Sometimes on the other hand, the context is a bit more narrow, a global context or a natural context. Lame Deer, for instance, really emphasized that the context of our lives that matters most is the context of nature. The context in which we figure is biological animals among other animals. The Dalai Lama emphasizes that the context of our lives is a social context, a context lived in which our primary responsibilities and our primary joys are social joys and that's a context that we saw Aristotle, Confucius, and indeed most early modern philosophers emphasize as well.

In each of these views, meaning emerges from contextuality, but notice again the contexts and vary and the contexts can be different. In each case, the key to finding the meaning in our lives is to first identify the context in which our lives make sense, and then to understand how we can make our small lives meaningful by connecting them to something much larger.

There's also a temporal context to life of course. The Stoics we saw emphasized the vastness of the universe that we live in, the eternality of the universe, the fact that it goes back to beginningless time, continues to be an endless future, and we are merely a blip in all of that. The time of the universe in which we exist is so tiny and bounded by infinite gulfs of our absence. That effemorality is what generates the problem of the meaning of life from a Stoic perspective. But notice that it also generates the answer, because part of the answer for the Stoics is that the reason that our lives are so valuable and that they're so meaningful is, A, that they are part of something so vast—such a vast history—but B, that they're so rare, they're so precious, our moments are so few and so they need to be valued all the more.

The same idea we saw developed in Buddhism, a constant awareness of impermanence and an awareness of the beauty of impermanence, and the urgency that impermanence gives to our lives. Impermanence can cause us anxiety and the fear of meaninglessness as when we push death to the background and allow it to condition our lives without being confronted. When we seriously confront our own impermanence and appreciate it, it gives a kind of urgency, beauty and meaning to our lives.

Tolstoy and Lame Deer, each in very different ways, pick up on this theme, the importance of mindfulness of death. The importance in each moment of our lives to be aware of our own mortality and our own finitude, and that this need not be something depressing. This isn't a kind of awareness of a catastrophe of something that's wrong with our lives, but an awareness of the finitude and context that means that every moment of our lives is important. That the novel that we're enacting in Nietzsche's terms is a novel that has an end, and we need to make sure that the structure of the entire life is one that we could look back at and say, yes, that was a work of art worth creating.

So often we've seen the question of the meaning of life addressed in the texts that we've examined in terms of an account of human perfection, a kind of larger sense of who we are. That began in the Gītā because the Gītā gave us an idea of perfection as involving a very deep kind of union of our own lives, our own consciousness, and our own purpose with a fully divine cosmos.

In the Gītā we saw this idea that the cosmos itself is permeated by meaning. It's permeated by significance. It's already fundamentally divine. That, if we can lead a life that is disciplined by concern for action, by knowledge and understanding of the nature of the world around us, and especially by devotion, devotion to the whole and a commitment of our lives to the benefit of the whole and to our own particular role and duty, that becomes a life of human perfection to the degree that we can strive for that ideal, we make our lives meaningful.

Aristotle again offered us an ideal of the perfect human life. When Aristotle characterizes eudemonia, or happiness, as the highest good, and then characterizes happiness as a life of activity in accordance with virtue, he characterizes a life in which we've cultivated a manifold of human virtues—all social virtues—in which we've cultivated a certain kind of moral strength, a certain kind of practical wisdom in which we have got a certain kind of relationship to those around us, deep friendships, and a membership in a culture that itself is valuable.

This for Aristotle is the perfect life, the happy life, the life of human flourishing. Again it's a life that we can attain or that we can at least aspire to obtaining an approximate. We can imagine a trajectory of our lives towards Aristotelian flourishing as one account of a life lived meaningfully.

Confucius too emphasizes this kind of socialized notion of perfection, a life in which we cultivate our humanity, in which we cultivate our propriety, in which we cultivate our virtue, in which we cultivate our sense of our place in the world, of our place in the universe. That life of the Confucian gentleman—or gentlewoman if we want to update Confucius—is again a life to which we can aspire, a life that we can understand and indeed a life that in a certain sense we can all admire, even if we don't accept all of the details. That again provides a trajectory that we can imagine our lives taking towards a certain kind of perfection and a trajectory that can give point and meaning to our lives.

The Daoists and the Zen Buddhists offered us another ideal of human perfection. The Daoist sage, the sage who was like water, not like the rock, the sage who is soft, the sage who pays attention to the empty spaces, not what's in the foreground and who lives completely spontaneously, effortlessly and who lives his life in the way one might cook a small fish, in a very delicate way, in a way that does not push too hard.

That's an ideal of perfection, maybe a more complex and a deeper and more aestheticized ideal, but again, an ideal of spontaneous life that we saw taken up very much in Zen Buddhism—Buddhism moves to China and engages with Daoism and again gives us a model of a trajectory that we could imagine our lives taking and the trajectory that could give a very different kind of meaning to our lives.

Śāntideva and *Bodhicāryāvatāra, How to Lead an Awakened life,* and the Dalai Lama who is such a close student of Śāntideva extend this account of perfection. They understand perfection in terms of the cultivation of a certain kind of compassion. Where again we understood this compassion as an altruistic commitment to action on behalf of others, action to relieve suffering, and his Holiness the Dalai Lama emphasized that this kind of compassion naturally extends to a universal concern and a universal responsibility.

On this view, again, we have an ideal of human perfection. The ideal of the bodhisattva, the idea of being committed to gaining awakening for the sake of all sentient beings, and who have cultivated this engaged kind of compassion that drives and motivates actions for the benefit of all.

Kant and Mill offered us an understanding of what human life is about. It's about reason, it's about knowledge, it's about discourse, it's about participating in liberal democratic societies in which we trade arguments, we trade reason, we freely express ourselves, we develop our individuality, we develop our creativity, we develop our ideas, we dare to know, and we express ourselves in this kind of freedom. That's another rich sense of human perfection, the perfection of the free citizen engaging in public discourse in an open society. We can understand that ideal. That's an ideal that many of us share, and so we can begin to see that our lives might be meaningful to the extent that they approximate that ideal. That ideal of course was challenged by Nietzsche who argued that this emphasis on reason is too narrow and focuses only on one and that is a highly abstract part of what it is to be human.

Nietzsche emphasized that what makes our lives beautiful, what makes our lives creative, is our artistry, our spontaneity, our ability to make something special out of our lives, to treat our lives as art or literature, to be courageous, to be authentic, to not accept the values of others even if those values are values that look well entrenched, like values of freedom, democracy, goodness; but to create our own values, to re-evaluate all values and to lead our lives in a way that is in harmony with values that we ourselves create, to be creative in our own existence. You can understand how that's another vision of human perfection, a trajectory towards which we might imagine our lives taking.

Lame Deer offers yet another kind of understanding of a perfect life. It's a life led in harmony with nature. It's not the life of action and service that the Dalai Lama suggests, that Gandhi suggests. These are lives of superhuman commitment to others. Lame Deer instead says, focus on your nature and on your relationship to the rest of nature. Live harmoniously with it. Live reflectively. Live thoughtfully. Don't push so hard. In that sense we have yet another vision of human perfection. Visions of human perfection can be part of what guides us to finding meaning in our lives.

Spontaneity: So many of the philosophers and theologians we've examined have thought hard about spontaneity and have urged that spontaneity is a feature of our lives we need to cultivate, that the spontaneous life is a life lived best, the life is not calculated, the life where we don't have to deliberate about each action we perform, the life in which we're not constantly offering justifications but acting naturally. That's important for several reasons.

One, it's a life of grace. Secondly, it's not just the aesthetic grace of a spontaneous life, it's the idea that our actions and our deepest values, the values that saturate us and make us who we are in complete harmony and don't need to be artificially brought together. Aristotle and Confucius we saw, each emphasized the need to work hard to cultivate spontaneity. The model here is the model of the artist, the performer who needs to practice, practice, practice. Developed skills, developed skills as Confucius put it—

cut, ground, polished—in order to achieve a second nature. A nature given to us by society and a nature which we then inhabit with complete spontaneity after arduous training and cultivation.

The Daoists share with Aristotle and Confucius this emphasis on the meaningful life as the virtuoso life, the totally spontaneous life. But they reject the entire idea of a second nature. They argue that what happens when we are socialized and learn all of the Confucian virtues, or we might imagine learning all of the Aristotelian virtues, we end up cultivating a way of being, but it's not a genuinely-spontaneous way of being from a Daoist perspective. It's an artificial, socialized way of being, that second nature isn't nature at all. The Daoists emphasized the need we have to pair off that artificial second nature and to return to our first nature which is in harmony with the nature of the universe.

This idea of a return to naturalness is inherited by Zen and stirred together with Buddhist ideas out of India. In Zen we found the emphasis on a return to naturalness that was based not on some sense of a great Dao or a particular way the universe is, but rather a focus on what's internal to us, on the nature of our own mind and the nature of our own experience, because what is urged in Zen is the spontaneity that emerges from immediate open experience, from presence, from living in perception instead of living through conceptuality, from acting spontaneously in response to what we perceive and to what we experience, not to the calculations that come afterwards.

In Zen we saw this enriched with a kind of deeply aesthetic approach to life, an account of spontaneity that emphasizes the beauty of life around us and the beauty of the spontaneous life.

Hume, though you might not think of Hume as somebody who's so involved in spontaneity, emphasizes a certain kind of spontaneity as well. Remember it was Hume who emphasized that it's our passions and our emotions that mediate so much of our lives and so much of our values. Hume is urging us not to govern our passions and emotions with reason, but rather to allow a kind of natural expression, cultivation, and extension of our passions in order to make us the kind of people we would like to be, that suppressing our passions suppresses our humanity.

Nietzsche follows Hume very much in this dethroning of reason and emphasis on our passionate, emotional, biological nature, and of course that intuition is perhaps expressed the deepest way by John Lame Deer and his emphasis that what we really need to do as human beings is to get away from the modernist notion that we're abstract rational beings who stand against a natural world, and to understand the fact that we are fundamentally biological, that we don't interact with the natural world, that we are part of the natural world. And that involves a kind of return to a life of circles rather than a life of squares, a life of continuity rather than a life of pausing, judging and prescribing, hence a different kind of spontaneity.

Freedom is so important as we think about the nature of a meaningful life. A meaningful life is a life that's not lived under constraint, that's not lived in prison. The Daoists we saw urge the need to free ourselves from social standards. The Gītā emphasized the fact that freedom emerges from discipline and the very reason for adopting the discipline to yogas in the Gītā isn't to constrain us but to free us from external constraint, from the constraint of the sensory, from the constraint of the immediate, from the constraint of the trivial.

Hume and Kant, each in their own ways emphasized in the context of the enlightenment, the need to attain freedom from authority, especially religious authority but also political authority. The meaningful life was the life of individual liberty. In Mill we saw the dramatic extension of this Kantian idea in the establishment of freedom, liberty, and an absolute kind of freedom of thought and political freedom as the absolute condition of the meaningful life and the very powerful articulation of that in terms of the harm principle.

Nietzsche was certainly critical of almost everything happening in modernity including almost all of the central ideas that Kant and Mill are defending. But Nietzsche is not critical of the idea of freedom, rather he reconceives it slightly. Nietzsche is worried, not so much about freedom from individual authority, the authority of the pastor, the authority of the king, the authority of the dictator, but rather the freedom from philosophical ideas, idols, or mummies as he calls them, the freedom from an intellectual tradition that makes it impossible for us to be creative in order to enable the genuine artistic creativity that could make a life meaningful.

Gandhi emphasizes self mastery, svaraj and insistence on the truth, but that self mastery is the self mastery of the Gītā, the kind of discipline that frees us from consumerism, that frees us from external constraint, that frees us from feeling that we need to obey another, and frees us to master ourselves and to obey ourselves. Lame Deer of course concurs with Gandhi in thinking that one of the most important things from which we need to free ourselves is consumerism, commodity fetishism, and this constant demand to acquire more things, to acquire more things thinking that that will bring us happiness.

Almost every account of the meaning of life that we've encountered has urged us to begin answering the question by thinking hard about the nature of reality and facing reality squarely. In the Four Nobel Truths, the Four Truths for those who would be noble as I prefer to call them, the Buddha asked us to face squarely the reality of universal suffering, the reality of impermanence, the reality of death, and the reality of the way that those are conditioned by confusion, attraction, and aversion, and that only by first understanding that reality could we begin to find liberation from suffering and move to something more meaningful.

Tolstoy echoes this emphasis on facing the reality of death and the reality of our impermanence. All of the Buddhist traditions emphasize as well understanding the reality of interdependence, the reality of impermanence, the details of interdependence, causal interdependence, part/whole interdependence, interdependence of conceptuality, gross impermanence, subtle impermanence, to really develop an analytical understanding because if we lead our lives in ignorance of the details of the reality in which we lead them, there's no way that we could ever make them meaningful.

Lame Deer of course emphasizes the need to understand our biological nature and to understand the symbolic nature of a natural world, to read those symbols, to attend to those symbols in order to live meaningfully.

Everybody we look at urges us to live authentically. For Kant and Mill that is to live in what we might call epistemic authenticity. There to know to really think hard, understand, identify with, and propagate the views that we take seriously, politically, morally, scientifically. Laozi, Dogen, and Nietzsche emphasize a different kind of dimension of authenticity. You might call it an aesthetic authenticity, to develop an understanding of what a truly beautiful life looks like, a life that's lived truly in harmony with the fundamental nature of reality and to lead that life.

We might say that there is a kind of answer to the question: What is the meaning of life? But it's not a single answer and it's not a simple answer. It's a deeply complex and deeply conflicted answer, an answer that requires us to integrate an understanding and an awareness of reality in all of its complexity and in all of its adversity, to understand the difficulties that the world poses for us, but also the ways in which each of those difficulties, each of those adversities, contains the seeds of our overcoming it.

We're called upon to lead our lives in a context. But it's a context that is at the same time cosmic, global, natural, and biological, and social, if all of these contexts condition who we are and what it is to lead a human life. We have to lead that life in a finite time. It's not something that we have all of eternity for. We lead a life that is bounded, and so if we're going to find meaning in that life, we can't wait, we can't postpone.

Finding that meaning is found in a commitment not only to our own individual excellence, but to making others excellent and to making other lives meaningful, and so to social service and that could only be understood by paying attention to our own roles in the social networks in which we figure, and a commitment to advancing understanding not only our own understanding of ourselves but the understanding globally that makes possible, meaning quite generally.

This requires us to achieve in some way, some how a kind of authentic virtuosity, the virtuosity that makes our lives effective, that makes it possible for us to say at the end of our lives when we finally are facing death that it was better that we were here, that we actually made a difference, and we made that difference happily, generously, spontaneously, creatively, and compassionately. I can't tell you how to make your life meaningful, but what we can say is that asking the question, what is the meaning of life, is a very good first step. A very good second step is to engage with the wide diversity of answers to that question that have been given throughout history and throughout the world's traditions. By engaging with that diversity and by engaging in constant conversation with others who ask that question, there's at least the possibility that we may come up with an answer.

I've really enjoyed the time that I've spent with you. I hope that you've enjoyed it as well, and I hope that it has been helpful to you. I hope that you'll read more. I hope that you'll pick up these texts, and I hope that you will continue to think about these questions. Perhaps someday we'll meet in person.

Glossary

ahimsa: Nonviolence, or refraining from harming others.

Analects, The: The collection of sayings and dialogues attributed to Kongfuzi (Confucius). It relies on a set of key philosophical ideas, including:

- *ren*: Humanity, warm-heartedness

- *li*: Ritual propriety, etiquette

- *de*: Virtue, integrity, moral rectitude

- *xiao*: Filial piety; respect for, and obedience to, one's parents, elders, and superiors

- *tian*: Heaven, or the order of the universe

- *wu-wei*: Inaction or spontaneous, effortless activity in contrast to studied, deliberate action

aretē: Virtue or excellence.

awarē: In Japanese Buddhist aesthetics, the particular beauty that derives from the impermanence of things, the beauty things have just before they fade.

being-time: The intimate union of existence and temporality; the fact that to exist is to be impermanent yet to have a past and a future to which one is essentially connected and the fact that human existence is always experienced in relation to past, present, and future.

bodhisattva: In Buddhism, one who has formed the altruistic aspiration to attain awakening for the benefit of all sentient beings.

Chaldeans (Book of Job): An ancient Near Eastern people who lived in Mesopotamia.

depersonalization: Abstraction from one's own personal interests or place in the world; taking a disinterested view of things.

dharma: A word with many meanings the root of which means "to hold." Meanings include duty, virtue, doctrine, entity, and reality, depending on context.

Epicurean: A school of Greek and Roman philosophy following the teachings of Epicurus (4th–3rd century B.C.E.). Central doctrines of the school were atomism, materialism, and an emphasis on the attainment of peace of mind through moderation and control of the emotions.

ēthikē/**ethos**: Behavior or conduct.

eudaimonea: Human flourishing, a good life, often translated as "happiness."

foundationalism: The doctrine that knowledge must rest on a basis. Examples of foundations of knowledge are perception and reason.

Jainism: An Indian religion in which nonviolence is the central value.

karunā: Compassion, the commitment to act to relieve the suffering of others.

kratē: Moral strength, the ability to stick to one's resolve in the face of temptation or fear.

Krishna: An Indian manifestation of divinity.

libertarianism: The belief that individuals should have the maximum personal liberty consistent with the liberty of others; resistance of the intrusion of the law into the private sphere.

metaphysics: The study of the fundamental nature of reality.

neo-Vedānta: A late 19th- and early 20th-century philosophical movement in India grounded in a revival and reinterpretation of the ancient Indian texts collectively called the *Vedas*. Prominent neo-Vedānta philosophers included Ramakrishna, Swami Vivekananda, and Sri Aurobindo.

phenomenology: Inner experience, or the theory of inner experience.

phronesis: Practical wisdom, the ability to deliberate wisely about how to accomplish one's goals.

postmodernity: An ideological outlook that rejects the fundamental tenets of European modernism—the unity of the subject, the fact that knowledge constitutes a unified system that rests on sure foundations, the conviction that civilization is progressive—in favor of a conviction that subjectivity is variable and often fragmented, a suspicion of unified systems and a conviction that knowledge is socially constructed and fluid, and a suspicion of a single narrative of human progress. The term also refers to the social conditions that reflect this view, namely, conditions in which fundamental claims are contested, societies are pluralistic, and values do not sustain a unified view of knowledge or progress.

Sabeans (Book of Job): An ancient Near Eastern tribe that lived near present-day Yemen.

Samaj **movements**: The Arya and Brahmo Samajs (*Samaj* means "society"); two prominent modernist religious reform movements that swept India in the late 19th and early 20th centuries. Both emphasized a return to classical Indian texts and ideas but also the abandonment of ritual, the rejection of caste, and an embrace of modernity and Indian nationalism.

Sanskrit: The language of classical Indian scholarship, as opposed to Prakrits, classical vernacular languages.

Sapere Aude!: Kant's motto of enlightenment: "Dare to know!"

satyāgraha: A Gandhian term: holding on to, or insisting on, the truth. A refusal to act in accordance with any principle one does not endorse and a commitment to principled action and honesty.

Sheol (Book of Job): The underworld, the place where the dead reside in the ancient Hebrew tradition.

śramana: A wandering ascetic of ancient India.

svadharma: One's own particular duty or role in life, often in India tied to caste.

swadeshi: Literally, one's own country. Commitment to the value and practices of one's own country or culture, to self-reliance, and to consuming only what is produced locally.

swaraj: Self-rule. This can mean individual self-mastery or the self-government of a people or nation. For Gandhi, these two senses were deeply connected.

theophany: Revelation of the deity.

Transcendentalists: A group of American philosophers, poets, and writers who looked to Asia for inspiration and who were oriented toward mystical values and concerns that transcend the mundane world. Emerson, Thoreau, and Whitman were prominent Transcendentalists.

Utilitarianism: A moral theory according to which actions are right to the degree to which they promote happiness or pleasure and wrong to the degree that they promote unhappiness or pain.

yoga: Discipline or spiritual practice. The *Bhagavad-Gītā* enumerates three kinds of discipline, representing three aspects of life:

- *karma* yoga: The discipline of action, the pursuit of divinity through action

Glossary

- *jñāna* yoga: The discipline of knowledge, the pursuit of divinity through knowledge

- *bhakti* yoga: The discipline of devotion, the pursuit of divinity through devotional practice

Biographical Notes

Aristotle (384–322 B.C.E.): Aristotle was born in Stageira and moved to Athens in his youth, where he was a prominent aristocrat. He studied under Plato at the Academy. After Plato's death, he traveled in present-day Turkey, conducting scientific research. In 343 B.C.E., he was appointed tutor to Alexander the Great. In 335 B.C.E., he returned to Athens and established the Lyceum, where he taught for 12 years, probably his most philosophically creative period. He left Athens to avoid prosecution for impiety and died at age 62 in Chalcis. Aristotle, like Plato, wrote philosophical dialogues, but none of his original works survives; what we have instead are lecture notes from his students. He wrote and taught on virtually every academic subject, including the natural sciences, rhetoric, poetry, metaphysics, logic, ethics, and political philosophy. Aristotle was enormously influential in the development of Islamic philosophy and medieval European philosophy.

Chuang Tzu (Zhuangzi) (perhaps c. 370–c. 300 B.C.E.): There is no consensus regarding the existence of Chuang Tzu, who may have been created as a fictional author of the text that bears his name. This text, however, may be the work of multiple authors over several centuries. It is said that he left a minor government position for a life as a hermit philosopher and that he once turned down a prime ministership.

Confucius (Kongfuzi) (c. 551–479 B.C.E.): Confucius was born in the Chinese state of Lu (the present-day Shandong province of China) to a military family near the end of the Spring-Autumn period of Chinese history, a period that saw a great deal of warfare between small Chinese states. His father apparently died when Confucius was young, leaving the young boy and his concubine mother in poverty. Confucius clearly studied the Chinese classics with great success and spent most of his life as a low-level civil servant. He became famous as a teacher and spent much of his life traveling from state to state, teaching philosophy and politics. The texts by means of which we know Confucius's thought are records of his conversations and teachings preserved by his disciples.

His Holiness the Dalai Lama XIV, Tenzin Gyatso (b. 1935): The Dalai Lama lineage in Tibet is regarded by Tibetans as a reincarnate lineage: Each successive Dalai Lama is recognized as a rebirth of his predecessor, and all are regarded by Tibetans as emanations of Avalalokiteśvara, the Buddhist celestial bodhisattva of compassion. Dalai Lamas are, hence, regarded by Tibetans as physical manifestations of compassion in the world. The Dalai Lama has traditionally been both the spiritual and political leader of Tibet. The present Dalai Lama was born in a small village in Amdo, in far northeastern Tibet. When he was 3 years old, he was recognized by a search party as the rebirth of the 13th Dalai Lama and brought to Lhasa for enthronement and education. In 1949, the Army of the People's Republic of China entered Tibet, and despite his youth, the Dalai Lama assumed, at the age of 14, political leadership of Tibet. Shortly after this, he completed his monastic education and earned the highest academic degree conferred in Tibet, the *geshe lharampa* (a Ph.D. with highest honors). For 10 years, the Dalai Lama attempted to cooperate with the Chinese government in order to allow Chinese authority and modernization while preserving Tibetan cultural identity. But as Chinese repression grew more severe, Tibetan resistance increased. In 1959, the Tibetans rose up against Chinese occupation, and the Dalai Lama was forced to flee into exile in India, followed by several hundred thousand Tibetan refugees. In India, the Dalai Lama has led a government-in-exile and overseen the establishment of Tibetan schools, orphanages, hospitals, social services, monastic institutions, universities, and finally, a democratic Tibetan government, stepping aside as head of government. He has opened a long-running dialogue with scientists and has published dozens of books, ranging from highly technical books on Buddhist philosophy to popular guides to happiness. The Dalai Lama has taught or spoken in countries around the world, always promoting nonviolent conflict resolution, interfaith harmony, and a humanitarian social identity. In 1989, he was awarded the Nobel Prize for Peace.

Dōgen (1200–1253): Dōgen was the illegitimate son of a high-ranking Japanese courtier, who died when her son was 7 years old. Early in his life, Dōgen joined the great Tendai monastery at Mt. Hiei. But he was dissatisfied with Tendai philosophy, bothered by the problem of the need to seek awakening if all sentient beings are primordially awakened. He moved to a Zen temple in Japan, studying under the great Zen master Eisai until the latter's death. In 1223, Dōgen traveled to China to search for teachings that would resolve his remaining concerns. After visiting several monasteries, he encountered the Zen teacher Rujing, under whom he had his awakening experience. In 1228, Dōgen returned to Japan with the Sōtō Zen lineage inherited from Ruing; he taught at several important temples and wrote hundreds of essays, laying the philosophical foundations of Sōtō Zen in Japan. He settled near the end of his life at Eiheji, which became the headquarters of the Sōtō Zen lineage in Japan.

Epictetus (55–135 C.E.): Little is known of the life of Epictetus, who was born a slave. He lived the first part of his life in Rome but was exiled to Greece. He studied Stoic philosophy in his youth and, at some point, gained his freedom. He was a popular teacher and widely respected both as a Stoic philosopher and an orator. None of his writings, if ever there were any, survives. The fragments that constitute his corpus are, in fact, lecture notes.

Gandhi, Mohandas K. (1869–1948): Gandhi was born in Porbandar, then a small princely state, in the modern state of Gujarat. His father was *diwan* of that state. Gandhi's parents were both devout Hindus, but much of the surrounding community was Jain; hence, he grew up in a context of great piety and commitment to nonviolence. He was married at age 13. At age 18, he left India for London, where he studied law. While in England, he was active in the Vegetarian Society and came into contact with theosophists; thus, he developed a broader interest in world religions. Gandhi also studied liberal political theory and read Tolstoy and the American Transcendentalists. He returned to India in 1891 and, after some desultory practice, accepted a position in South Africa in 1893. In South Africa, Gandhi encountered firsthand the racial discrimination that pervaded the British Empire. Most famously, he was thrown off a train at Pietermaritzburg when he refused to vacate the first-class compartment for which he had a ticket. This event and others led Gandhi to lead massive nonviolent protests against discriminatory laws. In this context, he formulated his principle of *satyāgraha*—insistence on the truth and principled nonviolence as the only ways to challenge overwhelming repression. Gandhi returned to India in 1915, joined the Indian National Congress, and became active, first, in the congress's efforts to resist unjust laws and policies, then in the independence movement. Gandhi led this movement to Indian independence through careful cultivation of nonviolent resistance and refusal to comply with British imperial rule. He led numerous public protests and was jailed regularly but maintained his pacifism and tolerance. Gandhi was deeply opposed to the partition of India and deeply saddened by that eventuality and the violence that came in its wake. He was assassinated by a Hindu fundamentalist terrorist as he walked to prayers in 1948. Gandhi has been a major influence on such subsequent advocates of nonviolence and insistence on truth as the Reverend Dr. Martin Luther King, President Nelson Mandela of South Africa, and HH the Dalai Lama XIV.

Hume, David (1711–1776): David Hume was a philosophical prodigy and a central figure of the Scottish Enlightenment. He entered the University of Edinburgh when he was 12 years old, rejecting the study of law for philosophy. After a brief career in business, he traveled to La Flèche, where in conversation with Jesuit philosophers and with access to an excellent library, he wrote his *Treatise of Human Nature*, published when he was 26 years of age. The *Treatise* is today recognized as one of the great masterpieces of Western philosophy but was ridiculed by critics at the time of its publication. Hume was undaunted and continued to publish philosophical essays, many of which were well-received, and his monumental *History of England*, a text that remained a standard history for more than a century after his death. He aspired to a chair in philosophy at Glasgow but was rejected as an atheist. Hume was widely admired as a humanist and as a scholar. He died in Edinburgh a very happy man.

Kant, Immanuel (1724–1804): Immanuel Kant is almost universally regarded as the greatest of all European philosophers. He was born and spent his entire life in Königsberg (present-day Kalningrad) in Prussia. Indeed, he never ventured more than 100 miles from that city. Kant studied at the University of Königsberg, then spent his entire career teaching there. He was a prolific writer, but most of the books of his early years are no longer influential. In 1781, however, he produced his masterpiece, *The Critique of Pure Reason*, one of the most profound philosophical investigations undertaken in the Western tradition. This was followed by both *The Critique of Practical Reason* and *The Critique of Judgment*, extending Kant's philosophical system from epistemology and metaphysics to ethics, then to aesthetics and a number of smaller but important texts. It is fair to say that

Kant completely transformed the face of European philosophy. He was the first professor of philosophy to be an important philosopher in his own right; he developed the first comprehensive European philosophical system since the Enlightenment; and he demonstrated that philosophy can take natural science seriously yet remain an autonomous domain of thought. Today, nobody can become a serious philosopher without first studying the work of Kant.

Lame Deer, John (1900–1976): John Lame Deer was a Lakota Sioux medicine man born on the Rosebud Reservation and educated in Bureau of Indian Affairs schools. In early adult life, he was a rodeo rider and led the rough life of that trade. After meeting the keeper of the medicine pipe of the Lakota people, he became a medicine man. The second half of his life was devoted to educating Lakota and other Americans about Lakota culture, to the revival of Lakota culture, and to the recovery of traditional Lakota land in the Black Hills.

Lao Tzu (perhaps 6th, 5th, or even 4th century B.C.E.): There is no consensus about whether Lao Tzu (Laozi) ever existed. Many scholars regard him as a mythical figure constructed as the author of the Daodejing, which may well have developed under the hands of multiple authors over several centuries. Putative biographies locate his birth in Chu (Henan province) and state that he spent much of his adult life in Zhou, near present-day Luoyang, working in a library. He is said to have left the court and disappeared into the West.

Marcus Aurelius (121–160 C.E.): Marcus Aurelius was the son of a wealthy, noble Roman family living in present-day Spain. Marcus was educated by eminent tutors and adopted, in 138, by the emperor Aurelius Antoninus (Pius), under whom he served as consul for some time. While in public service, Marcus continued to pursue his education, studying Greek, literature, philosophy, and rhetoric with some of the most prominent teachers in Rome. He also studied law, a subject for which he appears to have had little appetite. In 161, on the death of Antoninus Pius, Marcus assumed the throne as emperor of Rome along with his adopted brother Lucius, who died soon thereafter, leaving Marcus as sole emperor. His reign was marked by many border wars, all of which concluded satisfactorily for Rome. He was noted as a skilled legislator and judge and was apparently much occupied with administration. Marcus continued to pursue philosophy throughout his life and, on a visit to Athens, proclaimed himself "Protector of Philosophy." He died while on tour in what is now Vienna.

Mill, John Stuart (1806–1873): John Stuart Mill was the son of the historian James Mill, a close follower of the Utilitarian philosopher Jeremy Bentham. Bentham and Mill developed a rigorous system of upbringing and education for the young John Stuart, who was isolated from other children and taught Greek, Latin, Hebrew, and algebra from age 3. By the time he was 10, he could read Plato in Greek and composed poetry in classical Greek. In his teens, Mill studied logic, rhetoric, history, and economics, but by age 20, he suffered a psychological collapse. Mill married Harriet Taylor, a brilliant young woman, and with her was a forceful advocate for the rights of women, for political liberty, and for a social policy aimed at the benefit of the masses of ordinary people. Mill's essays on political philosophy were widely read in his own time and are still influential today.

Nietzsche, Friedrich (1844–1900): Nietzsche grew up in a middle-class Prussian family. He excelled in his studies, particularly in music and literature, and pursued theology and philology at the University of Bonn. Despite his parents' piety, he dropped theology and devoted himself to classical philology. Under the influence of Arthur Schopenhauer, he also developed an intense interest in philosophy and science. In 1869, Nietzsche was appointed, at age 24, professor of philology at Basle. Nobody before or since has held such a chair at such a young age. Nietzsche held the chair for 10 years, before his health declined, and during that period, he began his philosophical work. He was a close friend of the composer Richard Wagner during his early days at Basle but became estranged from Wagner later, breaking with him over political and cultural issues. In 1879, Nietzsche resigned his chair because of ill health, and for the next 10 years, he traveled Europe and wrote almost all of his most influential philosophical books. By 1889, however, Nietzsche descended into madness. From that time, his sister and mother cared for him, and he was frequently hospitalized. He died in 1900.

Śāntideva (8th century C.E.): We know almost nothing of the life of Śāntideva. All biographical sources agree that he was born a Brahmin, converted to Buddhism, and studied at Nalanda University in present-day Bihar state in India. He composed two principal works, *Siksasamuccaya* (*"Collection of Teachings"*) and *Bodhicāryāvatāra* (*"How to Lead an Awakened Life"*).

Seneca (c. 4-65 CE): We know little of Seneca's early life, although his was an influential family. One of his brothers was a proconsul, and Seneca himself became tutor to the emperor Nero. He studied Stoic philosophy with eminent teachers but seems to have been at odds with the court, nearly executed by Caligula and exiled by Claudius. Nonetheless, he returned to Rome to serve as Nero's tutor and counselor. Once again, however, he fell into political disrepute and retired to write. Seneca was later accused of participating in a conspiracy to assassinate Nero and was ordered to commit suicide, which he did. He was a remarkable writer, and his letters and essays have been widely read and have influenced many subsequent ethicists and moral psychologists.

Siddhartha Gautama (c. 500 B.C.E.–c. 420 B.C.E.): Siddhartha Gautama, more commonly known as Śakyamuni Buddha or just the Buddha, was born in Lumbini to the royal family in the small state of Kapilavastu, in present-day Nepal. The precise dates of his life are uncertain, and he may have lived as much as 50 years earlier or later than the dates indicated here. What we know of his life derives from the record of his teachings and from frankly hagiographic biographies. He was raised in the royal palace as crown prince, but in his early 30s, he abandoned the palace for the life of a wandering ascetic. He studied for several years under a series of teachers and finally set off on a solitary quest for understanding, culminating in his experience of awakening at Bodh Gaya, in present-day Bihar state in India. Following that experience, he taught for about 50 years, wandering through what is now northern India and Nepal, attracting numerous disciples and the patronage of several powerful kings, and establishing a monastic community. He died at the age of 80 in Kushinagar in what is now Uttar Pradesh state.

Tolstoy, Lev (Leo) (1828–1910): Count Leo Tolstoy was born into one of the most distinguished Russian noble families, but his own youth was undistinguished. He did poorly in school, dropped out of university, ran up huge gambling debts, and joined the army. Between 1857 and 1861, Tolstoy traveled extensively in Europe. During this time, he met eminent European writers and political thinkers, experienced the difference between liberal European states and the repressive Russian regime, and was exposed to new ideas about education. He returned to Russia an anarchist and a pacifist and with a passionate interest in the elevation of the serfs through education. He founded schools for his own serfs' children and began to write the magnificent novels for which he is so famous, novels critical of war, of the state, and of middle-class society. Tolstoy became a devout Christian and fused his Christianity with his commitment to nonviolence. He communicated with Gandhi and was influential in Gandhi's own fusion of religious fervor, nonviolence, and criticisms of modernity and the state. At the end of his life, at age 82, Tolstoy renounced his wealth and left home to become a wandering ascetic, but he died of pneumonia shortly after setting out.

Bibliography

Aristotle. *De Anima*. Hugh Lawson-Tancred, trans. New York: Penguin Classics, 1987.

———. *Nicomachean Ethics*. Martin Ostwald, trans. Englewood Cliffs, NJ: Prentice Hall, 1962. An excellent translation with a good introductory essay.

Black Elk, Wallace, and William S. Lyon. *Black Elk: The Sacred Ways of a Lakota*. New York: HarperCollins, 1991. A classic autobiography and exposition of Lakota religious beliefs and rituals.

Chödron, Thupten. *Taming the Monkey Mind*. Union City, CA: Heian International, 1999. An accessible introduction to Buddhist theory and practice aimed at a general audience and geared to showing the relevance of Buddhism to daily life.

Confucius. *The Analects*. Raymond Dawson, trans. New York: Oxford University Press, 2008. Includes a good introductory essay on Confucian philosophy.

Coventry, Angela. (2007). *Hume: A Guide for the Perplexed*. New York: Continuum 2007. A superb overview of and introduction to Hume's system.

Cox, Christoph. *Nietzsche: Naturalism and Interpretation*. Berkeley: University of California Press, 1999. An analysis of Nietzsche's program that demonstrates the role of science and of the theory of interpretation in Nietzsche's philosophy.

Dalai Lama XIV. *A Flash of Lightning in a Dark Night*. Boulder, CO: Shambhala, 1994. The present Dalai Lama's commentary on key passages of Śāntideva's *Bodhicāryāvatāra*, emphasizing the nature of moral cultivation and the role of metaphysics as a foundation for ethics.

————. *Ethics for a New Millennium.* New York: Riverhead, 2001. The present Dalai Lama's principal independent work on ethics, developing an account of interdependence as a foundation for an ethic of compassion and universal responsibility.

————. *The Universe in a Single Atom: The Convergence of Science and Spirituality.* New York: Broadway, 2006. The present Dalai Lama's discussion of the relation between contemporary physics and neuroscience and Buddhist philosophy.

Eagleton, T. *The Meaning of Life: A Very Short Introduction.* New York: Oxford University Press, 2008. A brief overview of approaches to the question of the meaning of life, principally drawn from the Western tradition.

Easwaran, Eknath, trans. *The Bhagavad Gita.* New Delhi: Nilgiri Press, 2007. Translation of the *Bhagavad Gītā* with an orthodox commentary.

Frankl, V. *Man's Search for Meaning.* Boston: Beacon Press, 2006. An existential psychological exploration of the problem of finding meaning in life in light of the European Holocaust.

Gandhi, M. K. *An Autobiography: The Story of My Experiments with Truth.* Boston: Beacon Press, 1993. Gandhi's autobiography, focusing on his *satyāgraha* campaigns.

————. *Hind Swaraj.* Cambridge: Cambridge University Press, 2009. Gandhi's manifesto for the Indian national struggle, emphasizing his critique of modernity and his insistence on individual self-transformation as the ground of political action.

Goodman, Charles. *Consequences of Compassion.* New York: Oxford University Press, 2009. An interpretation of Buddhist ethics as consequentialist in character, examining a wide swath of the Buddhist moral tradition.

Graham, Angus. *Disputers of the Tao: Philosophical Argument in Ancient China.* Chicago: Open Court, 1999. Classic history of the development of

Chinese philosophy, addressing the debates between philosophical schools and their role in the development of Chinese philosophy.

———, trans. *Chuang-Tzu: The Inner Chapters.* Indianapolis: Hackett Publishing Co., 2001. Superb translations of the chapters considered the core of this text.

Hansen, Chad. *A Daoist Theory of Chinese Thought.* Cambridge: Harvard University Press, 2000. A history of Chinese philosophy developed from the perspective of Daoism, taking Daoism as the background for the development of other schools.

———. *Tao Te Ching on the Art of Harmony: The New Illustrated Edition of the Chinese Philosophical Masterpiece.* New York: Duncan Baird, 2009. A beautiful new edition of this classic, with a completely new and provocative translation and stunning color plates.

Hume, David. *Dialogues Concerning Natural Religion.* Indianapolis: Hackett Publishing Co., 1998. Hume's classic attack on proofs of the existence of God and of a rational basis for theism.

———. *A Treatise of Human Nature.* New York: Oxford University Press, 2000.

Kant, Immanuel. *An Answer to the Question: 'What Is Enlightenment?'* New York: Penguin, 2009. Kant's defense of freedom of thought as the ground of liberal society and social progress.

Kasulis, Tom. *Zen Action, Zen Person.* Honolulu: University of Hawai'i Press, 1989. A lucid presentation of Zen philosophy in the context of earlier Buddhist ideas and of Daoism, with useful comparisons to European philosophy.

Kraut, Richard, ed. *The Blackwell Guide to Aristotle's Nicomachean Ethics.* Oxford: Blackwell, 2006. A collection of essays on Aristotle's ethics by leading contemporary scholars.

Lame Deer, John, and Richard Erdoes. *Lame Deer, Seeker of Visions*. New York: Simon and Schuster, 1994. An exposition of the Lakota vision of the nature of reality and human life, with autobiographical and historical insights from a Lakota medicine man.

Long, A. A. *Epictetus: A Stoic and Socratic Guide to Life*. Oxford: Oxford University Press, 2004. Translations of the works of Epictetus, with an excellent introductory essay.

Marcus Aurelius. *The Meditations of Marcus Aurelius Antonius*. A. S. L. Farquarson and R. B. Rutherford, trans. New York: Oxford University Press, USA, 1998.

McLynn, Frank. *Marcus Aurelius: A Life*. New York: Da Capo Press, 2009.

Mill, John Stuart. *On Liberty*. www.createpsace.com: CreateSpace, 2009. Mill's great defense of personal liberty, in particular the freedom of expression, in liberal democratic societies.

———. *The Spirit of the Age, On Liberty, The Subjection of Women*. Alan Ryan, ed. New York: W.W. Norton, 1996. An anthology of some of Mill's most influential essays on liberal society, with a fine introduction.

Mitchell, Stephen. *The Book of Job*. New York: Harper, 1992. A modern commentary on Job.

Nehamas, Alexander. *Nietzsche: Life as Literature*. Cambridge: Harvard University Press, 1997. An exploration of Nietzsche's philosophy, focusing on his aesthetic view of human life.

Nietzsche, Friedrich. *Twilight of the Idols and the Anti-Christ: How to Philosophize with a Hammer*. Michael Tanner, ed.; R. J. Hollingdale, trans. New York: Penguin, 1990. A reliable translation of the last two books Nietzsche wrote before descending into madness, with a fine introductory essay.

Norton, David F., and Jacqueline Taylor, eds. *The Cambridge Companion to Hume*. Cambridge: Cambridge University Press, 2008.

Plato. *The Republic*. G. M. A. Grube, trans. Indianapolis: Hackett Publishing Co., 1992.

Prebish, C., and M. Baumann, eds. *Westward Dharma*. Berkeley: University of California Press, 2002. A collection of articles by eminent scholars on the transmission of Buddhism to the West and the impact of that transmission on Buddhism and Western culture.

Queen, Christopher. *Engaged Buddhism in the West*. Boston: Wisdom Publications, 2000. An exploration of the ways that Buddhism has generated and inflected social activism in the West.

Rahula, Walpola. *What the Buddha Taught*. Chicago: Grove Press, 1974. An introduction to early Buddhist doctrine.

Red Pine, trans. *Lao-Tzu's Taoteching*. Port Townsend, WA: Copper Canyon Press, 2009. A translation of the Daodejing with the Chinese text and selections from canonical Chinese commentaries on each chapter.

Śāntideva. *A Guide to the Bodhisattva's Way of Life*. A. Wallace and V. Wallace, trans. Ithaca, NY: Snow Lion Publications, 1997. A fine translation of *Bodhicāryāvatāra,* with a good introduction and comparisons of the two major editions of the text.

Scheindlin, Raymond. *The Book of Job*. New York: Norton, 1999. A modern commentary on Job.

Schmidt, James, ed. *What Is Enlightenment? Eighteenth-Century Answers and Twentieth-Century Questions.* Berkeley: University of California Press, 1996. An anthology of essays by eminent scholars on the relationship between Enlightenment thought and contemporary issues in democratic societies.

Sellars, John. *Stoicism.* Berkeley: University of California Press, 2006. A scholarly investigation of Stoic theory.

Seneca. *Dialogues and Letters.* New York: Penguin, 1997. C. D. N. Costa, trans. A collection of Seneca's principal writings with a very good introduction.

Stambaugh, Joan. *Impermanence Is Buddha Nature.* Honolulu: University of Hawai'i Press, 1990. An interpretation of the philosophy of the Zen philosopher Dōgen, with comparisons to the work of Martin Heidegger.

Stoler-Miller, B., trans. *Bhagavad-Gita: Krishna's Counsel in Time of War.* New York: Bantam Books, 1986. Definitive translation of the Bhagavad-Gītā with an excellent introductory essay.

Suzuki, D. T. *Zen Buddhism.* New York: Three Leaves Publishing, 1996. An influential presentation of Zen by one of the first to propagate the Zen tradition in the United States.

Tolstoy, Leo. *The Death of Ivan Ilych.* www.createspace.com: CreateSpace, 2009. Tolstoy's short novel about the nature of death, our attitudes toward death, and the dangers of an ordinary life.

Wei-Ming, Tu. *Confucian Thought: Selfhood as Creative Transformation.* Albany, NY: SUNY Press, 1985. A scholarly examination of the Confucian account of personal cultivation, drawing on a range of classical Confucian literature, with thoughtful philosophical analysis.

Williams, Paul. *Buddhist Thought.* London: Routledge, 2000. An excellent textbook introduction to Buddhism. Fine scholarship and philosophical commentary addressed to an undergraduate-level audience.

———. *Mahāyāna Buddhism: The Doctrinal Foundations.* London: Routledge, 2008.

Ziporyn, Brook, trans. *Zhuangzi: The Essential Writings with Selections from Traditional Commentaries.* Indianapolis: Hackett Publishing Co, 2009.

Notes

Notes

Notes

Notes

Notes